Peoples *of the* World

OM

CONTENTS

COORDINATOR
Mirella Ferrera

WRITTEN BY
Mirella Ferrera
Gian Giuseppe Filippi
Marco Ceresa

EDITOR
Valeria Manferto De Fabianis

COLLABORATING EDITORS
Enrico Lavagno
Lara Giorcelli

GRAPHIC DESIGNER
Paola Piacco

TRANSLATION
Timothy Stroud

This edition published in 2003 by
Om Book Service
4379/4B, Prakash House, Ansari Road,
Darya Ganj,
New Delhi - 110002
Phone: 23263363, 23265303
Fax: 91-11-23278091
e-mail: sales@ombooks.com
Website: www.ombooks.com

ISBN 81-8710-717-0

Printed in Italy by Rotolito Lombarda
Color separation by Fotomec, Torino

1 Each year until marriage, the necks of young Padaung girls (Myanmar) are enclosed inside a new brass ring.

2-3 In Peru head coverings identify the wearer's provenance: for example, these two women are wearing the broad hats from the region of Cuzco.

4-5 The complex, delicate figures in the Legong Kraton (the Balinese dance of the divine nymphs) are taught during a long preparation period that begins at infancy.

6-7 A tradition of the Tuareg is that they never uncover their faces in front of strangers.

7 This small nomadic Tibetan girl is wearing traditional dress, complete with a heavy silver buckle.

8 The symbols traced on the forehead indicate the devotion of sadhus to Shiva, the supreme Hindu god.

9 Gujar nomadic shepherds winter on the plains of the Punjab and move in summer to the high valleys of Kashmir.

PREFACE

The aim of this book is to provide the reader with a description of peoples whose culture, different from our own, sheds light on the different ways of living human life and the contribution each makes to understand our shared existence.

What is a culture? The anthropologist Alberto Salza offers the simple definition that culture is the way in which an individual, belonging to a group, tackles and solves problems, using knowledge systems typical of the society in which he lives. And this is the definition that we have used in this description and representation of the many human cultures spread around the globe.

The book is divided into five sections that more or less correspond to the geographical continents: Europe, Africa, Asia, Oceania, America and the Arctic. Each section has an introduction that describes the peopling and origins of the groups that inhabit the continent, followed by an ethnographic description of each people. A particular people can be recognized in the first place by the 'name' used in scientific literature to identify the group it belongs to, and, second, by the cultural system it uses: a cultural system is a complex phenomenon that covers knowledge, beliefs, values, behavior, language, religion and folklore. The localization of the various peoples is indicated by a series of geographical maps.

Given the impossibility of describing even the greater part of human cultures, the need to make a representative selection was imposed, which was made on a basis of arbitrary choices such as direct knowledge, geographical localization and the availability of data and illustrations that would provide the reader with a wide and direct appreciation.

As a rule, preference has been given to peoples whose material and traditional culture has been and is still influenced, at least in part, by the environment in which they live. In consequence, the various sections of the book make wide reference to cultures of animal-breeders, hunter-gatherers and nomadic farmers.

The organization of material life, for reasons of sustenance, on the cycle of the seasons is a central nexus in the cultures of the peoples described. This cycle provides a central focus around which social and religious life is organized, with important implications for the relations between the different forms of life in nature and the relationship of individual peoples with the supernatural: for example, the purification rituals that are held before hunting expeditions, taboos that relate to certain animal or plant species among hunter-gatherers, ceremonies that celebrate a successful fishing expedition or the cycles of agricultural fertility (both sowing and harvest) or animal sacrifices made on ceremonial occasions by animal-breeding societies.

The selection of peoples in the continent of Europe required a different approach as there are few groups that live following either the rhythms of the seasons (as occurs, for instance, among the animal-breeding cultures in Sardinia and the Magyar horse-breeders in the Puszta) or a nomadic migrant culture, like the Rom. Moreover, although Europe has an enormous variety of ethnic groups and different languages, the culture of the peoples that inhabit the continent is substantially similar and their lifestyle has to a certain extent become standardized since the time of the Industrial Revolution.

Given this basic cultural uniformity, it becomes difficult to describe the culture of a certain group without risking falling back on descriptions of traditions, customs and behavior derived from a long distant past. In recent years,

however, this sort of 'disinterment' has become increasingly exploited as a means of establishing ethnic and cultural identities for political or territorial purposes, for example, by regional or national independence movements like the Bretons, the Northern Irish and the Andalusians.

Returning to this book, great emphasis (borne out by the number of photographs) has been placed on the 'ornamental' aspects that distinguish each group: elaborate hairstyles, face- and body-painting, jewelry, beads and feathers are in use all around the world, consistent with distinctive and fascinating criteria of beauty. There are forms of ornamentation that, once assumed, can never be removed, such as tattoos (popular among the Maori), scars (seen in many African populations), male and female sexual mutilation (circumcision, subincision, excision, infibulation), perforation of the earlobes so various objects can be inserted (practiced among the Maasai and some tribes in New Guinea), the insertion of lip plates (characteristic of the Surma in Ethiopia and some Amazonian groups) and the wearing of metal neckrings and necklaces (seen among the Ndebele women in South Africa and the Padaung women in southeast Asia). Ornamentation of this nature is used to emphasize social status, membership of a clan or the differences that exist between the sexes. They are 'indelible marks' that alter the individual's body permanently and which, for example, are performed during the initiation rites of adolescents into manhood or womanhood, when the experience of pain is considered necessary for the individual to understand fully the transformation that has taken place.

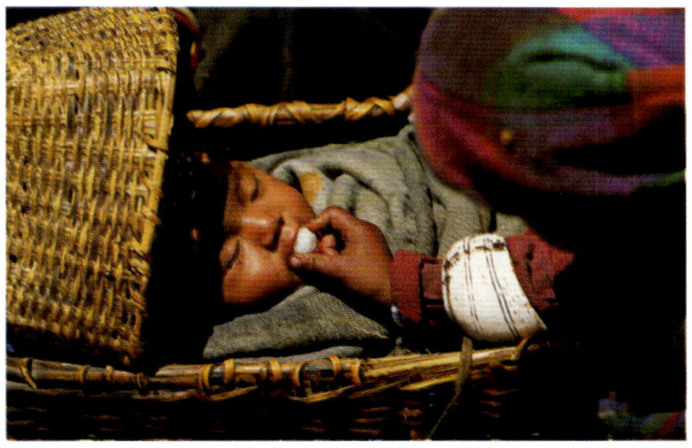

It is this dynamic, 'transformative' dimension of culture that we wish to underline in order to dispel the often common view that ethnologically interesting groups are 'immobile' – i.e., suspended in time and enclosed, isolated worlds – or worse, that they are 'primitive'. We seem to hold this view almost as though to give support to our desperate desire to compare ourselves with a more exotic existence. Peoples that we consider 'exotic' are no longer those described by anthropologists and scholars in the last century: as we are all well aware, their existences have been profoundly changed by globalization and emigration. We mention this fact to emphasize the right of cultures to a quality of dynamism and change: societies and the human groups of which they are composed are always in a state of change.

Finally, the description of the peoples in this book cannot be considered definitive given the complexity of dealing with human groups in continual transformation. This process of flux is the result of history and the constant pressure exerted by political, social and economic changes. It should also be borne in mind that no culture is 'pure' but the result of contact with other, neighboring groups. It is as a result of these exchanges that cultures evolve, being transformed by a continuous stirring and blending of information (and genes), building on the cultural traditions of the past but adapting them to the changes imposed by history. The 'transformative' component is expressed in the etymological background of the term 'culture', which is derived from the Latin word *colere*: all meanings of this verb (inhabit, cultivate, adorn) imply the idea of a transforming influence imposed by man, as it is man who, in the end, is the principal artificer of the transformations that take place within his individual, but communal, culture.

10 The harshness of the land in southern Ethiopia has determined the remarkable racial and cultural uniformity of local peoples like the Bale and Surma.

11 A Tibetan mother feeds her child in the cradle. On the Roof of the World the diet mostly consists of lentils, rice and yoghurt.

12-13 In February and March much of India celebrates Holi, the festival of color. On this occasion, Indians of every ethnic group and religion – oblivious to differences in caste – sprinkle each other with bright colors in enthusiastic and chaotic festivities.

14-15 The various Huli clans in Papua are identified by blue, white, black, yellow and red. Known as the 'wig-men', the Huli wear elaborate wigs (made generally from their own hair) adorned with feathers, flowers and bits of colored paper.

EUROPE

E U R O P E

List of peoples

Written by Mirella Ferrera

16 left On mounts decorated with rosettes, a group of horsemen prepares for the Sartiglia in Oristano, one of the many Sardinian festivals that has its roots in the pagan and rural rites of the past.

16 right Pilgrims from 80 or so different confraternities, and thousands of people from all over Spain, attend the romería in Rocío, one of the liveliest and most authentic celebrations in Europe.

17 The finely worked costume and severe profile of this old lady from Gressoney reveal the cultural wealth and material hardship of the Walser, a mountain people originally from Swabia.

NATURA SORRID NEI FIORI
DIO
NEI BIM

Introduction

The first peopling of the area that lies between the Ural Mountains and the Iberian Peninsula – what today is conventionally called Europe – probably occurred about a million years ago. It was with the end of the last Ice Age, around the eleventh millennium BC, that the principal ethnic and cultural traits began to form that still characterize the western end of the Asian landmass.

As we shall see, the history of the interleaving and mingling of human groups in Europe was extremely complex: the tangle of ethnic groups and cultural backgrounds lies in a certain sense at the origin of a fairly particular connotation of Europe, a region of the world in which man's activity has been of greater importance than the natural environment since earliest times. In general, the most significant cultural influences were derived from three regions: North Africa, the Near East and western Asia. With the improvement in the climate and consequent melting of the glaciers that had fragmented and isolated the region for tens of thousands of years, groups of nomadic farmers arrived from Anatolia. They mixed with the local populations of hunter-gatherers, who had probably also originated in western Asia. The Anatolian cultivators brought the 'Indo-European' languages with them that overlaid the idioms spoken by the Caucasian groups. Genetic studies suggest that the Caucasians were probably groups of anatomically modern *Homo sapiens* that had evolved in Africa and reached Europe roughly 40,000 years ago.

The isolation by glaciers of some regions of Europe at the height of the Ice Age around 20,000 years ago might explain the genetic differences that exist between the Iberian (including French Basques) and Caucasian groups. If this is the case, modern Iberians would be the descendants of the oldest inhabitants of Europe.

Migration from the Near East long continued uninterrupted with the result that, in addition to the Indo-European linguistic group and the proto-Mediterraneans in Iberia, Europe was also reached by the 'Uralic' group whose origins lay in the sub-Arctic regions around the Ural Mountains. In their case, the genetic typologies reveal a mixture of Caucasoid and Mongoloid characteristics. The peopling of the European sub-continent was therefore typified by the continual mixture of different peoples alternated by long periods of isolation.

Beginning a brief analysis from the west, the early Iberian peoples that had been present in the peninsula since the Neolithic period, and which were characterized by Mediterranean linguistic and physical features still found in the Basques, mixed with groups from widely separated geographical areas: from northern Africa (the Ligurians), central Europe and the Near East. Around the sixth century BC it was the turn of the Celts (Indo-Europeans from France) to migrate, whose example was followed by the Greeks, Phoenicians, Carthaginians and Romans between the fifth and first centuries BC. The fall of the Roman Empire at the end of the fifth century AD opened the gates for the barbarian invasions of the Iberian Peninsula. The term 'barbarian invasion' is generally used to refer to one of the cyclical, mass migrations of peoples from Eastern Europe who had been pushed in turn by the influx to their lands of nomadic groups from central Asia. It was the Wandalu tribe (the Vandals) whose name was adopted to signify the region of Andalusia. At the start of the eighth century, 250 years later, Arab-Berber invaders occupied the region and were to remain dominant until the end of the Middle Ages.

Moving east, the Italic Peninsula was also the setting for repeated amalgamations of local peoples with groups arriving from the Aegean during the third and second millennia BC, and later with Hellenic, Phoenician, Etruscan and Carthaginian groups from the Mediterranean, and with peoples from central, northern and eastern Europe like the Celts, Magyars and Scandinavians. In the eighth century BC, the ethnographic map of the peninsula shows the Etruscans

18 Embroidered with the saying 'Nature smiles through the flowers, God through children', a red cloth covers the cradle of a baby about to be baptized in the church in Fobello, a Walser village in the Mastallone Valley.

19 The pointed hoods of the penitent mix with incense fumes in a church in Seville during Holy Week. The atmosphere is filled with mystical tension. This is Andalusia, a region of strong passions and deep religiousness.

settled in central Italy, the Greeks in the south and the Carthaginians in Sicily and Sardinia. Later, during the fifth century BC, Celtic groups settled in the northern areas of modern Italy bringing with them knowledge of ironworking. After the end of the long Roman era, the barbarian raids were followed by invasions of Byzantines, Arabs and Normans.

To the northwest, the islands of the British and Irish archipelago were occupied in different stages between the fourth and second millennia BC by groups from every part of Europe. The primitive local cultures (of Iberian origin) responsible for the megalithic complexes in southern England were permeated by the Celts – therefore Indo-European – around the fifth century BC, then the Romans (first century AD), Germanic peoples (fifth century) and Scandinavians and Normans up untill the eleventh century. The name Britain (and consequently Great Britain) is Celtic in origin, whereas England meant 'Land of the Anglos', a Germanic people that invaded Britain in the fifth century AD. The ethnic and cultural influence of the invaders was less deeply felt among the population living in Wales, Scotland and Ireland, where the Celtic language and traditions survived.

The most notable characteristic of the peopling of modern France is the antiquity of the human presence there. The earliest traces found in the region date from the Paleolithic. Following a number of Iberian influxes during the second millennium BC (which also resulted in the construction of megalithic complexes), the most important immigration occurred between the tenth and seventh centuries BC with the arrival of the Celts. They brought with them both an Indo-European language and the culture of iron. After the fall of Rome, in the fifth century Celts fled to the region of Armorica following a Germanic invasion of Wales and Cornwall; as a result the corner of northwest France where they settled was also referred to as Britain, which has since evolved into Brittany. This region is home to one of the few peoples in Europe to have maintained for centuries several traditions – foremost their language – that are genuinely 'original'.

The Balkan region was for centuries affected by large migrations of peoples from central Asia, Ugrians, Greeks, Latins, Celts, Germans, Slavs, Mongols and Turks. The Hungarian plain, which for millennia had served as a bridge between internal Asia and Europe, was crossed by the Magyars in the ninth century, who set themselves over the Slav and Goth groups.

The Magyars were a Finno-Ugric people from central Asia beyond the Urals. They are related to the Finns who had traveled to northern Europe. Direct descendants of these Asian 'pioneers' of the European sub-Arctic areas are the Saami, a people more generally, but incorrectly, known as Laps.

Although this long history of migrations gave rise to an enormous variety of ethnic groups and different languages, there are in general currently no peoples of 'ethnological interest' in the Old Continent, not in the sense that there are in other regions of the world. The Industrial Revolution brought an end to the differentiation between European peoples, whose cultural and material lives are now mostly similar and dominated by the era of mass- and satellite-communications.

Where there do remain certain cultural traditions, these are often based on artificial 'folklore' traditions that, in recent years, have been exploited to invigorate ethnic and cultural identities for political and territorial purposes, e.g., regional and national independence movements as have occurred in Brittany and Ireland.

Nonetheless, on the pages that follow an attempt has been made to highlight the few human groups that still lead their material and cultural lives conditioned, at least in part, by the environment in which they live. This is the case for Sardinian shepherds, the Hungarian horsemen of the Puszta and those groups that retain certain cultural and religious practices that have deep connotations in their culture, such as in Andalusia.

20 *Wearing a clover-green shirt, and with pale skin and tawny hair, this girl is a perfect representative of the Irish, a people determined not to lose its identity.*

20-21 *A pause on the shore during a festival in Finistère. The Bretons are the descendants of refugee Celts who landed on the western tip of Armorica to escape the Saxon invasion of England.*

22-23 The rain is not enough to dissuade the Irish from going out in the jaunting-car. The mist shrouds the landscape of Killarney National Park, written Cill áirne *in* Gaeilge fem *(or Erse).*

22 bottom left Two men in Glencolumbkille thatch a roof using methods going back thousands of years.

22 bottom right Irish tinkers lead a nomadic life not dissimilar to that of the Rom, culturally and otherwise: even the barrel-shaped cart is fundamentally the same.

Irish

IRELAND

The Irish are a people of Celtic origin and the heirs of the island inhabited by ancient peoples whose native language was Erse, which is still the official language of the Republic of Ireland. The spread of this ancient language – which has been reassessed over the last few decades – is fundamental to the revival of the Irish ethnic identity.

Christianity was introduced into Ireland in the fifth century by Patrick, who was to become the patron saint of the island. The new religion was embraced by the Irish without cultural trauma, with the result that Christian heroes came to coexist without difficulty with the figures and legends of Celtic tradition.

It was the English king, Henry VIII, who introduced the Anglican church to the island. Under his daughter Elizabeth I, Catholics were outlawed as enemies of the State, persecuted and treated as inferiors legally and economically. The land of Ireland was confiscated by the English and ownership passed to members of the English nobility. Hunger and misery aggravated by continual famines that lasted decades stimulated enormous emigration of the Irish to the United States in the nineteenth century. Agriculture, on which the precarious Irish economy rested, was not enough to ensure survival of its inhabitants; the most valuable goods, like wheat and livestock, were exported to England. The basic foodstuff in the Irish diet was the potato, from which whiskey was also distilled. This humble diet was frequently rounded out in rural areas by the drinking of the blood of livestock, a practice that still exists in the animal breeding peoples of Africa like the Maasai.

Ireland was divided into two political entities in 1922: the Republic of Ireland (95% of which is Catholic) and Northern Ireland, which remained under British rule. The Catholic and Protestant churches more or less represented the ethnic and cultural divide between the British and Irish dominions: whereas the Catholics are generically associated with the Irish population, the members of the Protestant

23 top and bottom The Irish have always made the best of what nature offers them. The land is parsimonious with regard to cultivation but the climate and calcareous nature of the soil are suitable for the grazing and breeding of sheep and horses, which have long been traditional activities.

24 top left The ancient game of hurling – the forerunner of hockey – is here being played on a pitch of perfect green.

24 top right A young fly fisherman tests his luck in a river near Galway.

24 center left A group of children on their way to school where they also learn the Gaelic language.

24 bottom left Pubs are the traditional meeting place of the hospitable and naturally friendly Irish people.

25 The Irish are typically ruddy and red-haired but there are plenty of people with dark skin, eyes and hair who are probably the descendants of the pre-Celtic population of Iberian origin.

minority (on the island as a whole) emphasize their British ties. The two capitals symbolize this contrast, with the industrial, Anglo-Saxon Belfast representing modernity against the Irish city of Dublin, closely linked to tradition.

The traditional communities are mostly found on the northwest coast of the island where Celtic festivals are still held in rural areas to mark the seasonal agricultural cycle. The traditional fairs and festivals typical of times past are marked by music, dancing and competitive sports like hurling (the ancient forerunner of hockey) and horse racing. Right across the island pilgrimages are made to places of worship – usually sanctuaries – that attract tens of thousands of pilgrims and tourists each year. Ireland has an enormous wealth of popular traditional narrative that has been handed down over the generations by storytellers: ranging from the epic deeds of heroes to tales of magic and fairies, storytelling is a long and widely practiced art.

The existence on the island of a little known minority of wandering tinsmiths – tinkers – is worthy of mention. Tinkers are often confused with the Rom people (gypsies) due to the cultural similarities of the two groups.

Living in camps, tinkers are constantly on the move in horse-drawn carts or caravans and make a living from producing tools, selling and buying things, practicing divination and begging. The traditional barrel-shaped cart used for sleeping and a tent for performing daily activities have been replaced by modern caravans and vans that transport horses, bric-a-brac and waste materials. The origin of the tinkers is uncertain but they may be descended from a group of Celtic bards or Druids.

They are called tinkers (from 'tinsmith') for their ability to work with metal and for their custom of taking with them a small forge for shoeing horses and making tools. Naturally these characters figure large in traditional stories and ballads, two forms of art that the Irish have raised to a level of excellence.

Bretons

FRANCE

Settled in northwest France, the Bretons share direct descendency from the Celts with the Irish and Welsh. Their ethnic name (Bretons) links them to the ancient Britons who, between the fifth and eighth centuries, migrated to this corner of France from Wales and Cornwall to escape the Anglo-Saxon domination of their country. They took refuge in the region of Armorica ('land facing onto the sea') that was called 'Britannia' during the Roman era, from which the modern name of Brittany is derived. The exodus from Britain naturally brought the Old English language (which is distinct from the Celtic or Gallic languages of pre-Roman Gaul) and the religious customs of the island's Christianity, which led to the creation of a church of Celtic ritual.

The Celtic tradition of storytelling was carried forward for centuries with legendary cycles and epic-literary tales like those of Tristan and Isolda, and King Arthur and Merlin. Storytellers were important figures in Breton culture, the heirs of the Celtic bards (poet-priests) who lived at court and celebrated the exploits of their princes.

Until just a few decades ago, it was still possible to hear the traditional legends of ancient heroes in rural areas of Brittany during long winter evenings when families gathered around the hearth to listen to stories of those heroic figures. Hearths were the standard place for storytelling and were found in all the *penty*; these were typical Breton stone farmhouses with a single room divided into the cooking area, the fireplace (fitted with wooden seats for evening gatherings) and the sleeping area in which pallets were fixed in the walls and separated from the rest of the room by curtains or doors.

The Breton economy was traditionally based on agriculture and fishing. Farmers, tenant farmers and farm laborers in the coastal villages used to gather iodine-rich seaweed left by the tide that they used to fertilize fields of cereals and pulses. Fishermen used to risk their lives sailing

26 top and 26-27 Gonfalons sewn with silk and gold, finely sewn lace, a passion for local cultural roots and an almost nostalgic religious feeling are all elements of the Troménie in Locronan, the 'Pardon' in honor of St. Ronan Ronan was the Irish bishop who arrived in Finistère in the seventh century when the influence of the Druids was still strong.

26 bottom Young Bretons in traditional costume parade before the crowd during a pardon. Besides being strong tourist attractions, Breton ceremonies are important occasions for the whole population, which takes part with enthusiasm. The ceremonies are thought to be a legacy of Druidic liturgies.

27 bottom left Thousands of pilgrims follow the route in Locronan which, it is said, St. Ronan used to complete each morning in meditation.

27 bottom right The wide-brimmed hats, high caps and brightly colored velvet smocks are among the most clearly visible items of festive clothing.

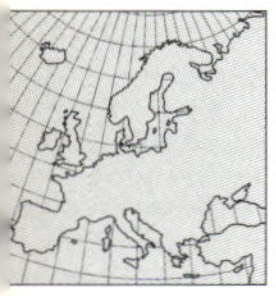

28 top and bottom The lace and costumes worn by the 'actors' in Breton festivals have been handed down over the generations or are made faithful to traditional models.

28-29 The embroidery and lacework in Pays Bigouden are famous for their decorative motifs and perfection. In the past the embroidery of the velvet was the work of a guild of men and the manufacture of the caps the work of the women.

right across to Iceland and Newfoundland in search of cod and to the coasts of Spain and Morocco for tuna. As in the rest of Europe, all work was regularly interrupted by religious celebrations depending on the season, for example, the 'Pardons', i.e., pilgrimages to ancient places of worship. The custom was that on the occasion of patron saints' feast days pilgrims would be rewarded with indulgencies ('pardons'). Even today thousands of pilgrims still make the journeys in traditional costume, carrying gonfalons, standards, statues of saints and crosses in procession. After the religious celebration, traditional entertainments are held such as Breton wrestling, dancing and music like the gavotte from Cornwall, which is played on the *biniou* (a small Breton bagpipe), the *telenn* (a small Celtic harp) and the *bouéze* (an accordion). The dances are accompanied by *ka ha diskan*, a typical form of Breton song in which two singers sing contrasting phrases.

The women wear wide black skirts with colored aprons, embroidered tops and white lace caps the styles of which vary from zone to zone and indicate the wearer's provenance. The most original are the tall cylindrical hats made of starched white lace (*beg*) worn in the Pays Bigouden or the ones that stand up like a cock's comb (*coq*) from Dinard. The men wear black jackets with buttons at the side, large, broad-brimmed hats and colored wooden clogs.

Today the linguistic minority of Brittany has fallen to roughly half a million, most of whom are old and live in Finistère ('Lands End') where the feeling of regional identity is strongest.

Here there exist several groups whose aim is to promote the study and conservation of Breton traditions: i.e., the language, customs, music, religious ceremonies and popular festivals.

Bretons

29 bottom left Every summer Lorien is the setting for the Interceltic Festival of Music in which groups interested in the legacy of Celtic culture take part in the dancing and wearing of costumes .

29 bottom right The embroiderers have their own festival at Pont l'Abbé, at which a 'queen' is elected. The symbolism of the embroidery is a subject of debate but may be related to concepts like 'life', 'pride' and 'strength'.

30 top left *In Seville the last days of April mark the start of the* feria de abril, *a sort of compendium of Andalusian culture. The noble Spanish tradition of equestrianism is the pivot around which bullfights and religious processions revolve, all to the background music of the* sevillanas *and flamenco.*

30 top right *'Make yourself noticed' are the watchwords for the enthusiastic participants in the* feria, *either by your behavior or the clashing of bright colors. Tasteful exuberance is the overriding characteristic here.*

Andalusians

SPAIN

The Andalusians live in southwest Spain in the region that the Vandals – a Germanic people from the Baltic coast – invaded in the early decades of the fifth century having been pushed out of their own lands by the Huns who arrived from central-eastern Asia. However, all trace of the Vandals shortly disappeared with the exception of their name, which forms the basis of the modern geographic name of Andalusia. Instead it was the Arab and Moslem occupation that lasted more than 700 years that left a lasting ethnic and cultural inheritance to the people of Andalusia.

To this can be added the Spanish and Christian contribution made as a result of the Reconquest which, starting in the north of the country, chased the last of the Moors out of Spain in the fifteenth century.

Andalusia is the home of the bullfight and flamenco. The contact between the local population and immigrant groups of Rom (gypsies), who settled here in the fifteenth century, lies at the basis of the music of the flamenco, which is a gypsy interpretation of popular Andalusian songs. Another feature of Andalusian culture is the many traditional festivities (fairs, feast days, religious processions, pilgrimages, etc.) held throughout the region that involve the entire community, whether at neighborhood or town level. As elsewhere in Europe, traditional festivals that were born in a rural setting and are associated with a rustic past have been handed down to the modern day and now involve large slices of the urban communities of cities like Seville, Granada and Cordoba. This is where one finds the cultural characteristics of Andalusian tradition, which includes the enjoyment taken in eating in company, the rituals of hospitality, singing and dancing, the wearing of traditional costumes and riding of horses.

A perfect example is the Andalusian *feria*, which had its origin in the annual livestock markets that have always been held in Spain. With the passing of the centuries, the festivities have got the upper hand over the commercial

30 center *Proud horses pose in front of the* casetas, *the multicolored tents where the public eats, drinks and, above all, dances. Dancing and traditional music are fundamental to Andalusian culture.*

31 *An Andalusian damsel rides 'sidesaddle' behind her escort. Despite its bulk, the* traje *(traditional women's dress) was designed as much for dancing as for horse-riding.*

32 top and bottom The traje de flamenca *was derived from much simpler nineteenth-century clothes but has undergone a complex evolution as the fashions and economic state of the country have changed.*

activities. The general arrangement is that a prescribed area is equipped with tents outside of the city area where groups of people (confraternities, flamenco groups, students, etc.) come together to form *casetas* or enclosed areas where they can celebrate and offer hospitality with music, food and drink. Between the *casetas,* there is a constant parade of men and women on horseback in traditional costume.

Andalusian folklore is also to be seen during religious celebrations and the many *romerias* (pilgrimages from the word *romero,* 'pilgrim') dedicated to the Madonna. These are probably developments of pagan agricultural festivals that the

33 right A team of three white steeds advances down an avenue in the campo de la feria, *the fairground built for the event populated by thousands of festival-goers. The* feria de abril *has a remarkably dignified history: its remotest origins go back to medieval agricultural fairs and, in particular, to a thirteenth-century edict of Alfonso X the Wise. Andalusian and Hispanic cultures owe much to this ruler, who earned his nickname for his vast, eclectic knowledge.*

Catholic Church 'Christianized'.

The most important and spectacular is the *Romería del Rocío* held every Pentecost when caravans of pilgrims in traditional costume from all over Andalusia set out on foot, horseback or in ox-drawn carriages for the sanctuary of Rocío. This is a village in the province of Huelva where an image of the locally worshiped Madonna is held. Roughly one million people take part in the festival, in the religious celebrations and in the singing and dancing of the *sevillanas* (a local dance performed either in the dusty streets of Rocío or in the *casetas*). The festival reaches its climax when the

32-33 Fitted out by private individuals, cultural associations and other organizations, the casetas *attract elegant dancers who perform spontaneously and instinctively. The flamenco – literally 'Fleming', a musical form of which the* sevillana *is an adaptation – has gypsy origins but has Arab influences in the melody and rhythm.*

34 top A huge crowd of pilgrims gathers in front of the white façade of the Santuário de la Virgen del Rocío *during Spain's most famous and popular* romería. *The epitome of Andalusian religious fervor, this magnificent celebration seems to belong to the past, when huge masses of people moved across Europe to assemble in places of divine salvation.*

34 center The romería *is also an opportunity to launch oneself into gypsy dances. Hovering between the sacred and the profane, the pilgrimage to Rocío has uncertain origins, divided between legend and fact, though it dates from the Middle Ages.*

34 bottom An endless parade of carts, cars, bicycles and pilgrims on foot: anything goes – the important thing is to arrive to worship the blanca paloma, *i.e., the white statue of Mary held in the sanctuary of Ayamonte.*

34-35 The extraordinary procession amidst the clouds of dust would seem anachronistic anywhere else, but not in Andalusia. Many people walk for days, often barefoot, to get there.

35 bottom One of the most important and emotional moments during the pilgrimage is the crossing of the Río Quemada, when canopies containing images of the Virgin (the carretas del simpecado*) are loaded onto rafts and floated to the other side. The* simpecados *are real works of art by famous masters. Each confraternity has its own, unique in design and decoration; all, however, are lined with hundreds of pounds of silver.*

E U R O P E

statue of the Madonna is carried shoulder-high from the sanctuary through the village to bless all the pilgrims.

Christian devoutness is also expressed in Andalusia in festive rituals, like during Christ's Passion before His resurrection at Easter. On these occasions the monks in religious brotherhoods throughout Andalusia process through the streets in their hooded costumes carrying religious statues and images on wooden frames. In Seville the official ceremonies are held on Thursday evening and Good Friday; the public applaud and cheer the parades of images and the bars of the city remain open all night. In Andalusia the blend of sacred and profane is a deep-seated feature of the local culture.

36-37 The procession of the Madonna del Rosario is particularly meaningful to the revival of the Walser traditions: celebrated for the first time in 1683, this celebration faded away with time but began to make a come-back three centuries later when the inhabitants of the Walser communities in Alagna in Valsesia began to rediscover their traditions.

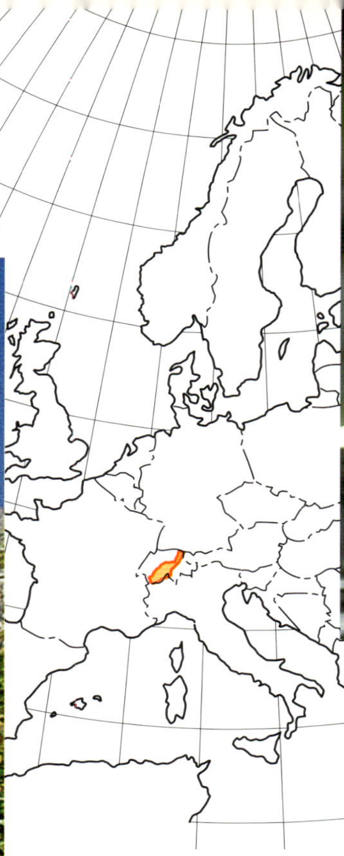

Walser

ITALY, SWITZERLAND AND AUSTRIA

The Walser are a Germanic people originally from ancient Swabia (what is today Bavaria) who moved south in the fifth to sixth centuries and settled in the Swiss valleys of the Wallis region. In the thirteenth century, several groups moved once more, colonizing the valleys surrounding Monte Rosa and settling in Valsesia and the valleys of Gressoney. Known as 'Walliser' or 'Walser' from the German name for the Wallis region (*Valais* in French), the people have also been called 'the Germans of Gressoney'. They lived in self-sufficient communities, growing barley, legumes and rye and breeding cattle, goats and sheep from which they produced cheese, fat, butter, wool and leather. They then exchanged these products for tools, wine and salt. Their lives followed the seasons: in May they herded their flocks up to the mountain pastures and in October brought them down again for the winter.

In the valleys around Monte Rosa, the houses in the compact Walser villages stand close to one another and share a communal oven, fountain and olive press. The lower levels of the mountain slopes are terraced with fields and the higher levels form the animal pastures. Typical Walser houses are built using a jointed structure of fir or larch beams that rests on a masonry base.

A large room on the first floor used to act as the stall, kitchen and storeroom for the farming tools. Warmed naturally by the body heat of the animals, the stall was separated by a wooden partition from the family's winter sitting area known as a *whongade*. The upper floors held the summer sleeping rooms, a weaving room and the *spicher*, which was both a pantry and an area used for storing hay. Outside the building on each floor ran a large wooden loggia fitted with racks for drying the hay. The roof was formed by large slabs of slate laid out using a technique that has almost completely disappeared.

36 bottom *The purbòus (typical Walser houses) are Nordic in style: made from stone at the bottom and with jointed wooden beams in the upper storeys.*

37 top *A strong religious feeling, verging on superstition and rooted in daily life, was a feature of the Walser community. The sign of the cross, the most important symbol, used to be pressed into the bread as a sign of thanksgiving.*

37 bottom *Celebrated at the start of autumn on the day of the Virgin, the procession of the Madonna del Rosario preceded the more important religious festivals that took place between December and March. During those months, most of the community's work was slowed by the winter weather.*

38 top *A natural consequence of progress is the disappearance of traditional activities. However, awareness of the value of tradition ensures that an increasing number of people has not lost the knowledge built up over the centuries.*

38 center *Brightly colored shawls contrast with the black of the typical Walser women's clothing. The design of the embroidered garlands of flowers varies from group to group.*

38 bottom *There are around 150 Walser communities in a mountain area that stretches for about 200 miles from the Monte Rosa valleys to Vorarlberg in Austria.*

38-39 *Geraniums brighten the schoflatte used to dry the hay on Walser houses.*

Rather more basic were the *stadel* (barns separate from the houses) and the shelters used during the transfer of the livestock up to the *maggenghi* (mid-mountain pastures that could be used in spring) and high altitude pastures. Dry-built from stone, these too were covered with a slate roof supported by massive architraves.

The seasonal cycle was marked by religious celebrations and feasts. The start of autumn was celebrated in early September with a bonfire called a *fraidfir* ('fire of joy'), followed by a feast that celebrated the end of the mountain grazing period and the return to the village.

Rye bread was cooked in the communal ovens and animals were slaughtered to prepare salted meat for *ubberlekke,* which was a filling traditional dish eaten in winter when the villages were covered in snow for six or seven months. St. Nicholas' day (December 6) marked the return of emigrants and the start of the winter season when the community would once again be back together and everyone would be able to join in the winter religious celebrations.

40 top A woman devotes herself to a local sewing technique in the half-light of a house in Carcoforo in Valsesia. As an indication of the Walsers' desire not to lose their traditions, this technique is now taught in special schools.

40 center and bottom left A band of lively geometric patterns takes shape in the hands of the sewer. The technique does not make use of drawings or sewing patterns. The origin of this tradition dates from the Renaissance but its provenance – perhaps oriental – is a matter of debate.

Walser

40 bottom right Weaving has been another household tradition in the central Alps for 400 or 500 years. This is the weaving of a rag rug, once a humble item created on a resistant burlap warp with weft made from simple rags.

40-41 By watching the elderly work, the young become the deposits of Walser culture. This young girl is observing the preparation of miacce, *which are wafers made from milk and eggs; animal products form much of the traditional Walser diet. These 'high altitude settlements' have always occupied the highest areas of the zones the people reached in their migrations and were therefore unsuited for cultivation. However, agriculture was practiced to provide cereals like rye and fibrous plants such as hemp and linen.*

42 bottom right Mògoro, near Oristano, is famous for its carpets and weaving. This art is based on techniques and patterns that are part of the region's cultural inheritance.

43 top The baking of bread for festivals is reserved to expert women bakers and the traditions are handed down from one generation to the next.

42-43 A fisherman baits large basket-like traps with old bread to entice crustaceans. This technique has been used in Sardinia for over 200 years.

42 bottom left The traps are handmade using easily obtained materials. They are much less costly and less harmful to sealife than nets.

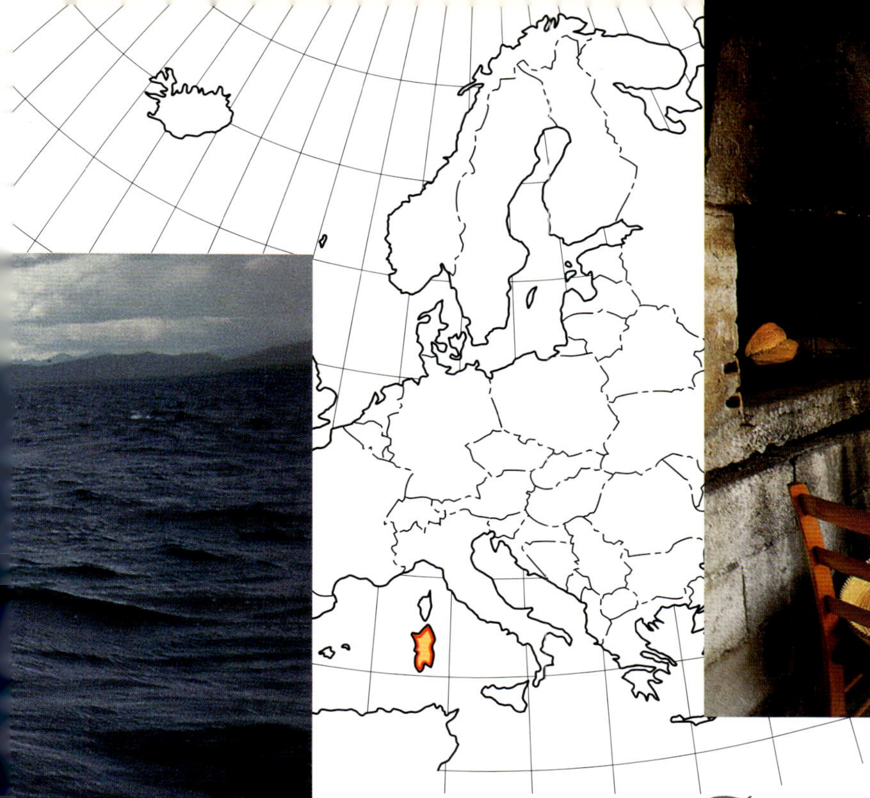

43 center and bottom *The fleecy sheep of Dorgali provide top quality wool used especially in carpet weaving. Animal breeding is the most deeply rooted of activities in Sardinia. Efficient animal and agricultural farming techniques were imported to the island as early as the sixth millennium BC, i.e., 45 centuries before the construction of the first* nuraghe.

Sardinians

ITALY

The Sardinians themselves like to stress that the insularity of Sardinia is not just geographic. For example, the island is also isolated linguistically as the Sardinian language is considered autonomous and derived from Latin like other Romance languages. One characteristic it shares with other islands – for example, Corsica and the Canaries – is the age-old practice of the inhabitants of abandoning their coastal settlements when threatened by pirates or invaders and taking shelter in villages hidden in the inhospitable interior.

Animal breeding is a traditional aspect of Sardinian culture and is well suited to the arid soil of the interior. The megalithic monuments of the *Nuraghi* civilization – found throughout Sardinia and dating from between 1500 BC and the conquest of the island by the Carthaginians in the sixth century BC – may have been associated with animal breeding. They were probably signal towers that marked the boundaries of the summer grazing areas and were used as shelters by the shepherds.

Seasonal grazing is still a feature of the coastal plains in winter and the mountains inland during summer. In the past the herdsmen used to drive their flocks of sheep and goats, and also herds of cattle, without the company of their families and would take shelter overnight in *pinnette,* which were a sort of hut with a conical roof and stone base. Today they travel in camper-vans but the image has remained of the shy, silent Sardinian shepherd who would spend long periods away from his home community without almost any human contact.

At one time an individual's subsistence was a communal affair: in Gallura, for example, if a herdsman lost his animals by natural causes, such as an epidemic or drought, he could recreate it by asking for a young animal from each of the other herdsmen.

Herdsmen and farmers also used to share the land and its benefits but in the nineteenth century the ruling Savoy family decreed the enclosure of property, which led to feuds

and clashes for control of plots of land. Since that time, stone walls and enclosures were put up across the island and animal-breeding activities began to wane; and it was at that time that banditry on the island began to increase.

Archaic traditions are relived in the many celebrations and festivals held across Sardinia. One of the most important is the *Sartiglia*, a thrilling tournament held in Oristano between Carnival Sunday and Shrove Tuesday. Organized since the seventeenth century by associations of farmers and carpenters – whose current existence is justified by this one function – the *Sartiglia* features the figure of the *cumpunidori*, a masked rider dating from a much earlier period. He represents a pagan king of the harvest and seasonal rebirth who ensures universal harmony. Chosen at the start of February on the occasion of the *Candelora*, the *cumpunidori* is meticulously prepared for the task he has to perform in the tournament: while at the gallop he has to pass his sword through a suspended metal star as the crowd watches on. Traditionally, the *cumpunidori*'s success or failure to do so is very important and represents the good or bad fortune of the months ahead.

Also at Carnival time, masked farmers and herdsmen dance in the procession of the *mamuthones* in Mamuiada in the province of Nuoro. Weighed down by enormous cowbells on

44 top left The equestrian acrobatics in the Sartiglia *in* Oristano *are thrilling but, in cultural terms, not the most important element in the event, which dates back to a much earlier time.*

44 top right A wooden mask is worn over the face of the cumpunidori *in the* Sartiglia. *Preparation for his task is carried out with great seriousness, in a sort of hieratic calm.*

44 bottom The climax of the Sartiglia *has been reached: the* cumpunidori *sets out at the gallop to thread his sword through a metal star. Should he succeed, the coming months will be auspicious; if he fails the* cumpunidori *is disgraced and the future augurs poorly.*

44-45 As occurs at Carnival all over the world, faces are hidden at the Sartiglia *with white masks, especially that of the* cumpunidori, *but here the purpose is different: the idea is to disguise a pagan entity from the eyes of a world that has been liberated of ancient gods.*

45 top This mask hides the face of a young child: the Sartiglietta *is a 'junior' version of the Sartiglia and held purely for children.*

45 right The seriousness of this young girl dressed for the Sartiglietta *matches the spirit of Oristano Carnival. There is of course fun to be had, but what is being evoked is not a laughing matter.*

46 bottom right Skilful riders perform dangerous stunts during the Cavalcata Sarda held on the last Sunday in May in Sassari. Unlike the festivities rooted in Sardinia's pre-Christian past, this celebration refers to a defeat inflicted on the Arabs in the early eleventh century by the Sardinians and Pisans.

46-47 and 46 bottom left The main characters at Mamuiada Carnival, the mamuthones, *have their faces covered by savage masks and their backs weighed down with cowbells. They offer an echo of one of the most common legends in Europe, that of the 'wild man of the woods', which perhaps harks back to the distinction between 'civilized' and 'primitive' peoples.*

47 top A parade of thousands of people from all over Sardinia dressed in traditional costume winds through the streets of Cagliari on May 1, the day of Sant'Efisio, in front of the statue of the martyr. This celebration is linked to a vow made by the inhabitants of the city in 1657 if the saint would clear the city of the plague, which had taken the lives of 12,000 people in Cagliari alone.

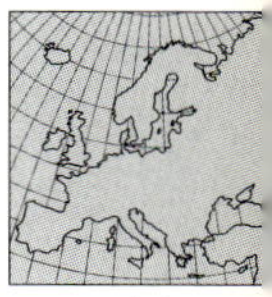

EUROPE

their backs and with smaller bells hung around their necks, the participants are made up to appear half human and half beast. This is a common element in many European ceremonies that refer to the 'wild man of the woods'.

Another attribute of Sardinian folklore is the round dance in which the participants dance in a circle around the musicians. The traditional instruments used on these occasions are the bagpipe and tambourine. Traditional Sardinian music includes *a cappella* chanting using four harmonic scales at the same time; this polyphonic style has its roots in very ancient times.

Time seems to pass more slowly on this very particular island: the conservation of ancient traditions – itself an unusual aspect – is matched by the longevity of some of its inhabitants. There are many people over 100 years of age who are currently the object of medical and scientific studies.

Sardinians

47 center and bottom
The variety of traditional dress in Sardinia is extraordinary: each of the 370 communes on the island has its own. Furthermore, unlike what happens in most of Europe where costumes are now brought out only for religious celebrations and festivals, in some parts of Sardinia – for example, the provinces of Oristano and Nuoro – it is not unusual to find old people wearing traditional dress.

Horsemen of the Puszta

HUNGARY

The word Puszta comes from the Slav *pust* ('desolate area'), which is a perfect description of the Hungarian lowlands. The strongly continental climate makes the *Alföld* ('lowland', the local name of the area to the east of Tibisco) very arid and completely without surface water.

In the not so distant past, the land was nothing but sand and steppe and there were very few inhabitants. Today the digging of artesian wells has changed the environment but not the principal subsistence economy: horse breeding. Several groups of breeders belonging to the Hungarian ethnic group inhabit this plain and are known as the 'horsemen of the Puszta'.

The Hungarians – or Magyars – are a blend of northern, eastern and alpine characteristics, with Turkic-Mongolian traces. This unusual mix is seen both in the people's distinctive facial features and their language; the latter is classified in the Finno-Ugric group and shows evidence of the Turkic, Slav and German languages. Yet the cultural characteristics of the herdsmen of cattle, sheep, horses and pigs in the Puszta are different, forged over the centuries by a material life that has almost completely isolated them from the rest of the Hungarian population.

The term Puszta refers generically to the lands of the

48-49 The csikós *are in charge of the horses and the unquestioned masters of the Puszta. They descended from a Finno-Ugric ethnic group that migrated from central Asia in the ninth to tenth centuries to what is today Hungary.*

48 bottom left Two csikós *pose on their obediently prostrate horses. Ancient authors referred to the Magyars as an 'equestrian people' for their extraordinary ability to work with horses.*

48 bottom right A horseman follows a group of colts during the Horse Festival. This is an important opportunity for the various groups of herdsmen to meet. It is held each year in Hortobagy National Park.

49 right Hortobagy is the region to visit to observe the spectacular riding feats of the horsemen of the Puszta. This steppe – the largest in Europe – is the only part of the Hungarian plain where traditional horse breeding is practiced.

Alföld used for grazing livestock. It is similar to the Argentinian pampas, which is also used for breeding horses and shares many characteristics with this inhospitable plain.

The traditional villages consist of a central square with radiating roads and a circular enclosure wall. The local houses – *tanya* – are built from sun-baked bricks and have three rooms: one for guests, one for cooking and one used for family life.

Next to the house stand the stalls, barn and animal enclosure. Behind the house lies the orchard. The herdsmen spend most of the year outdoors with their herds, sleeping at night beneath their leather capes that have now become a part of their traditional folklore costume.

Life on the Puszta is governed by rigid customs, which have resulted in the creation of a sort of hierarchy useful for ensuring the survival of the group in a very hostile environment. The category of horse-breeders – with its skilful riders and lasso throwers – represents the nobility of Hungarian herdsmen. Within this category there are various sub-levels: the *csikós* (grooms who look after the horses), *fószámadó* (the stockmen) and the *számadó bojitár* (grooms who look after the colts). Lower down in the overall hierarchy are the *gulyás* (cattlemen), followed by the *jahász* (sheep breeders) and lastly the *kondás* (pig breeders).

The various groups assemble in the summer at the annual stock fair when the herdsmen, in traditional costume, party with traditional music and dancing. The men wear an apron and long shirt over trousers, and the women wear a sleeveless jacket open over an embroidered shirt with puffed sleeves. Below they wear a short, pleated, bell-shaped skirt and high leather boots.

The traditional costume of the horsemen is worn on ceremonial occasions and consists of *szür-köponyeg,* which are broad felt capes embroidered with floral and geometric patterns that enhance the white or dark background of the material. A black three-cornered hat completes the costume.

Singing and dancing accomany the fairs, religious ceremonies and family festivals celebrated in the Puszta, which is why many Hungarian folk songs are based on the nomadic, free life of the herdsman. The tales of the horsemen draw on popular Hungarian folklore and feature spirits, dragons and witches. Many are dedicated to the Fata Morgana, who was born, according to legend, by the union of the sun and sea: two elements very distant from the Puszta.

50 top left Difficult to locate with accuracy, the Rom in Europe are most numerous in Romania, Germany, Italy, France, Andalusia, England and Ireland.

50 top right The Rom family unit reflects the strong sense of identity of the various tribes. The worst punishment for a Rom is banishment from the group.

Rom

A NOMADIC PEOPLE

Originally from northern India, the Rom (which simply means 'men') were chased out of the sub-continent around the eleventh century BC when the caste system was imposed. During a migration that lasted many hundreds of years, they crossed the Middle East and northern Africa and spread into Europe, Asia and, at the end of the nineteenth century, the American continent. Their many communities are divided into groups: the Kalderash and Khorakhané in eastern Europe, the Manush in France, the Gitanos in Andalusia and the Sinti in Germany and Italy.

The six million Rom around the world speak the Romany language, which is related to many northern Indian dialects derived from Sanskrit. Not having a written language, information regarding their history is provided by documents drawn up during their transit through the various countries where they have attempted to create an economic niche for themselves. The work they traditionally perform is typical of a nomadic existence: animal traders, metal workers (blacksmiths, pot makers, farriers, etc.), peddlers, street artists, musicians and fortune-tellers. Wherever they go they adopt the local religious beliefs, thus, in Catholic countries they pretend to be pilgrims on their way to Rome with special safe-conducts issued by the Pope, and in Islamic countries they convert to Islam. Such flexibility however has not saved them: their lifestyle has meant that they remained outside the control and laws of the nascent (and intolerant) nation states in Europe which, from the

50-51 A family of Romany gypsies walks alongside their characteristic barrel-shaped wagon: the nomadic lifestyle of this people has given rise to severe discrimination.

51 bottom left and right In some countries, like Romania, the life of the Rom seems to exist outside of time, based on moves and halts of varying duration.

50 bottom left The role of the Rom women is subordinate to that of their men but not in all fields: the handing on of cultural values, for instance, is their task.

50 bottom right Rom are not easily definable, not even their secondary facial characteristics. This blond boy is an Irish Rom.

52-53 From May 24-26, the village of Saintes-Maries-de-la-Mer in the Camargue is the setting for a large religious festival attended by Rom groups from all over Europe. The celebration is based on three figures: Sara la Kali (Sara 'the Black' or 'the Egyptian'), who is the patron of the Rom, Mary mother of James, and Mary sister of the Virgin.

52 bottom A group of selected men in the church of Saintes Maries carry the statue of Sara on their shoulders to the beach where the figures of the two Marys await in a boat.

53 top left A bishop blesses all those present and then, at the sea, gypsy music accompanies the prayers of the faithful.

53 top right The climax of the first day of festivities is the 'descent of the chests' when the reliquaries of the saints are presented to the worshipers.

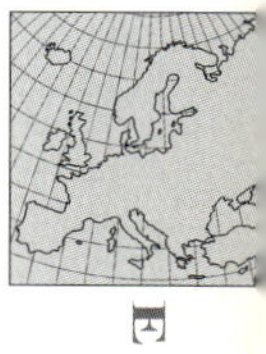

EUROPE

fifteenth century, have constantly kept them on the move or banned their presence. The tragic apotheosis of this reaction came in the twentieth century when no fewer than 400,000 Rom were put to death by the Nazis.

In reply to the discrimination they have suffered, the Rom have always kept themselves away from the settled *gajó* ('people attached to the earth' or 'farmers'). This behavior is founded on a strong sense of identity and group cohesion bolstered by the practice of endogamous marriages. To this should be added a sense of superiority over others that is supported by the myths of their origin. The best known of these myths explains why gypsies have dark skin: God created man by baking clay figurines, and one, which was removed from the fire too early, remained pale and became the forefather of the white race. Another, left to bake too long, became black and was the foremother of the black race. The third, however, which was taken out of the fire just at the right moment, was brown and became the originator of the perfectly formed Rom people.

Rom communities are composed of family groups under the guidance of a chief and a council of elders. The basic social unit is the extended family; strong blood ties bind the men to direct responsibilities held in the family group. Offences given and suffered result in instituted family feuds. The community exerts strong control over the individual, who is bound to conform to standards of behavior. Anyone who breaks the rules risks being punished with excommunication from the group, something the Rom consider the ultimate sanction. Within the family there is a clean separation of roles, with that of the male being predominant. The subordinate position of the woman, however, is reversed in certain aspects of daily life, for example, she has greater decision-making power through the control of her children, she is responsible for the transmission of values in the family, and she contributes to providing for the family with activities like peddling, fortune-telling and begging.

Many Rom communities from around the world gather each year at Saintes-Maries-de-la-Mer in southern France to take part in the pilgrimage in honor of Sara the Egyptian, their patroness. Sara was the servant girl who, according to the syncretistic religious tradition of the Rom, accompanied the two Marys (the mother of James and John, and the sister of the Virgin) who miraculously landed on this beach after the burial and resurrection of Christ.

53 center and bottom right
The origins of the celebration are debatable but nothing can dampen the enthusiasm of the thousands of people present – not just Rom – to acclaim the saints and Sara, whose statue can be seen in the bottom photo.

AFRICA

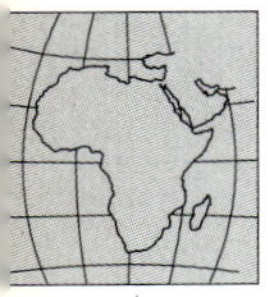

List of peoples

Written by Mirella Ferrera

54 left This man photographed in Kaduna State in northern Nigeria wears two gold disks – symbols of well-being – in his lips; the region has many gold mines.

54 center Very attentive to body care, the Himba sprinkle themselves with ochre and animal grease for aesthetic reasons but it also protects them from the burning sun of northern Namibia.

54 right A Maasai warrior is surrounded by his companions and young girls leaps in the dance that precedes the ceremony in which he will be recognized as a man.

55 Silver jewelry and colored beads adorn the face of a girl from Morogoro in Tanzania. Before the advent of plastic, beads were made from colored seeds.

56-57 Zulu women use a color code to communicate their feelings and desires. White, for example, has more or less the same connotations as in Europe, i.e., purity of heart and innocence. The Zulu are South Africa's largest tribe and, in the past, have also been its most powerful and aggressive. In the nineteenth century these famous warriors created an empire in the southern regions of the continent.

Introduction

Africa is the continent where the earliest fossils relating to human evolution (dating to four million years ago) have been found; it is also the site of the discovery of many items made by archaic forms of the genus *Homo* (from roughly two million years ago) from which the modern *Homo sapiens* descended 120,000 years ago. The hypothesis that has followed from these discoveries is that the origin of the human species may have been in Africa.

Studies by L.L. Cavalli-Sforza on the human genetic map of the original peoples of the continent offer very interesting material on how Africa was populated. According to the ethnocentric and racial approach taken by studies in the past that attempted to retrace the origins of the 'Negro race', the Khoisanids (Bushmen and Hottentots) were the original indigenes of the African continent. In fact this group has an Afro-Asiatic genetic inheritance and anatomic structures that lack the principal Negroid characteristics. It is probable that the Khoisanids originally lived in areas of northeast Africa where they mixed with Asiatic peoples, and that they spread to southern Africa where they have lived to this day.

The continual flow of genes between Africa and Asia would explain the substantial hybridization of African peoples. Groups in eastern Africa, for example, have a significant mix of genes with sub-Saharan, Nilotic and Asiatic types as a result of the interaction of different peoples along the Nile, from the land connection with Asia across the Sinai, and due to navigation across the Indian Ocean. Caucasoid peoples – from whom the Berber are descended (they have a pale skin similar to modern Europeans) – arrived in north Africa across the Iberian Peninsula around 20,000 years ago and from Asia around 10,000 years ago. They were attracted by the development of agriculture in the Near East and its spread westwards. Arabs and Bedouin arrived in more recent epochs when they mixed with the Berber. Around 7,000 years ago, prompted by the progressive drying up of the Saharan area, Nilotic peoples moved southeast to occupy the lands that lie between the southern Nile and the region that extends south of Mount Kilimanjaro where they mixed with Cushitic and Bantu populations. The representatives of a linguistic group that has its origins around Nigeria and Cameroon, the Bantu are comparable in some ways to the Latins of Europe, in that their colonization was essentially linguistic and cultural (ironworking) and of only slight genetic importance.

The peoples that spoke the Bantu language spread throughout sub-Saharan Africa from the sixth century BC and invaded the region inhabited by the Pygmies during their expansion into central Africa. The origin of the Pygmies remains a genetic mystery: a theory has been put forward that they came from the Middle East during successive waves of migration following the shrinking of the forest areas. In this theory, one group headed towards Asia where they gave origin to the Negritos (physically similar to the Pygmies) and another group reached central Africa where it remained isolated in the forest. Their physical structure (the average height of an adult male is 4'10", and their yellowish-brown skin differentiates them from the very black Bantu peoples) shows traces of complex hybridization that is atypical of an indigenous people.

The gene map of Africa confirms strong hybridization of the various peoples but does not throw any light on the origin of the 'Negroid type' whose characteristics are seen right across the continent. The rough division of the many human groups that inhabit the African continent according to their genetic inheritance corresponds in part to the distribution of the principal linguistic families. In Africa around 2,500 languages and dialects are spoken. Greenberg's (1963) linguistic classification was based on the following groups: Khoisanid (the language of the Bushmen and spoken in southern Africa), which is characterized by implosive and avulsive noises that sound like clicks; Niger-Kordofanian, which is divided into the Niger-Congo family (the largest African group and spoken from Senegal to the Congo and including, among others, Bantu subgroups like the language of the Ndebele) and the western Atlantic (Fulani) and Kordofanian language families; Nilo-Saharan (or Western Sudanic), which is spread between mid-Niger and the Nile (including the languages of the Nuba and Maasai); Afro-Asiatic (in the past referred to as 'Hamito-Semitic') which covers the Berber (including that of the Tuareg), Cushitic, ancient Egyptian, Libyan, Amhara and African Arabic languages; and Malayo-Polynesian, which is only spoken in Madagascar. Except for the ancient Egyptians and the Tuareg, no people in Africa has developed a written form of their language. Transmission of traditions is all oral.

The peoples above represent some of the African cultures that will be discussed in this section of the book. Their linguistic differentiation is matched by the different environmental conditions that they inhabit. Attention will be given to the Berber people that lives in northern Africa from the Mediterranean to the edge of the Sahara; the Tuareg "lords of the desert"; the Dogon in Mali, who have built their villages on the edge of a cliff 1,000 feet high; remaining in the desert environment, but in southern Africa, we will discuss the Bushmen of the Kalahari semi-desert and the Himba, who live in a mountainous zone on the edge of the semi-arid Kaokoveld; the Maasai, who tend their herds of cattle on the plains of eastern Africa; and the Pygmies, who inhabit the inhospitable rainforest of central Africa. A point to note is that although certain groups live in different environments – for instance the Bushmen and Pygmies – they may share the same subsistence economy based on hunting and gathering. It is the economic aspect of a culture that determines the way a people exploits its environment and adopts a specific strategy for subsistence. Some of the groups described share what is known as the 'livestock cultural complex', a term that refers to the lifestyle of nomadic stock breeders whose material, social and ritual existence revolves around the possession of animals. The groups that share this complex are the Berber of the Sahara (including the Tuareg), the Fulani (with the Bororo subgroup) in the Sahelian region, the Maasai warriors of Kenya and Tanzania and the Himba in Namibia.

The cultural traits that African herdsmen share, over and beyond their economic strategy, relate to the strong link these groups have with their animals, the possession of which is a source of prestige. Cattle are praised in songs, rarely eaten except on important ritual occasions, and used as a means of exchange in wedding transactions. Another element that herder groups share is the cult of beauty, which they express in constant care of the body and decorations with various styles of jewelry, ornamentation and body paint. The material life of these people also includes spiritual elements that are manifested in religious beliefs, ritual practices and speculation on the mysteries of nature and the world. When considering the religious aspects of the cultures described, an effort has been made to highlight the art and symbolism that exist within their ceremonial life (like the masks used in the ritual dances of the Dogon and the initiation rituals of the Maasai) though these may be simple everyday activities, as is the case in the polyphonic songs of the Pygmies and the decorations of the Ndebele.

The ancient religious beliefs of African peoples coexist with the great monotheistic religions introduced into the continent over the centuries. The Islamicization of the Berber occurred in the seventh century, and the foundation of the Christian Coptic church in Egypt and Ethiopia in the fifth. Then, a thousand years later, with the penetration of the Portuguese into western Africa, the gradual spread of Christianity took hold, spurred by missionaries from Europe and America and the foundation of many Catholic and Protestant missions as early as the beginning of the nineteenth century. Acceptance of the new religions, overlaid on the autochthonous religions, was facilitated by the introduction of social services like scholastic and religious education to the young, economic development projects and health services. Christian missionaries provided a substantial contribution to the spreading of Western culture in Africa, which has been further diffused by colonialism, modern tourism and the continual processes of acculturation in the name of 'progress'.

58 The custom of tattooing children's faces when they are still young is typical of the Sahara and sub-Sahara. The tattooed areas on the faces of Fulani women are generally the forehead, nose, cheeks and corners of the mouth.

58-59 Red turbans emphasize the dignity of the impassive guards of the Emir of Kano. Faithful to ancient Islamic traditions, the princes of this state in northern Nigeria continue to hold public audiences.

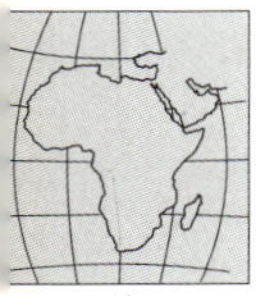

Berber

NORTHERN AFRICA

There are many groups of Berber across northern Africa. They are spread through Morocco, Mauritania, Mali, Niger, Algeria, Tunisia, Libya and Egypt. Generally speaking, the Berber inhabit a variety of environments: the coasts of the Mediterranean and Gulf of Suez, the Atlas mountains in Morocco and the desert expanses of the Sahara. The various groups have different physical characteristics depending on

the degree of Arab blood they have in them (most evident in Egypt and which slowly fades towards the west), but they share many cultural affinities, first and foremost their language. Berber represented the linguistic substrate of all northern Africa before the arrival of Arabic. It was 'Arabized' during the period from the eleventh to thirteenth centuries but also displays influences from the languages of neighboring peoples. The earliest information we have on the Berber reveals that they were influenced by the Phoenicians, Carthaginians, Greeks, Romans, Byzantines and Arabs, but that their geographic provenance was unknown. For that reason, the Berber are considered an indigenous African people. Some scholars have hypothesized that the Guanci people that once lived on the Canary Islands had a Berber descent. Notwithstanding the many invasions and Arabization of their culture, the Berber succeeded in maintaining specific cultural characteristics in their lifestyle, housing and ritual ceremonies. Sedentary Berber groups practice agriculture integrated with the breeding of cattle, sheep, mules, horses and dromedaries. There are few nomadic Berber herdsmen. Berber *fqiq* (spiritual leaders) celebrate ceremonies associated with agricultural and animal-breeding rites in a set of liturgies that includes the invocation of the rain. Their villages consist of typical Mediterranean houses

60 top right *Faithful to her duties, which include collecting wood for the fire, a woman in the valley of the Ait Bou Guemez tribe carries a heavy bundle on her shoulders while her companion watches over the children.*

61 top *A group of men from the Ait Bou Guemez tribe chat at the foot of the Atlas Mountains. Another element of their culture that they have retained is their language, which has quite distinct Arabic origins.*

61 center *The Berber have Mediterranean features, especially in the westernmost areas of their settlement, Tunisia and Morocco.*

61 bottom *Beneath a threatening sky, a group of armed herdsmen from the Ait Haddidou tribe leave Imilchil, in the heart of Morocco. In general, rural Berber villages are built from stone or* pisé *(a mixture of clay, stones and straw) near oases at medium altitude.*

60 left *Berber women collect grass for the livestock near Tabant at the foot of the Atlas Mountains. In the background are a group of buildings typical of the mountains: solid and almost closed, they are designed to retain the heat; in the past they also used to protect the villages from bandit raids.*

60-61 *A family in Ait Bou Guemez sets out on a journey on muleback. Berbers were converted to Islam in the eighth century but have maintained monogamy, one of their earlier customs.*

Berber

63 bottom left Despite her young age, this girl from the Ait Haddidou tribe at the Imilchil festival is either divorced or a widow, as the black dots on the red patches on her face indicate.

63 bottom right A government official confirms a wedding contract. The youngest girls are obliged to spend a 'trial period' of a year before the wedding but widows and divorced women can marry immediately.

62 With her face adorned with traditional ochre marks on a saffron yellow background, this young wife has just removed her veil. Berber women only wear a veil on their wedding day or from personal choice.

63 top A line of women wait by the gates of Imilchil for a possible husband. The town is famous for its bridal festival where young girls, divorced women and widows can find a consort.

64 top left A group of horsemen race through the dust and smoke in a field just outside Meknés during the Fantasia, one of Morocco's most traditional events.

64 bottom left The commemoration of a warrior past not so long left behind, the Fantasia is a thrilling event accompanied by the insistent trilling that Berber women give off to encourage their men in battle.

64 top right White burnous dazzle in the light before the cavalcade. The Fantasia only lasts a few minutes but for this reason is emotively intense.

64-65 In addition to the horsemen, the protagonists of this event are the horses. They are either magnificent Berber or descendants of Arab thoroughbreds imported during the seventh century. These steeds are small, fast and reliable.

65 An engrossed horseman clutches his heavy arquebus. The Fantasia is derived from an earlier contest disputed with crossbows, and, since the seventeenth century, with long-barreled rifles decorated with embossed metal.

with a terrace. They are generally fortified with towers and walls made from stone or compressed earth, and their most interesting architectural style is seen in the fortified towns of the *casbah*. The tents of the herdsmen are made from goatskin supported by wooden poles, and the floors are lined with rugs.

In Arab-Berber culture, the basic social unit is the extended patriarchal family. When they marry (using the Islamic ritual), women join the family group of their husband. Female adultery is considered a serious crime and an offence to the husband; in the regrettable event that a woman should be accused of adultery, she is repudiated and must return to her own family.

A series of related extended families that share the same progenitor form a *kharruba* (clan). *Douar* (villages) inhabited by different clans together form a tribal organization called a *cabila* headed by a *caid* (chief) who is chosen for his courage and wisdom. The authority of the *caid* is controlled by the Council of Elders and Assembly of Wise Men (*djemma*) appointed to run the village administration, oversee the oral transmission of tribal customs and regulate conflict or feuds. In cases of murder, the family of the aggressor must hand over 'blood money' of goods, livestock, services, etc., to the relatives of the victim as a symbolic recompense for the loss of a loved one. If the payment is not made, a family feud becomes inevitable and a vendetta may ensue until the parties reach an agreement. Important goods sectors of the Berber are wool rugs hand-knotted by women under the control of the men, the production of fabrics and crockery decorated with geometric patterns, exquisitely decorated metal objects, and finely engraved bronze and silver jewelry. In recent years the Berber culture has risen in estimation: the Western tourist industry has discovered the 'exoticness' of the Berber peoples and the places they live, whilst also offering them an acceptable means of economic development. In addition, the North African states where the Berber live are attempting to revive their cultural backgrounds, which they consider fundamental to the construction and strengthening of their respective national identities.

Berber

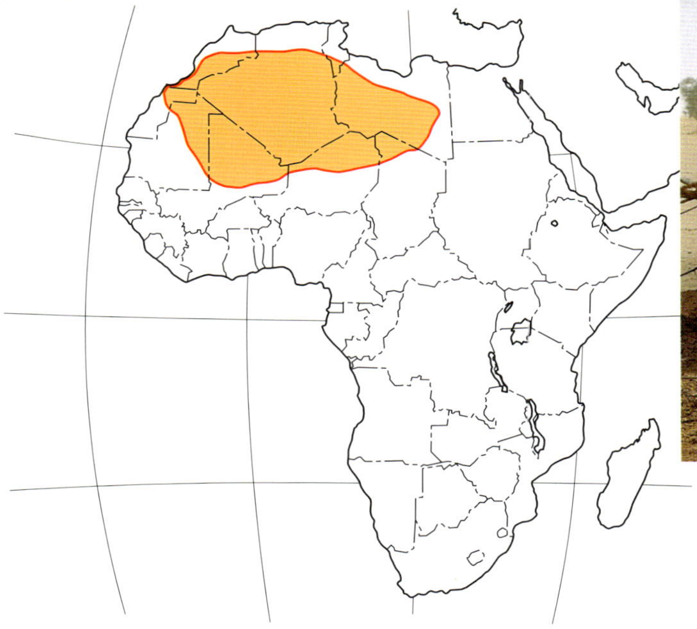

Tuareg

WESTERN SAHARA

Spread throughout the western Sahara, the 300,000 people that make up the Tuareg people live in Algeria, southeast Morocco, Libya, Mali and Niger. The different *kel* (tribes) speak variants of the Tamacheq language that was originally derived from Berber, and they still have their own form of writing called *tifinagh* that is similar to the ancient writing that used to exist right across North Africa.

Their different economic activities are mainly based on nomadic herding and reflect the three ancient strata of their society: nobles, freemen and slaves. The nobles, who once made up the ancient warrior class, breed dromedaries and entrust the breeding of goats and sheep to their vassals; their servants and former black slaves are responsible for performing the crafts, agricultural and domestic tasks for the benefit of their caste superiors.

66 A group of 'blue men' head into the desert from Merzouga oasis in northeast Morocco. With a longstanding reputation as robbers, today the Tuareg have now been partially integrated into the fabric of the various states in which they live.

67 top Wells are the crucial landmarks on journeys across the semi-arid Sahel, not simply for the provision of water but also for social contact between members of the caravans. Otherwise, they might travel for over a month at a time without encountering any other human.

67 center The Tuareg's 'black tents' meet their logistical requirements perfectly: they are easy to put up and take down and lined with dark clay to give the goatskins greater resistance.

67 bottom The greenish-brown eyes and black hair of this Tuareg girl show that she has Berber blood in her. Like many northern African peoples, the Tuareg have their roots in the Paleolithic period.

68 and 69 The taguelmust *is the characteristic turban of the Tuareg. It is often blue but might also be white or black. They are not just practical for protecting their faces from the sun and wind but also cultural as their use is related to the reluctance of Saharan people to show their mouths for fear of inhaling evil spirits.*

The nomadic lifestyle of the Tuareg requires light and easily assembled dwellings. For this reason they are made from goatskins colored with dark clay and supported by bamboo poles; alternatively, they are domed structures formed by branches covered with matting.

Tuareg culture shows many influences accumulated over a very long period. The heirs of the ancient Garamanti people cited by the historian Herodotus, the Tuareg are also called the 'blue men' for the *taguelmust* (indigo turbans) worn by the men that reveal only their eyes. The origins of the ancient custom of hiding their faces are obscure: some experts

70 top Another common form of shelter is the dome, formed by a frame of branches covered with matting.

70 center and bottom Life in Tuareg camps is very simple but not poor, either practically, culturally or educationally. In the picture at the bottom, a group of girls chants traditional verses under the guidance of a 'singing teacher'.

70-71 As usually occurs for nomadic populations, furnishing of Tuareg tents is reduced to the minimum: matting, rugs, a few plates and the tarija (drums to make the desert nights less solitary).

71 right The frame of the dome tent is made from reasonably flexible sticks of wood fixed with dromedary hide straps. The Tuareg in Niger and Chad more frequently use this type of tent.

connect it with the men's reluctance to show their mouths to women or strangers (a custom that is still common among many Saharan peoples). However, the women, even though they are mostly Moslem, do not cover their faces in any manner. Unlike other Islamic societies, Tuareg women enjoy a certain degree of freedom and remarkable importance inside the community; in particular, they are the only depositary of the people's oral traditions. The family structure is matrilineal, which is an inheritance from their Berber forbears, whilst the caste stratification system comes from the Arab-Moslem culture.

It was the Arab merchants that spread Islam to the Berber people when they entrusted trading across the trans-Saharan trading routes to the indigenous people. Thus the Tuareg used their dromedary caravans to transport gold, salt and dates, which they exchanged for millet, cereals and fabrics.

A hangover from the period of the desert crossings is the tea ritual that used to take place round the fire at the evening camp. The tea would be served three times: once for the guest, once for oneself and once for Allah. Each time the tea was boiled up it would be served with a different grade of sugar, each of which was associated with an emotion. They could be served in any order, depending on the pleasure or mood of the officiator of the tea ceremony: the first could be strong like love, the second bitter like life and the third sweet like death.

In recent times the Tuareg tribes have been pressured politically to submit to state structures but attempts to settle them are mostly in vain due to the reluctance, common to all nomads, of accepting any restriction on their movements. For this reason the Tuareg groups have been marginalized,

which has led to outright conflict with governments. Following the extreme droughts of the 1970s and 1990s, which seriously struck the Tuareg economy, refugee camps were built in Niger and Mauritania in which revolts were common. However, the expansion of tourism in Saharan countries has offered this people the possibility of integrating without giving up their independence. Having avoided the threat of urban migration, many Tuareg now work happily in the tourist industry. One of the few peoples in the world to retain an aura of myth, the 'blue men' seem destined to continue to cross the oceans of sand and time unharmed.

Tuareg

72-73 Every five days the mesmerizing, ochre-colored landscape of Sangha in Mali is enlivened by the colors and noise of a busy market. The main commercial products grown by the Dogon are tobacco, cotton and henna.

72 bottom left French and Arab lessons are held in the village school in Suan in Mali. To survive, the Dogon are obliged to accept modern ideas in parallel with their own, extremely rich culture.

72 bottom right Conical roofs of straw, towers and terraced houses made from dried mud and stone: Younga-Na is a typical Dogon village, one of the roughly 700 lining the foot of the cliff on Bandiagara Plateau. The architecture of this surprising people is all centered on a philosophical and spiritual concept of the human body.

73 Contrary to several fantastic hypotheses regarding an extra-terrestrial origin of the Dogon, the physical appearance of this people does not vary from the predominant one in western Africa. In this sense the 'official' history of this people confirms their oral tradition: that their forebears came from the west bank of the Niger.

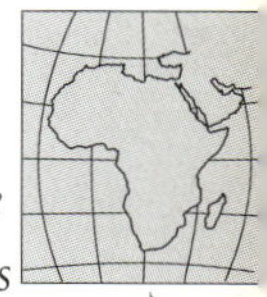

Dogon

MALI

In many ways the Dogon are one of the most remarkable people in all of Africa. This is also the case for where they live, perched on a sandstone cliff 1,000 feet high on Bandiagara Plateau, in a region that lies between Mali and Upper Volta south of the Niger River. The layout of the villages and individual houses is based on Dogon cosmology and the dual symbolism of the male-female principle associated with the couple and fertility. These are elements of absolute importance to the continuity of the family and the entire community. Granaries are built in a tapered parallelepiped shape next to the houses and covered with a conical roof. In the center of the village the *toguna* ('house of the men') is the meeting point for all the circumcised adult men and the seat of the Council of the Elders; it is also consecrated to the ancestors and where ritual sacrifices and ceremonies are carried out. The Dogon recognize the authority of a religious leader, the *hogon*, who also acts as a judge in the event of disputes. The *hogon* is the custodian of the myths of creation and responsible for their oral transmission; before the advent of Islam, he was also the village's supreme religious authority.

In the Dogon cosmogony, the creator of the universe was the god Amma, whose dual nature is emblematic of the fundamental dualist elements of nature (life and death, male and female, etc.) that permeate Dogon symbolism.

Their economy is agricultural and generally practiced in fields quite distant from the villages. They grow basic foodstuffs such as rice, maize and millet, but also commercial products like cotton, tobacco and henna. The Dogon calendar revolves around the seasonal cycle and the year begins with the harvesting of the millet in mid-October and is celebrated with a large feast.

In Dogon society the castes linked to crafts (blacksmiths, tanners and sculptors) are considered inferior to the extent that the men who belong to them are not circumcised. The blacksmiths are both feared and looked down upon at the

74 and 75 Dogon dances are not held in a particular place but are celebrated during processions down the rough, narrow paths from the top of the Bandiagara cliffs. Their traditional masks, some of the most beautiful in Africa, are carved by craftsmen who can never wear them: only circumcised men have the right to dance wearing a mask, and the woodcarvers, though a feared class, do not belong to that caste.

same time: its members understand the mystery of fire and are also healers. The tanners dye and decorate the skins bought from the herdsmen from whom they make sandals, bags and belts, but it is the sculptors who are the main figures in Dogon craftsmanship. They are some of the best-known African artists, with their magnificently carved masks, doors, door posts and various objects. Only uncircumcised men can be part of the 'society of the mask', which they enter in an initiation ceremony celebrated in the woods, when novices are admitted to the secrets and mythical beliefs of the group. Despite the strong Islamic influence in the region, the Dogon have maintained their traditional customs and the religious beliefs regarding their origins.

Their masks are used in celebrations and ceremonial dances dedicated to the ancestors, the fertility of the fields (held during sowing and harvest periods) and the honor paid to the dead, like the ceremony that celebrates the end of the mourning period with the conclusion of the social and eating prohibitions placed on the members of the deceased's family. The purpose of this ritual is to re-establish the order of things, upset by death, by recreating harmony between men. The ceremony may last for several days in its aim to accompany the soul of the deceased safely to the kingdom of the dead. Sometimes, however, it is celebrated long after the death of an individual due to the expenses that the family of the deceased must bear to offer food and drink to the guests. The dead are buried outside the living area in difficult to reach trenches among the rocks.

Stylistically and functionally the models of the Dogon masks vary from simple wooden representations of mythological creatures like the *walu* (oryx) to the *sirigi*, which is a sort of narrow, heavy frame nearly 30 feet high that dancers support with just their teeth.

In recent years migration from the villages to towns and cities has caused a depopulation of the Dogon's rural zones. Nonetheless, this fascinating people has an extremely varied and deep-seated culture: an attribute that alone will ensure the survival of any people.

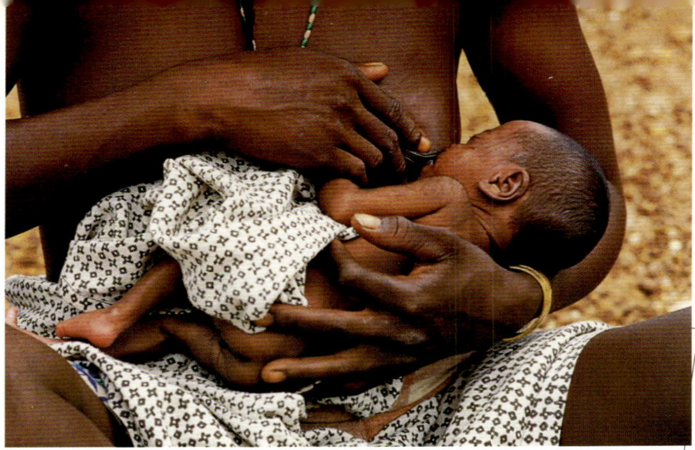

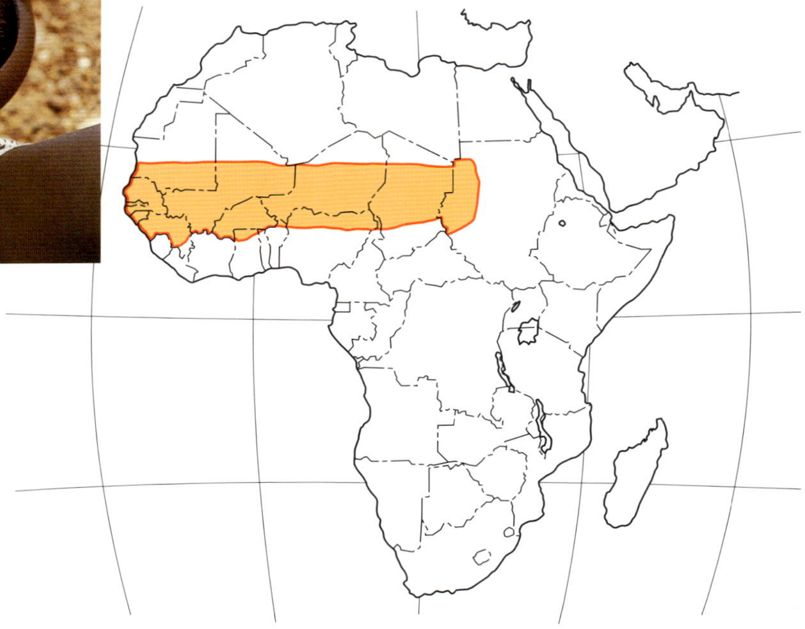

Fulani

SAHEL

Many groups of Fulani people are spread across the Sahel from the Atlantic coast of Senegal to Chad and even as far as eastern Sudan where the peoples of Arab origin refer to them as *Fellata*. Pastoral nomads also known as Fulbe or by the French term *Peul*, the Fulani speak the Fulaar dialect of the Fulfulde language, which is classified in the Niger-Congo linguistic group.

The origins of this people are thought to have been in Libya or southern Egypt from where, at some unknown point in time, they moved westwards towards the coast. Islamicized around the thirteenth century, the Fulani began to penetrate the interior around the same period, progressively occupying the areas that they now inhabit.

With strong warring traditions, the Fulani quickly set up powerful centralized states and expanded their influence until the early nineteenth century when several Islamicized groups of followers of Uthman dan Fodio subjected the Hausa kingdoms in Niger and founded the Moslem Empire of Sokoto. Subsequent European interference in the region led rapidly to the decline of Fulani power but they managed to retain many of their customs dating to the period of their greatest authority, including the traditional social division in classes. Fulbe society is still composed of castes, comprising the nobility, cattle-owners, herdsmen, the servile castes of the craftsmen and the cultivators who are descended from black slaves (agriculture is a scorned livelihood).

The Fulani are not Negroid in appearance and are the result of the mixture of the fair-skinned desert Berber people and groups from western Africa whose skin is much darker.

Their society is founded on the patriarchal family and the patriarch's ownership of all the land on which the blood group lives, as well as its livestock and buildings. For those who can afford it, marriage is polygamous and based on the 'bride price', which is a sort of reverse dowry in that it represents the sum paid to the family of the bride by the family of the groom.

Though profoundly Islamicized, in some isolated areas the Fulani still retain beliefs from remote times of their history founded on the cult of Mother Earth.

76 top left Traditionally a warrior people, the Fulani have retained several racial and cultural characteristics of the Libyan-Berber peoples. Exclusively pastoral, they leave all other jobs to neighboring peoples.

76 top right A Fulbe woman suckles her child. The Fulani are currently estimated to number around 15 million, two-thirds of which live in Nigeria.

76 bottom The facial features of this herdsman, with his tattooed face and few hair braids, are very different to those of the Negroid peoples with which his people share the sub-Saharan region.

77 The hair of this young girl is styled in typical Fulani fashion with strips of cotton worn above the forehead. The Fulani are tattooed during infancy.

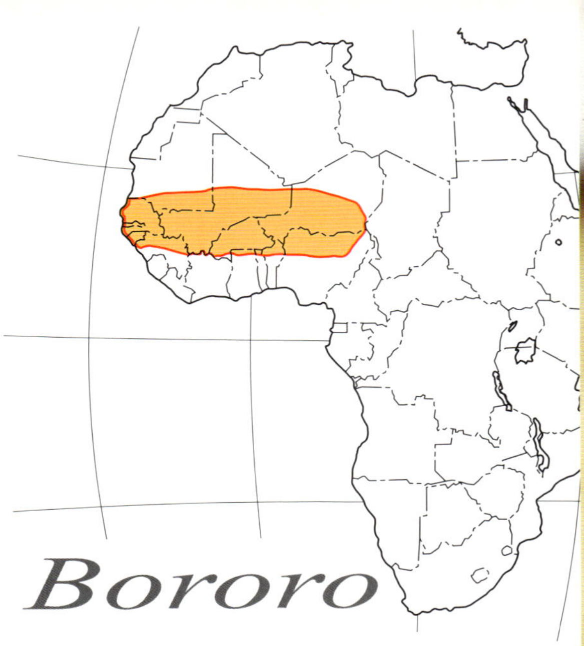

Bororo

SAHEL

The Bororo are nomadic herdsmen who live between Senegal and Niger and belong to the largest ethnic group of the Fulani (or Fulbe) people distributed throughout western Africa. The Bororo refer to themselves by the name Wodâabe and speak a dialect of the Fulfulde language, similar to Bantu, that is classified as part of the Niger-Congo linguistic family. Most of the Bororo live in Niger where small groups settled at the start of the nineteenth century in the areas conquered by

followers of Uthman dan Fodio, the founder of the Moslem Empire of Sokoto.

One of the last peoples in Africa to live a fully nomadic existence, the Bororo breed *zebu* (Djibouti oxen used as beasts of burden), goats and camels. They drive their herds as they follow the seasonal grazing pattern. Like all pastoral tribes, their livestock is of great importance to them as the prestige of a man and his family is directly represented by the number of head he owns. The women are responsible for milking the animals and selling the products in the market place.

Individual families are formed by a man, his various wives and unmarried children; they live in simple dome-shaped huts grouped in villages. Each village is a stable camp under the authority of a spiritual leader. The Council of Elders makes the decisions affecting the good of the entire community and negotiations with settled communities regarding the transit of the Bororo. Polygamy is widespread among the Bororo, particularly among richer

78 top right Bororo social life is based on widespread participation, including the maintenance of children: a mother with many children may entrust the care of some of them to a sterile woman.

78 left A herdsman with long-horned Djibouti zebu*. This is the animal most bred by the Bororo and a fundamental element of their economy. The number of head owned by a man determines his social prestige.*

79 top right *The large gold rings worn in this young girl's ears are one of the most highly prized ornaments among Bororo women. When they realize they are being observed, Bororo women are expected to lower their gaze.*

79 bottom *Traditionally preoccupied by beauty, both Bororo men and women never neglect their appearance, which is an unusual characteristic for a warrior people. Bororo morality is founded on virtues like strength of spirit, modesty and patience.*

78-79 and 79 top left *Milk is collected in large gourds and either drunk fresh or treated and dried. It forms almost all of the herdsmen's diet. Deep knowledge of the territory through which they travel allows the Bororo to select their grazing sites shrewdly in order to benefit the reproductive capacity of their livestock as much as possible.*

80 *With his face sprinkled with saffron, his eyes and mouth marked with kohl and a vertical line to render his nose longer and slimmer, this young man is ready to demonstrate the most appreciated aspects of beauty among the Bororo.*

81 *top left Highly symbolic and codified ceremonial tunics provide a sort of graphical narration of the history of the family of the wearer.*

81 *top right The turban worn during the beauty dance is created using a strip of fabric nearly 12 feet long.*

81 *center and bottom right The dancers line up shoulder to shoulder and begin a pantomime of exaggerated smiles, eye-rolling and snorting that the jury (lined up in front and composed only of women) assesses carefully.*

men who can afford more than one dowry. The dowry is generally made in the form of cattle.

Generally, marriages are agreed between families and are endogamous, i.e., the choice is made among the members of the community. The preferable arrangement is for marriage between patrilineal cousins, i.e., the children of brothers of the head of the family. After the ceremony the bride moves into her husband's hut and is welcomed by the women of the village with a festive ritual.

Marriage confers great dignity on the married couple, in particular if they have children. Paternity makes a man to all effects an adult member of the group, and motherhood increases a woman's social status, especially if she gives birth to male children.

The Wodâabe attribute great importance to the cult of beauty, which they celebrate in traditional songs and dances. The care they pay to appearance is clearly evident in the *gerewol* ceremony that marks the end of the rainy season. This is a beauty competition in which the young men of different tribes participate, attempting to win with elaborate hairstyles and facial decoration and by how they exhibit themselves in the dances. The purpose of the *gerewol* is for the men to attract a wife, as the young women use the competition to choose a future husband. For this reason the young Bororo men spend hours preparing their faces with particular attention paid to the elements that are considered the most important in masculine beauty: their eyes and teeth. During the competition itself, the men roll their eyes and force their smiles into exaggerated positions, a tactic that seems to bring success with the girls. Once a young man has been chosen, the girl in question drags him off into the undergrowth for a prematrimonial trial, in which he may or may not live up to his personal beauty.

Though Islam exists among the Bororo, the tribe enjoy a certain sexual freedom, a characteristic that would appear to go straight against the name that this people has chosen for itself: Wodâabe actually means 'people of the taboos'. The term refers to the social code they have inherited from their forefathers in which the most important elements are loyalty, modesty, discretion, foresight and patience.

82 top left *Created by manual application of lime and ochre dissolved in water, the body decorations of the Surma use many forms, most of which are idealized and inspired by nature, for example, snakes, waves or sun disks. The patterns are purely for aesthetic reasons and have no ritual symbolism.*

Surma

ETHIOPIA

The Sua and the Mursi are the two autochthonous tribal peoples that inhabit the Omo Basin in southern Ethiopia. The term 'Surma' is used by neighboring groups belonging to the Cushitic ethno-linguistic group (i.e., coming from northeast Africa), for example the Sidama, Borana and Gabbra (Oromo groups), to refer generically to the 'black' tribes in southern Ethiopia distinguished by clearly apparent Negroid physical features.

Settled in an isolated area that is not easily reached near the Omo River (a tributary of Lake Turkana), the Surma live in villages of huts dispersed in the undergrowth. Their economy is predominantly pastoral but they also indulge in hunting, gathering and the cultivation of maize, beans and sorghum due to the relative fertility of the alluvial soil between the Omo River and Lake Chew Bahir. The Surma use the sorghum to make an alcoholic drink called *borday* that they traditionally drink at funerary celebrations. They hunt large game (mostly elephants and hippopotamuses) in groups and with the help of trained dogs.

The other peoples that live in the alluvial Omo Basin – with which the Surma share many customs and ethno-linguistic similarities – are the Nilotic groups of the Arboré, Bume, Dassanetch, Hamer, Karo and Tid peoples. The culture of the Surma comprises a number of overlapping elements: the Surma have maintained various archaic cultural traits typical of the Paleonegritic culture of the area such as the ancient Omotic language and the almost total nudity of

both sexes. A very evident feature of their culture is the custom of inserting a large balsawood or terracotta disk in the lower lip as a sign of tribal identity and ornamentation, but it is also a useful means of indicating the size of the dowry paid by the family of a husband to that of the bride. The size of the disk (or sometimes wedge) is directly proportional to the number of cattle that are generally used as payment in this type of transaction.

All these elements have been overlaid with cultural aspects of Cushitic and Nilotic origin as a result of contact with pastoral groups in the zone.

Examples of the pastoral cultural system are the class structure based on age, the initiation rites at puberty of circumcision and the insertion of the disk in the lower lip and the practice of carrying a spear, wooden or leather shield and the horseshoe-shaped armband-cum-knife common among Nilotic warriors.

Another feature of the Surma's existence is the theist

82 top right *The large disks that Surma women use as earrings and lip ornaments are made from baked clay colored with ochre.*

82 center *The first disk is inserted at the age of 20. It is small and replaced by larger ones at regular intervals.*

82 bottom *Lip ornamentation is partly aesthetic (the Surma consider them attractive) but also 'economic' as the size of the disk represents the size of the dowry (in head of cattle) asked by parents for their daughter as a bride.*

82-83 *Body paintings are used to extol beauty and attract the opposite sex (and in the case of men to intimidate adversaries) but also stress friendships: adolescents in particular paint themselves with the same patterns as their best friends. The most skilful artists (generally males) often help to decorate other members of the group.*

84 top left *Women are obliged to wear their lip disk even when eating and drinking, only in the presence of men or during ritual ceremonies.*

84 top right *One of the functions of body painting for men is to emphasize physical strength.*

84 center *The staffs used in stick fights are being raised in the center of this group. Over eight feet long, they are very strong but only weigh about two pounds.*

84 bottom *Sometimes the lip disks are wedge-shaped; in this case they are not made from clay but balsawood.*

85 *As the intact lower lip of this girl indicates, she has not yet reached marriageable age.*

religion and their belief in good and bad spirits in animals, trees and mountains; both these aspects are typical of other pastoral cultures in the area.

The Surma are also known for their body decorations made using colors obtained from lime and ochre dissolved in water and applied with the fingers. Both men and women, but especially the former, spend hours decorating themselves with spirals, concentric circles and patches of color. The aim is primarily aesthetic and even the occasional symbolic motif is more likely to be inspired by its artistic patterns than its value in cult purposes. For the Surma the body is a means of expression, and practically the only one available to them given that this people hardly wears clothes or ornaments.

The most remarkable ceremony in the Surma culture – considered one of the most impressive in all Africa – is the fighting with *donga* (staffs) for the purposes of winning a wife. The champions from the different villages meet in an agreed location where they fight one another for hours using long staffs carved at the end in the shape of a phallus. The aim of the fight is to floor the opponent and the only rule in the contest is that killing is not allowed.

At the end of this cruel clash, the bruised and bloodstained winner is carried in triumph before the young girl spectators who decide between them who gets to marry the victor.

The extension of the tourist industry into the more inaccessible areas of Africa and elsewhere in the world has inevitably brought the Surma beneath the curious and intrusive gaze of adventurous travelers. Outsiders such as these come with their invasive cameras in search of 'sensational' photographs of exotic or primitive tribes. Although these visitors are most probably unaware of the fact, their repeated visits contribute in part to accelerating the Surma's cultural break-up.

The point has been reached where the Surma demand payment to be photographed and are seemingly unwilling to accept visitors who arrive without a camera, as they bring no gain to the group.

86-87 The soft light of dawn enflames the dust raised by the large herds the Maasai drive to the grazing areas. Herdsmen since time immemorial, until a few decades ago the Maasai were also warriors and today, given their traditional attitude to weapons, many youngsters work as armed guards in the parks.

86 bottom left The term kraal *refers to the livestock enclosure but has been extended to signify the settlement of round huts (sometimes brightly decorated like this but near Lake Baringo) that circle the animal pen.*

86 bottom right Maasai women clean and arrange in the pack-saddles the hydrous sodium carbonate that they have collected around Lake Natron. The salt is sold as caustic soda and is an important resource for the local peoples.

Maasai

KENYA AND TANZANIA

Traditionally a warlike people, the Maasai probably originated in the Nilotic region of northern Africa from where, around the fifteenth century, they moved down to the region crossed by the Great Rift Valley in Kenya and Tanzania. The Maasai speak the Maa language, which is classified in the Niger-Congo group, and breed *zebu*, cattle, goats and donkeys. Their livestock is kept in their villages inside large *kraal* (enclosures formed by thorn-bushes and, by extension, also the name for the village itself), and the huts are arranged in circles around the *kraal*. The huts are formed by a framework of branches lined with mud and cow dung, which together form an effective insulator against the heat and the rain.

The Maasai's daily life revolves around the possession of livestock, which is their only source of sustenance. During seasonal migration, the herds provide most of the Maasai's diet in the form of milk and blood (and more rarely meat). The blood is drawn from the animals by making a hole in the jugular vein with an arrow and then collected in a bowl; the wound is then closed with mud and grass. The cattle provide the Maasai with a series of useful products: horns provide tobacco boxes and containers, the skins are tanned and used to make sleeping mats and the dung is used to make the material the huts are lined with.

In general, the livestock is used in exchange for agricultural products cultivated by nearby farming peoples (*kikuyu*) and, in exceptional cases, sold. One of the main purposes of the herd is to pay the 'bride price', which is a sort of remuneration in kind paid by the future husband to the family of the bride.

Cattle are always at the center of the most important ceremonies, as these require the sacrifice of a number of animals and the distribution of their meat to the community as a whole. The Maasai traditionally raids herds and flocks, as, for the Nilotic herdsmen of eastern Africa, cattle-rustling is a way of life, and each group justifies it with its own creation myth. The Maasai myth says that God gave cattle only to them and that, in consequence, all the other peoples

87 top *A group of herdsmen from the village of Olonana (visible in the distance) lead their livestock across a ford in the Mara River. The river flows into Lake Victoria on the Tanzanian shore.*

87 bottom *Maasai children spend much of their time playing freely. A typical game is to look after pretend herds in which the cattle are represented by colored stones.*

88 top left A herd of work animals are left free to graze outside a kraal while others are loaded with pack-saddles.

88 top right The morning mist is brightened by the bright red capes of two Maasai. Red is typical of the fierce pride of this people.

88 bottom left A Maasai woman makes a bead ornament. Bracelets and necklaces of this kind are typical of the Maasai and refer directly to the age and status of their wearers.

88-89 A barrier of wood and shrubs protects the perimeter of the circle of mud and straw huts in a typical Maasai settlement. The huts ring the kraal (animal enclosure) formed by irregularly shaped poles.

89 top In a region that offers little construction material, thorn-bushes offer the best defense for the settlements and, even more important to the Maasai, for the livestock.

89 right Wrapped in typical Maasai red capes, a woman and herdsman chat facing towards the entrance to the kraal.

Maasai

90 *Before undergoing clitorectomy, young Maasai girls enjoy a certain freedom. Inseparable from the warriors, they are recognized as 'official' girlfriends even if, due to their age, their relationships are chaste.*

91 *top and center left The elders, both men and women, generally wear a simple wool blanket instead of the* chukka *(red cape) and always wear earrings and beaded ornaments.*

91 *bottom left Ears are pierced in both boys and girls when very young. The holes are gradually widened until they reach a remarkable size.*

91 *right The Maasai preference for red – also common to similar peoples like the Samburu – is probably connected to the color of animal blood, which to them is a source of life and an important form of nourishment.*

92 top Maasai warriors help each other in the long and laborious business of 'making up', when they sprinkle their bodies with a mixture of ochre and lamb fat.

must be thieves. Rustling therefore becomes necessary to 'retrieve' what has been taken from them. Myths apart, rustling and breeding are fundamental to the livelihood of the herdsmen, who organize raids on the herds of neighboring tribes in particular to build up herds that have suffered from drought, illness or raids by others. Rustling is considered a test of courage and a way for *murran* (warriors) to demonstrate their personal value to the defense of the community and its assets.

Maasai boys can only become warriors by undergoing initiation rites and, between the ages of 14 and 30, by studying as warriors under the guidance of the elders. During this period, they mostly live isolated in the savannah, far from the care and support of their families, where they must pass several tests of courage. During periods of drought it is the duty of the apprentice warriors to take the cattle to mountain grazing areas.

The end of the *moranato* (a sort of military service) is

92 bottom Thick ochre ointment is rubbed into a warrior's hair. The length of their braids depends on the time that has passed since their passage from one age group to the next. At the end of the Eunoto (the celebration that marks the end of the Maasai warrior 'apprenticeship'), the head of the murran (warrior) is completely shaved by his mother and he enters the circle of adult men. Each passage brings new and greater responsibilities.

celebrated in the village with animal sacrifices and dances in which the Maasai warriors demonstrate their extraordinary leaps. Once this ritual is completed, the young men are recognized as adults and can enter the life of the community and form their own family. Only after these ceremonies – celebrated by the *laibon* (spiritual leaders) – is it possible to inaugurate a new class of warriors. Analogous to other Nilotic herdsmen, the Maasai are organized in a class system based on age: for example, one class is filled by young circumcised boys to which they belong for a period of 14 or 15 years. Bonds between the members of the group are formed that may last an entire lifetime.

The initiation ritual of the young girls requires circumcision of the clitoris, which is considered indispensable to marriageability and the passage into the life of the adult women.

Maasai society recognizes the authority of the elders, who are respected and looked up to by all. The spiritual leadership of the group and administration of justice are the functions of the Council of Elders, which judges cases both at an individual level and for the entire community.

Currently the governments of Kenya and Tanzania are attempting to cut down on the pastoral activities of the Maasai and other nomadic herdsmen by confining them to reserves and introducing settled agriculture. The most direct consequence of this measure is that many youngsters choose to abandon the villages and pastoral life and search for work in the cities or tourist industry. In the latter they often end up participating in meaningless shows of ethnic folklore for the benefit of Western tourists.

92-93 The moranato *is a sort of military service inaugurated by circumcision around the age of 15 or 16. However, the* murran *are only considered 'real men' at the end of the* moranato, *which lasts for 14 years.*

93 right Under the critical eye of his moranato *companions, a warrior makes a characteristic leap in the Maasai dance known as* empatia. *Athletic ability and courage are highly considered virtues among this proud and physically strong people.*

94-95 *In a dugout canoe, a group of men leave to gather food. It is probable that the Pygmies, who arrived in the area before the Bantu, were the earliest human inhabitants of the inhospitable forests of Zaire.*

94 bottom *A fisherman armed with a bow waits to pierce a fish with an arrow. Fishing and gathering are the most important sources of food for the various Pygmy groups.*

95 top *The smile of this adolescent shows the effect of a highly painful rite: the filing down of the teeth which all Pygmies undergo before being considered adults.*

95 center *Two women select the most suitable leaves in the forest near the Komo River to cover a* mongolu, *the Pygmies' dome-shaped hut.*

95 bottom *When completed the* mongolu *is almost indistinguishable from the undergrowth. In addition to other tasks, the women are responsible for construction of the camps.*

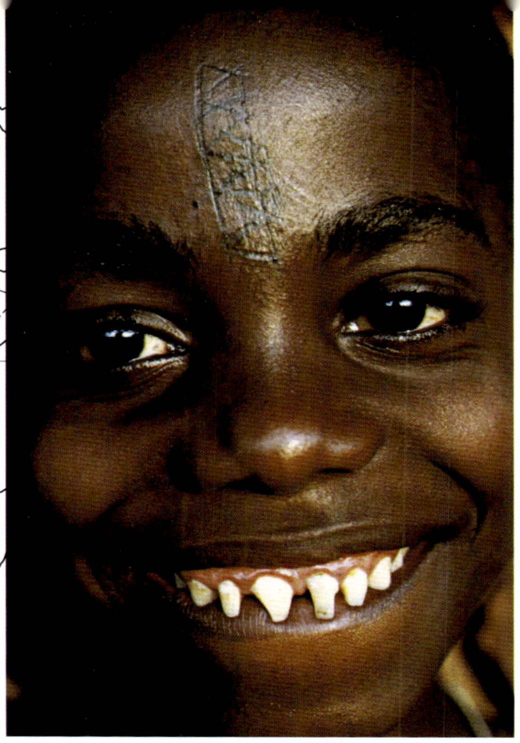

Pygmies

ZAIRE

The 200,000 Pygmies that currently live in the forests of central Africa are descended from an indigenous people that lives in the same region in ancient times. Certain Egyptian documents mention their existence in the area 4,500 years ago and refer to them as 'inhabitants of the forest and dancers of the gods'. Divided into different groups, they are profoundly different physically from other central African peoples. So noted for their short stature that the word 'pygmy' has entered vocabularies to mean a small person, they have yellowish-brown skin and are markedly steatopygous; they have always been discriminated against – if not exterminated – by neighboring peoples who consider them inferior and untrustworthy. For their part, the Pygmies have a sense of aesthetics that considers their neighbors – as tall as they are black (Tutsi or Watussi herdsmen for example) –clumsy and graceless due to their size; the Pygmies think them 'as large as elephants'.

Pygmies are hunter-gatherers organized in family groups who have always had relationships with the nearby agricultural or pastoral peoples, obtaining agricultural products, metal tools, alcohol and tobacco from exchanges and adopting their languages. The Pygmies view the forest as a mother's womb, a source of protection and nourishment. It provides all they need for survival, from materials for the construction of their domed huts covered with leaves to their hunting requirements. The collection of tubers, larvae, honey and termites – which provide 70% of their nourishment – is the job of the women, while hunting – prescribed by such requirements as sexual abstinence – is the duty of the men and provides the remaining 30%. Before starting out on a hunt, in which women and children sometimes take part as drum beaters, propitiatory and purification ceremonies are held with the lighting of a ritual fire.

Apart from these rituals and the commemoration of ancestors, Pygmies pass little time in ceremonies, but music and dance are parts of daily life. Songs accompanied by drums and other percussion instruments are associated with important events like preparing for a hunt or the celebrations at a birth or wedding and with everyday situations like gathering food, evenings around the fire and the domestic setting. The Pygmies speak the Bantu languages used by their neighbors but also have their own 'language', which is expressed in a wordless song of isolated sounds and shouts woven around a principal melody intoned by the singer. The song is therefore a 'language without words' and is a means of expressing the secret language of the forest. Using it, the Pygmies communicate with the spirits of the forest whom they ask to be generous. Their polyphonic songs are handed on from generation to generation orally, i.e., by listening, learning and repeating.

Deforestation for wood-felling or to create space for coffee plantations is reducing the Pygmies' capacity for hunting and gathering, but even the programs instituted to protect them are counteractive as they oblige the Pygmies to abandon the areas transformed into reserves or national parks and to adopt a settled farming lifestyle favored by the authorities. And this, sooner or later, could silence forever the ancient melodious voices of this threatened people.

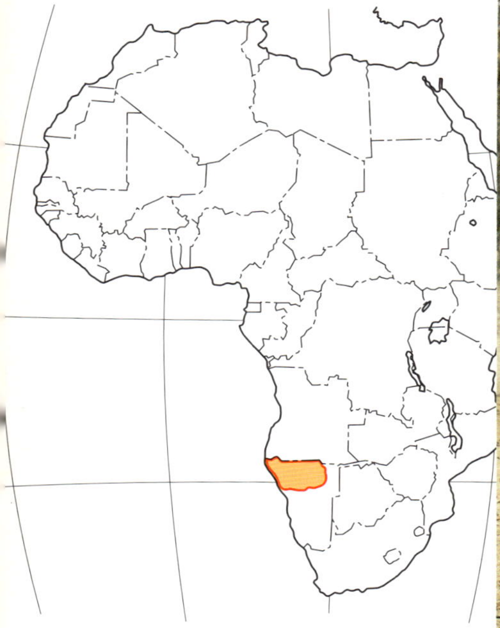

Himba

NAMIBIA

A people of Bantu origin, the Himba live in the Kaokoveld semi-desert in northern Namibia just inland from the famous cemetery of ships and sailors known as the Skeleton Coast. Estimated to number around 10,000, the Himba are in fact a subgroup of the Herero, the dominant people of the steppes of northwest Namibia, from which they separated around the end of the nineteenth century when they were forced by the hostile Nama (Hottentots) of Namibia to seek refuge in Angola. Reduced to destitution and forced to beg for survival, from then on they were called the 'himba', a term that means 'forgotten' or 'beggars'. After retaking the Kaokoveld in 1920, the refugees returned to their homelands and began their pastoral life once more, but they did not abandon their name even though it does not do them justice. The Himba, in fact, like all other pastoral groups, are very proud and indulge in a cult of physical beauty.

Himba culture blends elements of the sedentary agricultural lifestyle of Bantu origin with aspects of the 'livestock complex' probably derived from contacts with groups of Nilotic herdsmen. Recognition of a bilateral ancestry is unusual for a tribe of herdsmen because, according to tradition, livestock is inherited through the maternal line, but in fact property is owned by men. Indeed, after the morning milking, the milk is offered to the head of the family and only after he has tried and approved it can the others drink. Moreover, the head of the family inherited the sacred oxen from his father.

The cult of the ancestors is a cultural element of agricultural origin, typical of the forest Bantu people.

Himba villages are formed by round huts surrounded by a thick hedge of thorn branches referred to by the Dutch word *kraal* (from the Spanish word 'corral' meaning enclosure) within which an extended family, its animals and ancestors live. At the center of the *kraal* lies the enclosure for the cows and calves, while the goats and sheep are kept in a smaller, separate enclosure. All around the *kraal* stand the dome-shaped huts, made from a framework of branches covered by a lining of mud and cow dung to protect them against the sun and rain. The entrances to the huts face inwards towards the *kraal* and the enclosure for the sacred cows lies behind them. The adult children of the head of the family sleep in a hut inside this enclosure whilst the head of the family himself has a separate hut close to the sacred fire. This is generally kept permanently alight in memory of the ancestors and is the place near which the sick are looked after.

The Himba community is ruled over by the Council of Elders, which is formed by the various heads of the families. A representative of the Council has the right to sit in the national parliament to voice the petitions of the community.

Like all African herdsmen, the Himba devote a lot of time to their physical appearance, making use of body ornaments of different types. The women cover their bodies with fat

96 top left A herdsman follows his livestock in the sparse undergrowth of Kaokoveld. Once the Himba owned the largest herds in Africa but the past and present vicissitudes of this people, including the effects of guerrilla warfare, have drastically reduced this wealth.

96 top right Functional aesthetically and as a protection against the dust and sunlight, the mixture of ochre and fat that gives the bodies of the Himba a reddish hue is used on children from the first days of their lives.

96-97 A row of curious children faces the entrance to the hut of the head of the family, which is separate from the others in the kraal. *The most powerful member of the group has exclusive ownership of the tribe's sacred cows, and their milk, equally sacred, is contained in the gourd at the top of the picture.*

97 top Himba villages are centered on the kraal, *the thorny enclosure for the livestock also used by other peoples in western Africa. What is different is the 'special' enclosure for the 'sacred cows'.*

97 bottom Himba huts are very simple but perfectly adequate for nomadic herdsmen that do not carry their housing with them. When they move in search of greener pastures, the families use the huts as temporary bases.

98 top Made from twisted copper or iron wire tied with leather strips, Himba necklaces are only taken off if the skin begins to suffer.

98 bottom left During a feast, a young boy claps his hands to the music. His ornamentation is covered with ochre and coal as a sign of protection.

98 bottom right Government-backed development of the area where the Himba are settled is opposed by the elders, who are aware of how fragile their culture is in the face of progress.

99 The headdress of this young groom hides his ozonya *hairstyle. This consists of two parallel braids that run from the top of his head to his neck.*

and ochre and wear metal ornaments and beads on their arms and legs; those women who have had their first child wear a shell suspended around their neck. Much attention is paid to hairstyles, which are used to denote social status. Girls who have not yet reached puberty wear *ozondato* (braids) while those during puberty have their hair tied back and above their forehead shaved.

Small children have their heads completely shaved except for a single braid worn like a 'tail'. Girls of a marriageable age wear an *ekori* headdress, which is a sort of cocked hat in the shape of a leaf; it is made from goat or sheep hide and decorated with iron beads. After a year the *ekori* is replaced by the *erembe*, which is a hide taken from a goat's head and tied at the nape of the neck beneath the hair. Adult men wear two braids tucked up under an *ombiya* (leather cap), as are the backcombed hairstyles sprinkled with sawdust of the influential elders. Natural braids are often added to with hair cut from the heads of women or children. The cut hair is cleaned with ash and then plaited into another's hair mixed with mud and ochre.

The Himba have a highly unusual funerary ceremony in which, for an entire day, the deceased is hurriedly carried around so that he or she may choose the place of burial, which is then marked by a pile of cow skulls.

100 A young mother is milking a cow. The physical features of the Himba are markedly Negroid but various traits suggest an eastern African involvement. The Himba share certain institutions like bilateral ancestry with Nilotic and sub-Saharan herdsmen and also a concern for physical beauty.

101 top left A Himba woman surrounded by her collection of calabash (empty, dried gourds). These are used by the Himba as containers, bowls and, after suitable preparation, rattles in magical and therapeutic rites as they believe that their sound will frighten away evil spirits.

101 top right In a harsh environment like northern Namibia, children are always close to their mother or another woman in the family group. The national government has set up peripatetic elementary schools for Himba children; if they should wish to continue studying, the young are obliged to leave their family and abandon Himba traditions.

101 bottom With her braids pasted with ochre, this young Himba girl wears a heavy metal necklace encrusted with red earth. Although the base material is one of the most abundant in nature, the ochre the Himba use for cosmetic reasons has a certain value, and it figures among the gifts that members of a group offer to newlyweds.

102-103 Like all the Bushmen's goods, their weapons are very rudimentary but not inefficient: poisoned with a substance taken from a beetle, their fragile arrows are deadly hunting instruments.

102 bottom left During hunts that might last several days, the Bushmen mostly move in pairs or small groups. Despite familiarity with their hunting lands having lasted millennia, the poverty of the region does not provide the skilful San hunters with the necessary nourishment for the community.

102 bottom right The elders are treated with great respect. Authority is recognized in those with apparent personal qualities and, in particular, in those of advanced age.

103 top and bottom The future is uncertain for the young. Long discriminated against by other African peoples and Europeans, in South Africa the Bushmen are already considered extinct. In the Kalahari they are on the verge of extinction, having been absorbed genetically by other peoples.

Bushmen

SOUTHERN AFRICA

The Boschjesman (Bushmen), as the Dutch referred to the San people, live throughout southern Africa in the semi-desert areas of the Kalahari in Botswana, Namibia, Angola and South Africa, and numerous prehistoric rock carvings provide evidence of a much wider distribution from the southern tip of Africa to Chad. The ethnic name give by the Boers to these nomadic hunter-gatherers of ancient origin corresponds to the name 'San' used by the Hottentot peoples and has the same derogative sense.

Khoisanid, known as the 'click' language, is spoken by the Bushmen and the Hottentots and is unique for its series of implosive sounds.

The Bushmen are physically short, with pale ochre-colored skin and frizzy 'peppercorn' hair; the women are steatopygous, i.e., they have a large accumulation of fat around their hips and buttocks.

Up until the 1980s the Bushmen practiced hunting and the gathering of wild plants. As with other tribes, hunting was an exclusively male pursuit. Using a simple bow and arrows tipped with deadly poison produced from a powerful toxin taken from a beetle, the hunters caught large wild animals (antelope, gnu and warthog) and small game (hares, porcupines and birds).

The gathering of plants and small animals (ant larvae, beetles, worms and bees), which are essential for rounding out the Bushmen's protein intake, was the job of the women, who were also responsible for gathering firewood. They would place their findings in *kaloss* (canvas sacks) that belonged to the family, whereas the result of the hunt would be divided up between all the members of the group. For all hunting and gathering activities, the Bushmen would split up into bands, each of which had a particular area to exploit marked by precise boundaries. There were also 'free zones' in which exchanges took place, alliances and marriage agreements were drawn up with other groups and dances and ceremonies were held. Not having a particular leader, the bands recognized the authority of the eldest member of the group or of the individual with the greatest hunting experience.

The Bushmen's traditional religious beliefs include the cult of a beneficent creator goddess who bestows *kaggen* (rain), and to whom the souls of the dead go, and the cult of a destructive god (*Gauab*), the lord of the spirits and the dead, whom they supplicate with offerings and sacrifices so that he keeps sickness and ill-fortune away from the group.

Supernatural entities, like the spirits of the dead, are contacted during trances reached during dances around the fire. Lasting throughout the night, these ceremonies grow in emotional intensity under the power of the music and hand-clapping until the dancers reach paroxysm. The *shaman* are also able to make contact with the spirit world during a state of trance when they 'capture' a spirit in order to use it, for example, to cure the sick or perform a harmful action against someone.

During the 1980s, of the 70,000 Bushmen in southern Africa, only a small percentage of the hunters remaining in the Kalahari reserve led a normal nomadic life. When they were expelled from this last refuge, the survivors (the exact number is not known but a 1995 estimate put them at 15,000) mostly worked as stockmen or laborers for neighboring tribes like the Tswana or on farms belonging to whites.

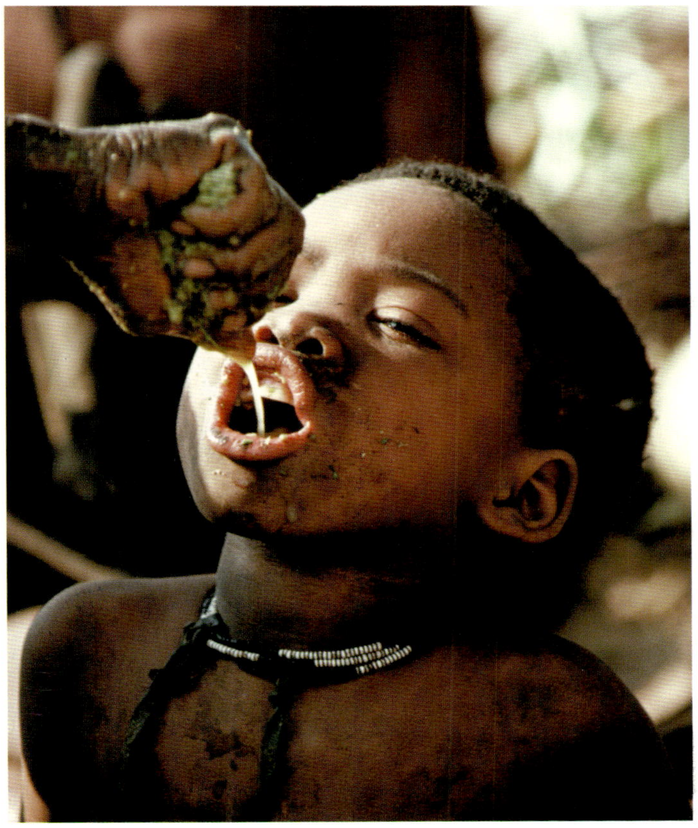

104 top A woman collects water with a cracked gourd. It is a source of pride to the San women – responsible for gathering foods – to nourish the families in the group in just three days of gathering each week.

104 bottom left Besides gathering plants, wood and water, the Bushmen women catch small animals, including snakes that are anything but small: watched by her child, this young woman prepares to cook a python.

104 bottom right One of the fruits most commonly gathered is the mongongo (Ricinodendron rautanenii), which is a highly nutritious nut that can be kept for months.

105 Bushmen society is founded on the principle of altruism and ignores classes of all types and even competitiveness. Only the elders, who are esteemed for their wisdom, are given titles of respect.

Ndebele

ZIMBABWE AND SOUTH AFRICA

106 top left and 107 With their necks adorned with heavy idzilla, *these proud Ndebele women are wearing the* ingubo, *the blanket that indicates their status as married women.*

106 top right A weaver at work on a simple loom. Women are the only depositaries of traditional Ndebele ornamentation.

106 bottom The birth of a child is essential to the happiness of married life: if no children are born, the husband's family may ask for the return of the 'bride price' they paid.

The Ndebele or Matabele are currently settled in western Zimbabwe and northeast South Africa but their origins are to be found in the Nguni people, who historically inhabited the South African province of KwaZulu-Natal on the southeast coast of the continent. According to a recent census, the Ndebele population numbers between one-and-a-half and two millions, a much more reassuring figure than that of the early 1980s, which put their total at less than 800,000. Such an increase is especially remarkable because the Ndebele have had a tormented history, marked since the early sixteenth century by feudal wars, diasporas and forced migration, which culminated negatively in the Boer conquest at the end of the nineteenth century. The Dutch invasion of southern Africa deprived the Ndebele of their lands and forced them to work in conditions of slavery on the Boer farms. After a revolt put down quickly by the British, in 1896 the Ndebele abandoned their arms and devoted themselves to live-breeding and agriculture, activities at which they are today pre-eminent.

In general, agriculture of cereals, legumes and tobacco is women's work whilst herding and milking fall to the men; however, the number of Ndebele men working in the cities and mines is on the increase.

Their traditional villages are formed by the animal enclosure at the center ringed by houses built from mud brick mixed with goat dung. The most remarkable feature of Ndebele villages is the brightly colored geometric patterns painted by the women on the walls of the houses and enclosure. Probably the wall paintings are derived from the more ancient ornamental tradition of decorating women's clothing: both forms of expression make use of abstract forms, symmetry, differences in color and the combinations of vertical, horizontal and diagonal lines. Both artiforms are practiced and handed down to the next generation by women.

Wall paintings and traditional costumes are displayed on

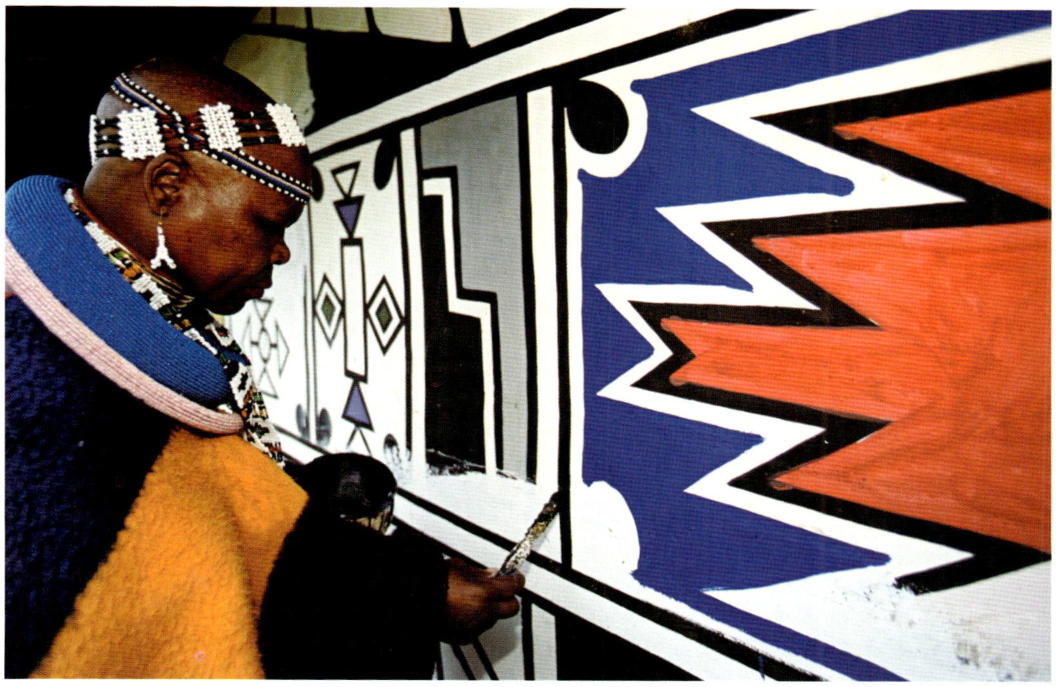

108 Mother and daughter pose in a welter of brightly colored geometrical patterns. In addition to the ingubo *and* idzilla, *the woman is wearing* isigolwane *and* ingolwane *(the cumbersome bead rings on the ankles and wrists) and an* iphotho *(the white bead apron with geometric patterns). Each detail in the complicated Ndebele women's clothing is associated with a particular status; the apron, for instance, indicates which age class the girl belongs to, whether she is a mother or expecting children and her desire for chastity and purity.*

ceremonial occasions like initiation rites or social events. *Ukuwela* (male circumcision) is performed late, between the ages of 18 and 22. The young men spend a training period away from the village and, under the eye of the elders, are required to perform tests of courage and strength; they are also given an education on the customs of the group.

During the absence of the young men, their mothers repaint the walls of the *umuzi* (house enclosure) and receive visits from relatives and friends. At the end of the period of apprenticeship, the youngsters who have become men return to the village where the women welcome them in festive spirit, dressed in traditional costume and dancing to the sound of whistles. The occasion is marked by the sacrifice of several calves, and eating goat meat cooked by the women.

Analogous in some ways, *isiphephetu* (female initiation rites) require the girls to live isolated for three months during which time they learn from the older and more expert women the techniques and secrets of painting and how to make the cloth used in traditional dress. A characteristic that is peculiar to the Ndebele, clothing 'grows' with the individual, in the sense that it is constantly integrated with new or larger elements as time passes or the individual's status changes.

Also typical of the Ndebele are the *idzilla* (metal rings worn around the neck, ankles and arms), *lighabi* (an apron made from tassels and beads, on occasion worn by males, which is replaced by larger versions as the individual grows) and *isigolwane* (large rings of beads on an iron or straw core worn in increasing number on the hips and legs). The only function of the cumbersome *isigolwane* is to imitate rolls of fat, which the Ndebele consider attractive. After initiation, girls replace the *lighabi* with a rigid rectangular apron mounted on goatskin or canvas; married women are distinguished from unmarried women by the greater number of rings they wear and their more elaborate costumes. It might be said that the jewelry and ornaments of Ndebele women are collected throughout their lives.

109 top An artist in the museum village of Botshabelo to the east of Pretoria is completing the restoration of a wall painting. Often the patterns are based on schematized architectural forms, but also on objects like bulbs or a razor blade; the latter can be seen on the right in the picture.

109 center A smiling Ndebele woman poses at the window of her house with a traditional doll.

109 bottom The entrance to Mabhoko church in South Africa is a sort of anthology of the most typical Ndebele patterns.

ASIA

List of peoples

110 left The Balinese have for centuries mixed with the peoples of Indonesia, which embraced Islam in the tenth century, but have strenuously retained their Hindu religion. This often takes the form of splendid rituals.

110 right The name Bedouin means 'people of the steppes'; it was used to differentiate the nomads from the settled peoples. What the two have in common is their material rather than ethnic culture.

111 The Miao inhabit southwest China, Laos and Thailand. They live in groups in which each of uses a different predominant color in their women's clothing: black, red, white or floral pattern.

112-113 Monks from Spituk monastery in Kashmir are engaged in one of the most surprising and fascinating Indo-Buddhist and Lamaist practices: the creation of a mandala *or spiritual model of the cosmos. The technique is complex: colored powders are applied using straws and are not glued. Buddhist doctrine emphasizes the impermanence of the world so, when the* mandala *is finally complete (which may take months of work), it is immediately destroyed.*

Introduction

Owing to the vast expanse of the continent of Asia, the many peoples that inhabit it have considerable genetic, cultural and linguistic variations. This variety imposes the need for a division of the continent as a whole into regions: the Near and Middle East, southern Asia, northeast Asia, Southeast Asia and island insular Asia.

The expression Middle East came into being at the start of the twentieth century when it was used to describe the political and military interests of Great Britain in the area of the Persian Gulf, but this book uses the term in a wider meaning: as a cultural area that includes the Anatolian Peninsula and Syria to the north, the countries around the Persian Gulf (Jordan, Saudi Arabia, the Yemen and Oman) to the south, Lebanon and Israel to the west, and Iraq, Iran, Afghanistan and Pakistan to the east.

The idea of the Arab and Moslem East is generally linked to religion – i.e.; the spread of Islam – however, this region includes very diverse linguistic, religious and cultural islands; for example, the Kurdish people in Turkey, Iran, Iraq and Armenia, the Jews in Israel and the Christians in Armenia.

Southern Asia covers the Himalayan regions of Nepal, Tibet, Sikkim and Bhutan and the Indian sub-continent, itself just as culturally and linguistically varied. The principal countries that fall within the boundaries of northeast Asia are China, Japan and Mongolia. The expression Southeast Asia was also coined last century, during the Second World War when it was used to denote a strategic military zone covering Burma (now Myanmar), Laos, Thailand, Cambodia and Vietnam. Insular Asia represents Malaysia, Indonesia and the Philippines.

The peoples of the Middle East share a certain uniformity as they are united first and foremost by the Arab-Islamic culture, but also genetically the peoples in this area show a relatively modest internal variation. This uniformity can be explained by the development of agriculture in the Fertile Crescent around 9000 BC, which permitted a degree of stability and uniformity to occur in the movements of the peoples, with the exception of internal migrations. Groups of Caucasoid origin – similar to Europeans – who had a pale skin and rounded skull are present in the western part of Eurasia, whereas peoples of Mongoloid origin generally inhabit the eastern region of the continent. The forefathers of the Caucasoids may reach back to a people of African origin which, around 10,000 years ago, began to spread into Asia across the Sinai and into southern Europe after crossing the coastal area of northwest Africa.

Different remains of *Homo sapiens neanderthalensis* and *Homo sapiens sapiens* dating from 120,000 to 50,000 years ago have been found throughout the Middle East (Syria, Lebanon, Israel and Iran). It seems equally possible that, around 70,000 years ago, another migratory wave of hominids from eastern Africa crossed the sea on light boats to reach the Arabian Peninsula, India, Indonesia and even Australia, making use of the chain of islands across the Indian Ocean like stepping stones. Around 10,000 years ago, groups of farmers living in the Fertile Crescent began to migrate in different directions. Heading northwest they populated Europe, bringing with them farming techniques and Indo-European languages; going southwest they reached north Africa across the Sinai; to the east they reached what is today Iran and the Indian sub-continent; and northwards they reached the steppes of central Asia, which were unsuitable to cultivation. It was in this last area that they developed live breeding stock and the domestication of the horse. The horse became the 'means of transport' of the nomadic herdsmen that began to migrate around 4,000 years ago, spreading Altaic and Indo-European languages. Generically known during the classical era as 'barbarians', this group included the Huns, Mongols and Tibetans.

Isolated to a greater extent and, in consequence, more homogeneous genetically, are the many Chinese ethnic groups and Korean-Japanese peoples. China was probably the land of origin of the Mongol peoples that would have formed around half a million years ago. The population and diffusion of agricultural techniques had varying outcomes: in southern China rice was domesticated around 8,500 years ago and, about 1,000 years later, millet was cultivated in northern China. This north-south separation is also reflected in culture. With the unification of China marked by the construction of the Great Wall in the second half of the first millennium BC, the only true unification was linguistic.

Caravans connected the Iranic regions to the west with China along the Silk Road, the trading route along which goods and communications between the West and East traveled. Chinese society and culture exerted its influence throughout eastern Asia, including Japan, and even reaching Mongolia and Southeast Asia. This last region is also known by the name IndoChina for having received equal ethnic and cultural influence from India and China.

Tribal groups from southern China (like the Thai and Meo) and from India attempted to colonize Southeast Asia around 1000 BC and began to spread stable cultivation of rice among the aboriginal cultures of indigenous inhabitants (the Negritos) who had until then known only a hunter-gatherer lifestyle. In general, the groups that existed prior to the migrations from India and China were forced towards the mountain zones and into the forests, i.e., into the more inhospitable and isolated areas where survival depended upon hunting and gathering and the primitive itinerant agricultural technique of slash-and-burn.

The distribution of the main linguistic groups in Asia can be seen in the ethnographic descriptions of the peoples represented in this section of the book. The Semitic languages include Arabic, spoken by the Bedouin and Palestinians, and Hebrew, but the language spoken by the Mongols belongs to the Ural-Altaic linguistic family. The language of the Kurds, with other Iranic languages like Persian, Osseto, Pashto (spoken in Afghanistan and Pakistan) and Hindi (used by various groups in the Indian sub-continent) belong to the Indo-European family.

The Tibeto-Burmese language spoken by the Padaung and the languages spoken by the Miao, Nepalese and Tibetans belong to the Sino-Tibetan family, whereas Balinese is part of the Malayo-Polynesian (or Austronesian) group. Lastly, the language of the Ainu people is from an isolated group.

In conclusion, Asia is home to the principal religions of the world – Islam, Buddhism, Hinduism, Taoism and Christianity. Islam is worshiped across the entire continent from the Middle East to southern Asia, Indonesia and the Philippines (in India Moslems represent 11% of the population). Islam pervades the cultural, social and, in some cases, also the political life of the people in the Middle East where, historically, the other two great monotheist religions are also present: Judaism and Christianity. Christianity exists in Syria, Israel, Armenia, Turkey, Iraq and among the Maronite communities in Lebanon. Judaism, historically the oldest of the three monotheist faiths, had its origins in Palestine and was spread across the world with the Diaspora; today it is the national religion of Israel.

Hinduism is widespread even in areas that are diverse from a cultural and social viewpoint, and in India it coexists with Buddhism. Buddhism developed in the sixth century BC as a reaction to the rigid caste system of the Brahmans and spread to the Himalayan area, Tibet, Southeast Asia, China, Korea and Japan in the eighth century. The form of Buddhism practiced in Japan, and which is the state religion, is Shintoism.

In addition to the large and widely practiced religions, there exist across all of Asia ancestral creeds of animistic or shamanic origin – such as cults of fertility, animal sacrifices, the cult of the spirits – that have nearly always been integrated into more advanced forms of worship.

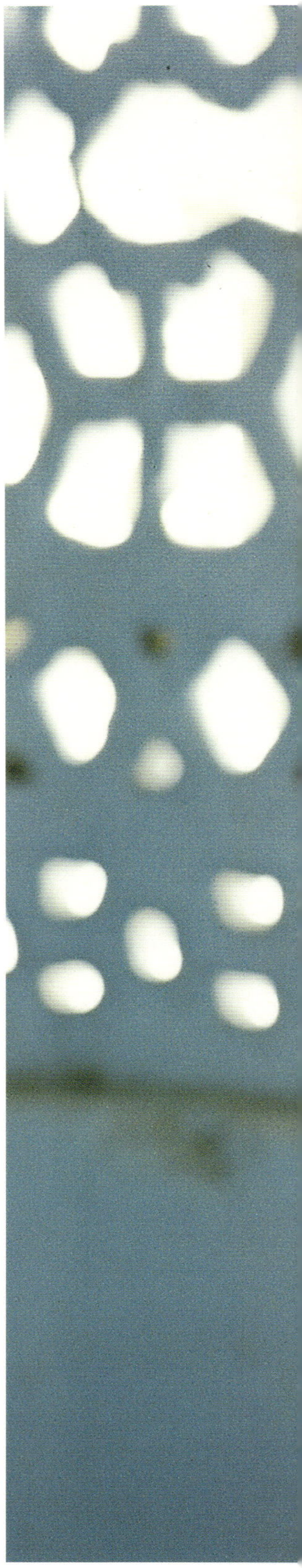

114 A group of women gathers in the court of Devnarayani Temple in Pushkar. The origin of this divinity is linked to the women's practice – opposed by the government – of suttee, *self-immolation of a widow on her dead husband's pyre.*

114-115 A Gujar farmer on pilgrimage rests in a daramshala *(lodging) in Pushkar, the holy city in Rajasthan. These lodgings are generally reserved for members of a particular caste or ethnic group.*

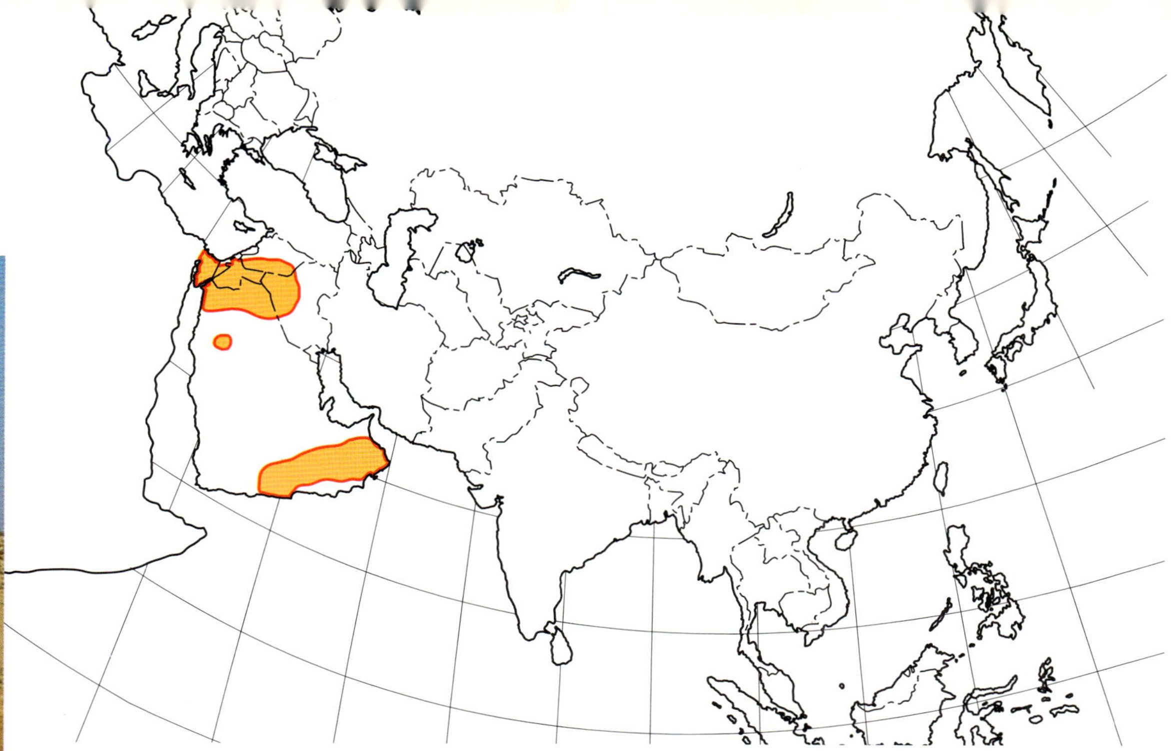

ASIA

Bedouin

NEAR AND MIDDLE EAST

The Arab word *badawi*, from which the name Bedouin is derived, means 'inhabitant of the desert'. The description is very generic but effectively portrays the many culturally varied tribes of settled, semi-nomadic and nomadic Bedouin across the immense deserts and steppe-like lands of the Near and Middle East. The Bedouin are mostly Sunni Moslems though there still exist pre-Islamic beliefs and practices relating to evil spirits, witches and divination among the various groups.

Some tribes, especially those in Saudi Arabia, practice dromedary breeding and are continuously on the move with their herds except during the blazing summer months. They follow a set route through *dirah* (established tribal territories) from wells to oases to grazing areas. The dromedaries are predominantly female as they provide a greater quantity of milk (almost two gallons a day). The diet of the Bedouin herdsmen consists principally of camel milk, cereals bartered with groups of settled farmers and dates picked in the oases. Tribes that breed goats and sheep practice a semi-nomadic existence migrating seasonally in search of water and grazing.

The Bedouin also provide the transportation by caravan of various commercial products like cereals, cloth and the jewelry that Bedouin women love to wear.

Extended families are the basis of the *qabila* (Bedouin tribes), which are united by a common forebear. Social cohesion is maintained by strong ties within the families and a precise code of honor and loyalty based on concepts like generosity, obedience and – the most appreciated virtue – hospitality.

Important features of Bedouin society are the clear distinction between individual responsibilities and the separation of males and female roles. The dwellings are made from goatskins and goat wool and have separate living quarters for the men, women and children. In general the males are responsible for the care and use of the dromedaries, which, in the past, included rustling. It is

116-117 and 116 bottom right A group of Bedouin water their dromedaries in a pool in northern Sinai.

116 bottom left To the Bedouin the desert is a sort of bastion against the tide of progress.

117 Individual roles are rigidly established and delegated based on sex and age: smoking a narghilé, *for example, is a male privilege, while one of the tasks children perform is serving food to the tribesmen.*

interesting to note how this activity, today almost non-existent, was codified: practiced above all during periods of drought, it was conducted with the minimum bloodshed possible and could be avoided by caravaners and sedentary livestock breeding through payment of a sort of protection money.

The women are responsible for looking after the smaller children, watching the flocks, caring for the camp and performing domestic work and weaving.

Marriage is generally endogamous, i.e., it occurs within the family group, but, if not, the possibility exists to make strategic alliances that establish ties and cooperation with other groups, thereby facilitating access to resources in distant territories.

Each group is run by a sheikh who is chosen for his courage, generosity and wisdom. The sheikh is supported by a council of men who dispense justice. Internal conflict is dealt with in accordance with tribal custom, which takes into account the criterion of 'joint responsibility'. This

118-119 and 119 top Fundamental to the Bedouin economy, the flocks of goats and sheep, generally 20 or so head, are the property and responsibility of the tribeswomen.

118 bottom A Bedouin woman gathers grass near Bir Taba not far from the Gulf of Aqaba in the Sinai. In harsh regions like this it is essential to prevent livestock from damaging the thin vegetation. Animals left free to graze will devour anything they find, contributing substantially to the desertification of already arid zones.

119 center Rings and other forms of soft pita are arranged around an oven to bake. Pita bread is not new to the West and is used as a plate on the Bedouin table.

119 bottom left The most traditional Bedouin tent is formed by hand-woven cloths of sheep's and goat's wool. The rooms are mostly furnished with rugs and cushions and number between one and five.

119 bottom right Two Bedouin on dromedaries almost blend into the bare landscape of the Sinai. The Bedouin of the Negev desert concentrate use of the sparse winter rains in restricted areas to increase fertility.

ASIA

120 *Women's clothing conforms to the dictates of Islam, which prescribes the veil for adult females. The women's condition is changing quickly, however, under the influence of settled habitation but not always for the better: in this society structured rigidly around individual responsibilities, the preclusion of women from performing one of their main tasks – care of the flocks – threatens to remove some of their personal dignity.*

121 *Considered in the West as a punishment, in reality the veil for Bedouin women is an accessory that can provide a degree of elegance, as proven by this magnificent hijab that hides the face of this woman from the Sinai. For this nomadic people, attachment to traditions (in the widest sense, e.g., religious beliefs, eating customs, clothing, social roles, etc.) is the only means of survival in inhospitable environments like the desert; this prevents confusion overthrowing the order that has existed for centuries.*

means that the entire group is responsible for the actions committed by an individual member.

In recent years, governments have attempted to limit the autonomy and movements of the Bedouin using forms of control and prohibition that forbid them to carry out their traditional activities.

The result is a gradual process of settlement. Many Bedouin, however, have succeeded in benefiting from their experience of the desert and have become drivers over difficult terrain, tourist guides, soldiers, farmers or employees, often turning to advanced studies.

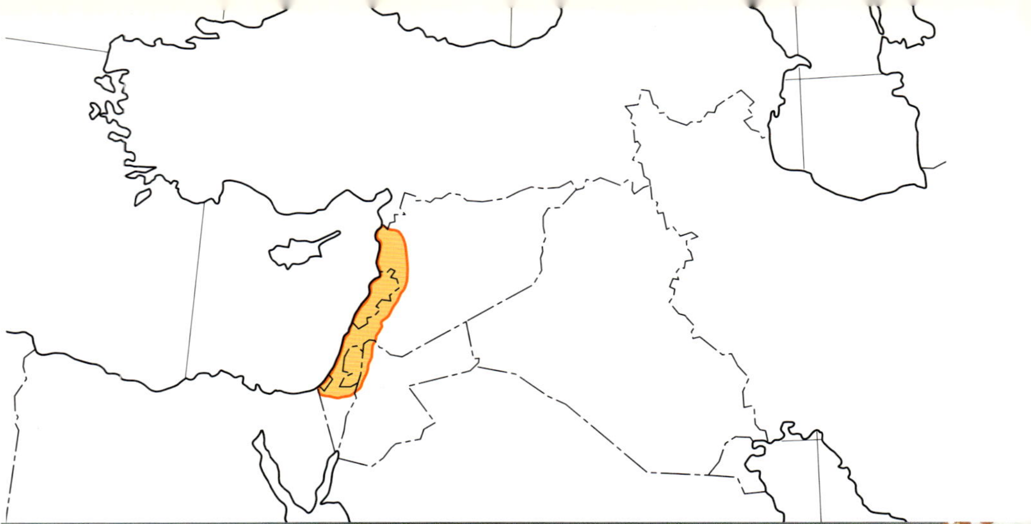

Palestinians

NEAR EAST

The name 'Palestinian' is an ancient one but common to all who are familiar with the Old Testament. It is derived from the word Pelishtim (Philistines) that was used to describe one of the peoples of obscure origin (the 'Sea Peoples') that invaded the eastern coast of the Mediterranean around the twelfth century BC, in other words, about a century after the arrival of the Israelites in the region. The history of Palestine, as the Bible tells us, is a chronicle of upsets from earliest times. This in part is attributable to the territory, which makes it difficult to define as an individual geographical region. The only certain and immovable boundary in Palestine for millennia has been the Mediterranean Sea to the west.

This ambiguity has made identification of territory and ethnic groups particularly difficult and it is quite logical that Palestine has been the theater of innumerable invasions, from the times of the Egyptian pharaohs of the Middle Kingdom until the Ottoman sultanate. Nonetheless, perhaps the most consequential cultural transformation, in that it still characterizes modern Palestine (the most correct definition of this people is 'Arab-Palestinian') was the Moslem invasion of the seventh century AD. The first people to be overrun by the Arab expansion, the Palestinians adopted the Arab

language (part of the Hamito-Semitic family) and the Sunni persuasion of Islam. There are currently six million Palestinians spread across the Near East, where they emigrated following occupation of their territories that began with the constitution of the state of Israel in 1947-48. In Jordan, Palestinians form 70% of the population and enjoy full liberty and sovereignty, whereas in Syria, Lebanon and the territories occupied by the Israelis they live in refugee camps. There are also many Palestinian communities in the United States.

Today both Palestinian men and women make up part of the specialized labor force in countries in the Persian Gulf

122 and 122-123 The kefia *is the red-and-white or red-and-black headdress that has become a symbol of Palestine and, in particular, of Islam.*

123 top left A man reads peacefully on a rug in a mosque. Palestinian culture has a long tradition, especially in the field of poetry.

but the rural population continues to practice agriculture, including the women. As a result of the conflict that has raged in the region for so long, the overall condition of Palestinian women is highly unusual. Due to the frequent absence of men, they are often obliged to run the villages, to work as laborers in the clothing industry or to be teachers and nurses.

The basic unit of Palestinian society is traditionally the nuclear family, i.e., the married couple and their children. Marriages are generally monogamous and arranged with a preference for first cousins. The authority of the head of the family is exercised on questions of education, work,

123 top right This Palestinian shop in Jerusalem, overflowing with fruit and vegetables, almost closes off the alley in one of the old city's three bazaars. Contrary to the common image of this harsh land, Palestine is generally fertile and productive, having been worked by man for thousands of years.

123 bottom right The souk *is where Palestinians prefer to do all their shopping. These markets are traditionally organized into areas by types of goods sold. There are* souks *for dyers, blacksmiths, wood carvers and the highly perfumed spice market.*

124 top *Female students with their hair covered in a school in Gaza. Education at secondary school and university levels has been available to women for a number of years and is taught in 12 Palestinian institutes.*

124 bottom *This symbolic picture shows two youngsters in Gaza watching life in their contested city from behind a window. Do we see a wink, a smile? Peace is rare in these places but hope springs eternal.*

marriage and the spatial separation that often divides members of the group.

Parental groups in Arab-Palestinian rural communities refer to an important traditional institution that has survived the increase in personal mobility and urbanization: the *hamula* is a group of individuals who live in the same district or village and claim ancestry from the same forebear, or who are bound by a sense of mutual social, economic and ritual solidarity. The social and political organization of the villages has experienced changes under the various political powers that have succeeded one another over the years, bringing about changes that have influenced the structure and function of the *hamula*.

During the Ottoman Empire this organization protected the villagers' common interests regarding the agricultural subsistence economy that was based on the shared ownership of the land between all members of the village.

Under British rule, it lost its cooperative nature as the land became personal property, thereby creating social differences between members of the *hamula*. With the creation of Israel, the new work opportunities offered by migration within and outside of Palestine have finally recreated the balance that existed between parental groups as the *hamula* has reactivated its promotion of social cohesiveness. This is in part a result of the requests for autonomy from Palestinians who live in the occupied territories.

124-125 Wife, daughter-in-law and grandchildren are seated next to the eldest man in the family, and therefore the one with the greatest authority. Palestinians are mostly Sunni and therefore strictly bound by sharia *(Islamic law) and* fiqh *(jurisprudence).*

125 bottom The conflict has helped to change roles and customs. In recent years many Palestinian women have assumed new responsibilities and taken jobs in industry and the education and health sectors.

127 center right *With his head covered by the tallit, this worshiper wears tefillin ('prayer belts') on his forehead and wrist. They contain verses from the Torah that remind him to observe the commandments.*

127 bottom right *Orthodox tradition distinguishes between joyous and sad commemorations. The latter includes the days dedicated to the memory of the two occasions on which the Temple was destroyed, in 587 BC and 70 AD.*

Haredim

ISRAEL

126 *Dressed in accordance with the precepts that govern morning prayers, an Orthodox Jew in Jerusalem recites a sorrowful prayer in front of the Wailing Wall (Hakotel Hama'araui), the last vestige of the Temple destroyed by the Romans.*

127 top left *Men and women pray in separate areas both inside the synagogues and, as here, in front of the Wailing Wall.*

127 top right *At the age of 13, a young boy becomes a 'son of the commandment' or Bar Mitzvah. He takes on full religious responsibilities in the presence of the sacred rolls of the Torah and in the eyes of the community.*

127 bottom left *The beard of the Jewish worshiper should not be cut according to Leviticus, the third book in the Pentateuch, which contains standards and prescriptions relating to sacrifices, offerings and the ministry.*

According to the Pentateuch, the father of the Jewish people was the patriarch Abraham and his place of birth Ur, in Chaldea, on the south bank of the Euphrates close to the Persian Gulf. In historical terms the first definite localization of the Jews and their unity as a people is known to have occurred during the thirteenth century BC when they conquered Palestine – the Promised Land – and they divided themselves into the 12 tribes around a single temple.

Over the millennia the Jews have suffered continual and bloody persecutions on religious, political or economic pretexts that have forced them to emigrate around the world. Consequently, modern Jewish society is extremely composite, as they have integrated into different cultures around the world despite retaining a strong sense of identity and belonging. This has been manifested wherever they have lived by preservation of their religion, which has found the symbol of their reunion, rebirth and freedom in the city of Jerusalem.

For this short description, however, it is necessary to make an arbitrary choice within the Jewish people as a whole, and the selection falls on the Haredim, the Orthodox Jews of Jerusalem and the representatives of the deep-seated Jewish adherence to tradition. It is worth stressing that, considered overall, Jewish culture is exceptional around the world for its depth and complexity. Jewish orthodoxy recognizes in the books of the Torah the revelation of Yahweh, the only God and creator of Heaven and Earth, and in the Talmud a parallel revelation handed down orally. One of the most important prayers is the Shema Israel ('Listen, O Israel'), which is intoned at the start and end of each day. It contains a basic profession of faith in the uniqueness of Yahweh. The revelationary texts are flanked by the Mosaic Law, which is a vast body of prescriptions expressed in over 600 commandments that govern individual and social behavior, lay down ethical standards and define the rules governing purification and eating. With regard to this last point, great importance is placed on ritual washing and *kosher* foods, i.e., the treatment of meat and permitted

128-129 and 128 bottom right A frugal meal in the refectory is all that pupils in an Orthodox school in Jerusalem receive. In institutes of this type education begins at the age of three with the teaching of the Jewish alphabet and continues for 10 years until the Bar Mitzvah. Almost all teachings are based on knowledge and understanding of religious texts.

128 bottom left and 129 top right The teaching of texts like the Torah in Orthodox schools requires the use of Hebrew and its script but students are also taught Yiddish, the language developed by the Jews in eastern Europe during the Middle Ages.

129 top left and bottom The Book of Leviticus prescribes long curls at the sides of the head, like these two Orthodox students. In juridical terms, membership of the Jewish people is only open to the children of a Jewish mother or those who have converted to Orthodoxy by means of circumcision and full acceptance of the Mosaic Law.

foods and the list of those that are prohibited.

Another important element of Jewish Orthodoxy is the holiness of the Sabbath. This is a day of celebration and prayer from which all work must be excluded. In the past, non-observance of this precept was punished by stoning and is still so significant that it is included among the mortal sins.

Many religious festivals mark the Jewish year, for example, *Shavu'ot* ('weeks'), which is celebrated seven weeks after Easter (Pesach) to commemorate the gift of the Torah offered by God to Moses on Mount Sinai. This celebration coincides with the harvest, so that it is customary to decorate the synagogues with flowers and to offer coffee, sweets and cheese-based foods.

Important ceremonies mark the stages of an individual's life. Circumcision (*Berith milah*) occurs on the eighth day of a baby boy's life and sanctions the covenant (*Berith*) the Jewish people made with God. The operation is performed by a *mohel* (circumciser) whilst the *sandak* (godfather) holds the baby on the seat of the prophet Elijah who, it is said, is present at the ceremony. It is also the occasion on which the newborn is officially named.

At the age of 13 a boy celebrates his Bar Mitzvah ('son of the commandment'), which marks his reaching of religious maturity and passage to adulthood and means that from that moment on he can participate at the reading of the Torah in the synagogue.

Mixed marriages are not permitted but, if it should happen, the children of the marriage are considered Jews only if the mother is Jewish.

The wedding is celebrated by the rabbi and takes place in a *huppah* (wedding canopy) that symbolizes the house the married couple will live in. The groom places the ring on the bride's finger then, after reading the *ketubbah* (wedding contract), he breaks the glass from which he and the bride have drunk wine. This act is to evoke the destruction of the Temple in Jerusalem in 70 AD by the Romans, an event that is still painfully alive in the memory of this extraordinary people.

Kurds

TURKEY, SYRIA, IRAQ, IRAN AND ARMENIA

The Kurds are a people who speak an Indo-European language derived from the West Iranian branch. Their origins are fairly obscure but are connected by some to the Kardaka people mentioned in the Sumerian texts from the second millennium BC. Today, however, they are indigenous peoples living in the region that lies between the Black Sea, the Caspian Sea and northern Iran. Certain information about the Kurds only exists from the time of the Arab invasion in the seventh century AD when documentation refers to tribal groups strongly desirous of independence who stirred up insurrections and revolts. This fiery and independent nature has characterized the history of the Kurds until the modern day and facilitated the conservation of a remarkable degree of cultural uniformity. Their number is difficult to calculate but it is estimated that there are at least 20 millions distributed across Syria, Turkey, Iraq, Iran and Armenia. The collapse of the Ottoman Empire and its formation into independent political states broke up the mountainous region of Kurdistan where communities of Kurds either lived in isolated mountain villages or were seasonally nomadic herdsmen.

The traditional organization of Kurdish society was founded on the tribal group led by a hereditary *agha* (chief) who guided the nomadic tribe's movements and mediated in internal conflicts. A powerful and cohesive figure in the community, the *agha* was a landowner and received rent for his land leased by others. His prestige was measured by the generosity he showed during community assemblies, which were customarily held in his house. Given the importance of blood relationships, the position of the chief was less important in settled than semi-nomadic groups as the inhabitants of a village might belong to different family groups, and therefore the authority of a single representative of one family line was not always respected.

The tribal structure was founded on the territorial unity of the group and on blood relationships but it progressively went into crisis following the absorption of

130 top *Flour without yeast, water and salt are the ingredients in* yufka *(traditional flat bread), which is cooked on a flat stone and can be kept through the winter.*

130 bottom *Kurd houses are built of stone and set out on different levels like terraces.*

130-131 *The first floor of a Kurd house is used as a stall, and the upper one, reached through the ceiling, is where the family lives.*

131 bottom *In Turkey, clouds of dust rise as the herds invade a Kurd camp during the seasonal migration.*

the region by nation-states after the First World War. The setting up of frontiers blocked seasonal migration so that the majority of Kurds were obliged to give up their pastoral activities and practice settled agriculture or to emigrate to cities to look for work in the state economy. Tribal organization only exists today among a few nomadic groups that have resolutely remained isolated in the mountains.

The Kurds are for the most part Sunni Moslems but some groups in the rural zones belong to confraternities or the mystic and ascetic Sufi orders that search for *ridâ* (divine love). The syncretic Yazidi sect, founded in the twelfth century by Sheikh Adi of Mesopotamia, still has various followers. The Yazidi recognize the existence of two supernatural entities – one divine and beneficent, the other evil – and they practice a series of cults associated with fire, water, the moon and the sun. In every village there are different spiritual chiefs: the *mullah* is responsible for Koranic education and officiates over religious ceremonies, the *sheikh* is the head of the Sufi religious confraternity and the *sayyd* is the prophet.

Kurdish women enjoy greater freedom than women in other Moslem communities and have always been active in society. They are not obliged to wear the veil and have the opportunity to receive education and take on political responsibilities in the community. A Kurdish form of poetry known as the *laùk* is composed and sung exclusively by women.

In addition to the Islamic religion, which they adopted in the seventh century, the Kurds still retain several pre-Islamic principles, in particular, the cult of the ancestors and animist beliefs based on spirits associated with natural objects (stones, trees, water, fire, etc.). In sacred sites it is customary to build mounds of stones associated with ancestor worship as a sort of altar on which offerings of bread and sweets are made.

132 top According to Islamic custom, the men eat separately from the women. Externally quite rough, inside Kurd houses are comfortable and cool.

132 bottom A line of women enters the gate of a residential area carrying the food for a feast. A Kurdish speciality is kibbeh, *very spicy beef rissoles.*

132-133 Traditional dances enliven the festival on May 1 in Ruwanduz. The corresponding month in the Kurdish calendar is gullan, *which runs from April 20 to May 21.*

133 bottom left The guests dance at a wedding in northern Iraq. In this case the group includes women who do not wear the veil, in keeping with Kurdish custom.

133 bottom right In the shade of a tent a herdsman clips a tightly bound goat. One of the uses for the wool is for weaving Kurdish rugs.

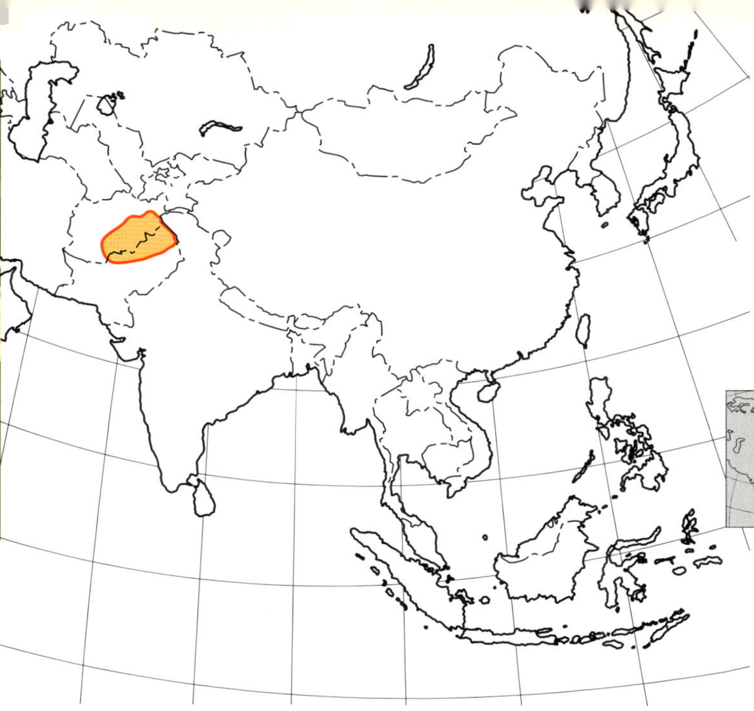

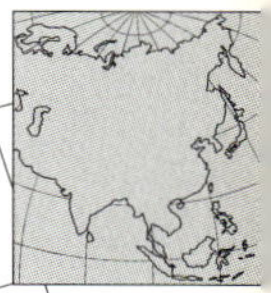

Pashtun

AFGHANISTAN AND PAKISTAN

The Pashtun speak Pashto, which is a language belonging to the West Iranian branch of the Indo-European linguistic family. They live in southeast Afghanistan and northwest Pakistan. Before the war with the former Soviet Union (1979-89), the Pashtun tribes (Durrani and Ghilzay) in Afghanistan represented a political tribal elite that had been assimilated into the state administration. It was from this group that the Taleban emerged.

The Pashtun are divided into tribes formed by clans, which in turn are composed of extended families under the leadership of a *malik* (chief). The chiefs, elders and male adults in a group form the *jirga* (assembly) where questions relating to the community and internal disputes are discussed. Disputes are regulated by the levying of sanctions that the family of an offender is obliged to pay as recompense to the family of the plaintiff in keeping with the criterion of 'joint responsibility' in use among pastoral cultures.

A code of traditional behavior known as the *pukhtunwali* regulates the sanctions and is founded on concepts of honor, hospitality and the protection of women; in other words, the women are excluded from public affairs and kept so that they are not subjected to the gaze of strangers. Nonetheless, it is not uncommon for bloody vendettas to involve entire families and even clans, and so an extended assembly (*loya jirga*) of tribal chiefs and religious leaders exists to oversee the most serious of intertribal conflicts.

The Pashtun are Sunni (as are 90% of the world's Moslems) and follow the Moslem liturgical calendar. Spiritual leadership is provided by the *mullah*; these are religious leaders that direct Koranic schools and preside over ceremonies, for example, those that mark the stages of life: birth, circumcision (which takes place at the age of seven), marriage and death.

Funerary customs in part reflect the customs of another Middle Eastern people of pastoral origin, the Jews, who wash the coffin and cover it with a white shroud. The main difference in the customs of the Pashtun is the positioning of the deceased, who is buried facing Mecca. In addition to the Moslem religion, the Pashtun profess pre-Islamic beliefs such

134 and 135 top The Pashtun are of Iranian stock; their heads, faces and noses are long and narrow and they are medium-tall in stature. Moslems, having been Islamicized in the ninth century, though they were invaded by the Arabs two centuries earlier.

135 center As dusk advances, a man recites the evening prayers on Salang Pass north of Kabul. The Pashtun are mostly Sunni

135 bottom An essential element inside their simple traditional houses is the charpoy, the sofa-bed used for discussions and rest.

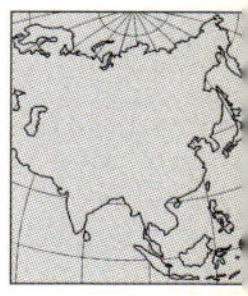

136-137 and 137 bottom Schooling is a painful topic in Pashtun and Afghan culture in general. The chronic lack of teachers, books and educational materials caused by the war is worsened by the restrictions imposed on females, who have been excluded from education for centuries. The efforts of the current government, however, are directed at radically changing this situation.

136 bottom There are no shops in the villages, so sellers sit in the street. The traditional meeting places of the tea-houses (right) are slightly more organized.

as the superstitions regarding *jinn* (evil spirits), *ruh* (the spirits of the dead), fairies, witches, angels and demons.

The Pashtun practice sedentary agriculture, seasonal migration of herds and trading following caravan routes, but these activities are being increasingly substituted by the development of small companies or farming using advanced irrigation systems. The consequence of this transformation is the generalized settlement of Pashtun groups, the recent history of which has reflected a crisis in traditional values; these are threatened by risky and constrained development, for example, the cultivation of opium for the international drug market and the consequent clashes between groups for control of the underground market. The most serious threat to this people, however, is the state of war that seems to have no end in the country. Only with peace and international collaboration will the ancient roots of the Pashtun be able grow into a modern society.

137 top left The recent past: a group of women wrapped in white chadri flees from Kunduz during a Taleban attack. Shortly after the Taleban took power, the fundamentalist government found support from the traditionalist Pashtun.

137 top right These large hanks of boiled wool will be used to make carpets and cloth. Before being sold, the finished product will be cold-washed in river water to fix the colors.

Rabari

INDIA

[RAJASTHAN AND GUJARAT]

Semi-nomads in the Thar Desert in the Indian state of Rajasthan, but also present in northern Gujarat, the Rabari are a tribe of about 12,000 people divided into small village communities. Though they speak a neo-Sanskrit language (a variant of Rajasthani), very probably their origins are from elsewhere but unknown. The most probable hypothesis is that they are the last line of the Hephthalite (white) Huns that overturned the Hindu Gupta Empire at the turn of the fifth century AD. These fearsome warriors from the heart of Asia swept down into Rajaputana (modern Rajasthan) where many became sedentary, were absorbed into the local *kshatriya* caste of warriors and married into the princely houses of the rajas and maharajas. Some, however, still live a semi-nomadic life retaining cultural and religious characteristics typical of central Asia and falling into the rank of herdsmen. With the passing of the centuries they gradually succumbed to Sanskrit culture and their foreign village gods (which still remain) were overlaid by the Hindu pantheon. In addition, their language was replaced by the variant of Hindi known as Rajasthani. From the Middle Ages their livelihoods were based on the breeding of horses, camels, cattle and goats and on trade, as they supplied the caravans that carried goods from one city to another on the edges of the Thar Desert. Finally, they used their notoriety as fearless and ruthless horsemen – a last resource in times of peace and shortages – to enrich themselves through banditry.

Although they always had humble or illegal occupations, the Rabari were recognized as distant but poor relations of the aristocratic Hindu caste and were considered an undisciplined class of rajput. Marriages between Rabari rajput and aristocratic city rajput are not uncommon, and for this reason the Rabari do not think of themselves as a tribe but as an authentic Hindu caste.

They live in small villages of mud and brick houses with thatched roofs. Periodically the men leave the village and

138 top The features of this man seem to resemble those of an ancient rajput. In fact, the Rabari have had very close contacts with this exclusive caste of noble-warriors; they have assumed some of the rajput culture and mixed it with their own traditions of steppe nomads.

138 bottom Rabari crafts are some of the most appreciated in India. Silver is alloyed with zinc to increase its malleability, enabling them to produce elegant and complex designs.

138-139 A group of women form a circle of grace and color as they dance the Rasada to the sound of four drums and the melody provided by the jodja pava (double-flute). At the more than 1,500 fairs in Gujarat each year (without counting the festivals), Rabari women display their famous bharat kaam (embroidery).

139 bottom Wearing jewelry and her best clothes, a Rabari girl participates at her name-giving festival, which is a sort of Hindu baptism.

140 and 141 top Rabari children are dressed very elaborately during festivities. Those shown here are participating in the Namakaran, the name-giving festival, which is considered very important for providing a child with 'a good start' in life. During this occasion the father whispers into his son's ear the names his son will be called: the first is chosen on the basis of zodiacal criteria, the second according to the month and the less formal third, will be the child's everyday name.

141 center and bottom Even from the cradle children wear elaborate Rabari silver jewelry: earrings with pendants, large silver necklaces, bracelets and anklets. These items are generally old, as they are passed down as heirlooms. In the various villages of Kachchh – the westernmost region inhabited by the Rabari – craftsmen have specialized in particular products for centuries. One theory is that this highly wrought means of expression is a reaction to the monotony of the desert.

Rabari

leave it in the hands of the women to drive the herds to new grazing grounds. It is interesting how desert life has given the Rabari a similar lifestyle to the Bedouin or Tuareg, including several traditions that differ from the religious or juridical customs of the environment in which they have settled. The autonomy of Rabari women has always been considered improper by Hindu society, which considers their natural self-possession unbecoming. Even today the Rabari women are thought of as wicked and practitioners of magic and sorcery. Their notoriety as having been the bloodthirsty companions in their men's raids has not died away.

Little remains of their ancient religion of the steppes, but it is not uncommon for an oracular form of shamanism to occur every now and then. However, these spiritualists, who easily fall into a trance, also practice as oracles in Hindu temples, which proves that they have been absorbed by the dominant religion.

Tall, lean and strong, Rabari men wear high turbans and like to be armed. The women wear colored saris with gaudy metal jewelry which resembles gypsy dress when observed close up. Like many peoples of nomadic origin, they love music, song and dance, which both men and women indulge in during festivals. Skilful wood carvers, the Rabari are famous for the elaborately carved doors of their modest houses. Other typical features are their icons of village gods, the richly ornate *charpai* beds and their musical instruments, the style of which is reminiscent of this warrior people's central Asian origins.

142 top left and bottom The perak (a typical Ladakhi hat) is similar to Tibetan models. The traditional clothing in this part of India begins to diverge from that in the sub-continent on the lush slopes of Kashmir.

142 top right and 143 A young Ladakhi girl wears a turquoise cascade in her hair, brocade clothing and strings of coral beads. Ornaments of this kind are of great traditional and material value and are part of a bride's dowry. It is widely thought that women are better off in Ladakh than anywhere else in India, but recent studies have demonstrated inequalities in education, work and income. Men earn much more than women.

Ladakhi

INDIA

[JAMMU AND KASHMIR]

The Ladakhi are a mixed people of both the Buddhist and Moslem faiths, but who all speak a southern variant of Tibetan. The Ladakhi language seems an archaic Tibetan dialect with many contributions from Sanskrit.

The ethnic composition of Ladakh is a complex one and difficult to unravel. It is known that in the second to first centuries BC the Seleucid influence in the zone was replaced by that of the Greek-Bactrians, who represented the easternmost representatives of Hellenism. Then, in the first century AD, these were overrun by the Kushana tribe from central Asia who were related to the Scythians. During this period Ladakh was part of the cultural area known as 'Gandhara' that was considered 'Greek-Buddhist' for its extraordinary cultural mix of the Hellenistic west and Buddhism.

The Kushana Empire, which extended from central Asia to northern India, was defeated at the start of the third century by Huns from central Asia. All these varied peoples overlaid and intermixed with one another to an inextricable degree.

In 842 the king of Tibet, Glang-dar-ma, was assassinated. Some of his successors fled with their supporters and guards towards the region of the sacred mountain Kailash, where they carved out the small kingdom of Nga-ri. This, at its southern tip, included the area of Ladakh. The kings of this region naturally looked to Tibet as the political and religious center but, having contacts with India through Ladakh, they were aware of the cultural attraction of their large southern neighbor.

It should be remembered that India was the birthplace of the Buddha and that in this period the famous monastic universities of Nalanda and Vikramashila flourished there. The advent of Islam in the eleventh century and the

144 top *The* yak *and* ghi *– respectively the male and female of the Himalayan ox – have been one of the Ladakhi people's most important resources for centuries. These patient animals provide wool, milk and meat and are the traditional means of transport in the highest mountains in the world.*

144 bottom *The position of women has changed greatly in Ladakhi with the development of the region. Accustomed to heavy work – compounded by the altitude – they are obliged to work even harder when their children are at school and their husbands have steady work.*

Ladakhi

consolidation of a powerful Moslem dynasty in Kashmir did not represent a danger to Ladakh, but the kingdom of Ladakh eventually came into existence when Nga-ri lost its trans-Himalayan territories as a result of the Guge family coming to power in Tibet. In the fifteenth century Ladakh became a vassal of the kingdom of Kashmir and had to resist being Islamicized.

Two hundred years later, Ladakh was the theater of a struggle between the Tibetan army of the fifth Dalai Lama, who was attempting to conquer territory towards the plains of the sub-continent, and the troops of the Grand Mogul in Delhi, who was defending Indian territory.

Ladakh risked being swallowed up for the last time. From that moment on, the Ladakhi Buddhists lived in peace with Ladakhi Moslems, even to the extent of interfaith marriages. The Moslems continued to use the Ladakhi-Tibetan language and it was only recently, following fundamentalist Moslem pressure from Pakistan, that the Urdu language was forcibly introduced.

Ladakhi villages perch on mountain slopes, preferably facing south. The houses are similar to their Tibetan equivalents and structurally comparable to the houses of any mountain people.

They have two or three floors of which, as is customary in cold environments, the first acts as a stall, wood store and barn and the vast single room on the second floor as a living and sleeping area for the whole family. It also has a corner dedicated to the family's private altar. The third floor is used as a store for foodstuffs.

Skilful tradesmen, the Ladakhi depend on caravans to purchase and transport foods from India and Tibet. The land is stony and dry so little cultivation is possible. Consequently, livestock breeding and seasonal grazing are two of the principal activities of this country. Perhaps more frequently even than in Tibet, in Ladakh there is a presence of popular shamanism, which is tolerated by the Buddhist monks as long as it is limited to healing.

144-145 *A specialty of Ladakh and Tibet, the famous salted tea mixed with ghee that they drink is very refreshing. The photograph shows preparation of unleavened bread, which is eaten with the tea.*

145 bottom *The basis of the diet in Ladakhi valleys is made up of cereals, which are used in soups (left), roasted barley flour and* tsampa *(right). Although the region is covered with snow for much of the year, it has a chronic lack of water resources.*

146-147 The Gallong sacrifice the mithun (a large ox that lives in the sub-Himalayan strip), however, traditional religious practices are withering away in the face of Donyi-Polo, an 'artificial' religion created to counter external cultural influences.

146 bottom left Two women make offerings to the spirits, represented by raffia simulacra.

146 bottom right Another means of beseeching divine favor among the Gallong, besides animal sacrifice, is by means of traditional dances.

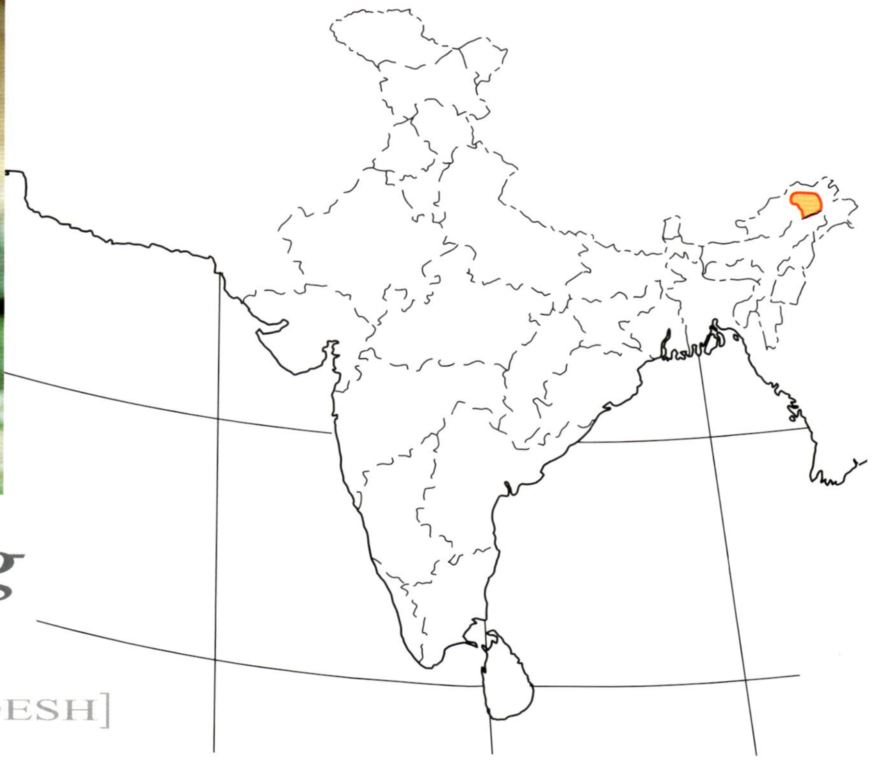

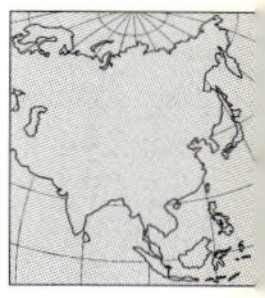

Gallong

INDIA

[ARUNACHAL PRADESH]

Settled in West Siang in the Indian state of Arunachal Pradesh, the Gallong are also known as the Western Adi to distinguish them from the Southern Adi (or Padam) with whom they form a vast Tibeto-Burmese language tribe. The Adi probably came from the Brahmaputra Valley, as their songs narrate, and arrived in the area where they now live around the seventeenth century. The Gallong practice exogamy and consider marriage between members of the two basic entities that form their society - the subclan and the family - to be incestuous. At the same time, they do not practice marriage between the two Padam tribes, which has resulted in the two becoming separate nations. The family is patriarchal and patrilineal and polygamy is occasionally practiced. When the father dies, the inheritance goes mainly to the eldest son and the widow generally goes to live with the younger son.

The patriarchal family, from grandparents to grandchildren, includes unmarried members and lives together in a long house divided into sections for the various nuclear families. All residents of the house eat together but the lighting of a second fire inside the house heralds the separation of the family into two parts in the near future.

The main forms of livelihood are hunting and fishing, with subsidiary economic activities being a low level of agriculture and livestock breeding. In the past this rather bellicose people used to organize expeditions to capture prisoners and enslave them in their villages. This occurred until 1961 when the Indian government succeeded in purchasing and liberating the last of the unfortunate prisoners. The Gallong claim they are descended from the Heaven and the Earth, the two primordial gods from whom the entire universe resulted after a number of divine generations. Since the late 1960s, a new religion has sprung up even among this people so tenaciously attached to tradition: developed as a reaction to Christian, Hindu and Buddhist proselytism, it is a monotheistic belief called Donyi-Polo that is founded on the unity of the god Sun-Moon. The new faith is causing the disappearance of ecstatic shamanism and the sacrifice of the mithun (a huge sub-Himalayan ox) and, in addition, is bringing the two branches of the Adi together and sowing the seeds of a national consciousness among them together with other local tribes.

147 top A Gallong poses in hunting attire. His rigid headdress is made from reeds, which is the most widely used material in Arunachal for making tools.

147 center The village chiefs, wearing red as a symbol of authority and harmony, talk politics.

147 bottom A line of Gallong youngsters do the sword dance. The female dancers, in traditional muted dress, wear long bead necklaces, the colors and shininess of which have different meanings. Sometimes ornaments of this kind, used by both women and men, are so large that they entirely cover the chest of the wearer.

148 top *Carrying bamboo baskets using a band across the forehead, a group of Nishi women follow the controlled movements of the harvest dance. Many tribal dances in Arunachal Pradesh are dedicated to fertility.*

148 center *This warrior is wearing a* bopa*, the close-fitting headdress adorned with a feather and the tinted bill of a hornbill. The frame of the slightly conical hat is made from reed fiber.*

Nishi

INDIA

[ARUNACHAL PRADESH]

148 bottom *Long like all the houses of peoples living in central Arunachal Pradesh, those of the Nishi are spacious and comfortable and have a huge verandah at the front.*

149 *The vaguely threatening gaze of this Nishi man seems to reflect a characteristic of this people who are known for their pride and quarrelsome nature.*

Numbering 55,000, the Nishi are the largest tribe in the district of Subansiri in Arunachal Pradesh. This Tibeto-Burmese ethnic group probably originated in the eastern Himalayas and the first documentation that relates to them dates from the early nineteenth century. The tribe is divided into three subtribes – the Dopum, Dodum and Dol – that, according to their mythology, were named after the three sons of the first man. Each of the three subgroups is divided into 10 exogamous clans.

Their economy is based on slash-and-burn agriculture that forces them to move on in search of unexploited land every 12 years or so. This periodic wandering keeps alive the art of hunting and retains the importance of the hunter in Nishi society; the hunter is a potential warrior and his authority is recognized immediately after that of the village chief and the shaman.

Sheep, pigs and fowl are raised almost in the wild state, while marked mithun (oxen) are left free to wander in the forest and hunted when a religious festival is to be celebrated.

Nishi villages consist of a small number of stilt-houses – generally between four and 20 – built from bamboo fairly distant from one another. A rather warlike people, the inhabitants of a house (which can number up to 80) are more loyal to their family head than the village chief. Quarrels between the inhabitants of different houses are not uncommon and these can degenerate into outright battles. Bearing in mind the pride, individualism and confrontational nature of the Nishi, it is understandable how the *nyat* (peacemakers and judges) are particularly respected.

The religious life of the Nishi is strongly typified by ancestral shamanism, with the result that their attention is more directed towards the spirit world than that of the gods. Knowledge of the gods is passed on orally through stories and songs that recount how the supreme god – the God of the Forest – created first the tiger, then man. The gist of the myth, however, focuses on the respect that the hunter has for the tiger rather for the god, and this point reflects on the religious and social importance in Nishi society of the shaman, who is able to control the spirits when he is in a trance.

ASIA

150-151 This young man is smoking an elaborate silver pipe – a typical and renowned Nishi product. His features reveal the eastern Asian origin of the roughly 25 tribal peoples of Arunachal Pradesh, the 'Country of the Morning'.

151 The Nishi are always armed with a long sword, which they wear almost horizontally below the left armpit, and carry a bag of rushes covered with coconut fiber over one shoulder.

152-153 A woman sprinkles millet seeds in front of her house to dry them. The Atapani have different features to the other tribes in Arunachal Pradesh: they are more advanced and educated; they use the Latin alphabet for their own language (sometimes with an attempt at literature) and enjoy a stable economy.

152 bottom A shaman (a group that are disappearing) officiates over a funeral. The Atapani believe in a new life after death.

153 top The custom of inserting bamboo knots in the nose has been explained as an attempt to make Atapani women look ugly so that they would not be taken as slaves by the nearby Nishi; however, it is more probable that the purpose is to imitate the nostrils of a wild animal.

153 bottom The tight bun worn by adult Atapani began to disappear in the early 1970s.

Apatani

INDIA

[ARUNACHAL PRADESH]

The villages of the Apatani people have existed for at least four centuries around the town of Ziro on the Apa Tani Plateau. This area in the district of Subansiri in Arunachal Pradesh is completely surrounded by Nishi territory, the Apatani's traditional rivals. A people in the Tibeto-Burmese language family, the Apatani number about 17,000 and are the most technologically advanced tribe in the region. They are an agricultural people who developed their own irrigation system several centuries ago, with the result that they have become successful rice-growers and have organized a sales network to sell their product to other tribes. To defend themselves from the raids of the bellicose Nishi, the Apatani have organized themselves in seven large villages, in each of which an area is allocated to each of the 13 clans that make up the tribe. The villages therefore have a development plan, with larger streets that separate the clans' districts and smaller streets and squares within the separate sections. In the center of each square stands the totem pole of each clan.

The tribe's enduring ancestral religion requires the sacrifice of mithun, which is carried out at the end of every winter for the community or privately during funerary rituals. The Apatani cosmology is complex and populated by gods and spirits. The soul of the deceased is thought to escape into the atmosphere and travel to the underground world of the dead where it remains for eternity. Some priests state that, with the approval of the gods, it is possible to be reborn on Earth. However, these ancestral beliefs are being modified by the spread of the new Donyi-Polo religion and bringing about the disappearance of the Shamans.

Wancho

INDIA

[ARUNACHAL PRADESH]

154 top The warrior-like Wancho make strong, attractive headdresses like battle helmets. They are decorated with the beaks of toucans, boar tusks and colored feathers.

154 bottom left and bottom right Fish are trapped in a section of the river current and speared or killed using the wide bladed dao *swords. In the past* dao *were used to cut off human heads.*

The Wancho are a Naga tribe who speak a Tibeto-Burmese language. They migrated from northern Thailand to settle in the district of Tirap in Arunachal Pradesh in the fifteenth century. Known for their aggressive nature and custom of hunting human heads, the Wancho used to organize expeditions to procure macabre trophies in order to increase the fertility of their fields. The struggle against this custom was fully successful towards the end of the nineteenth century thanks to British opposition and the work of missionaries. Today there are roughly 30,000 Wancho and they practice rotation cropping on a slash-and-burn basis. They learned a good deal from the Christian missionaries as the Wancho now cultivate not only rice and millet, but also potatoes, tomatoes, tapioca and hot peppers.

The family forms the basic social entity, comprising only the parents and children. When the eldest son marries, he remains in the house (which he will inherit) but when the other sons marry, they are obliged to leave and build their own houses. Families are strictly patriarchal and patrilineal and form the pillars of the village. More so than in other tribes, the men's hut is of utmost importance because young boys leave their families to live communally with all the other boys where they learn the tribal traditions under a strict military discipline.

The Wancho's traditional religion used to be based on a pair of supreme gods – Rang, the beneficent creator, and his brother Bau Rang, the wicked destroyer – and the future of the universe depended upon the eternal struggle between the two gods. The conduct of the Wancho towards their gods was not moral and the worshiper could strengthen his relationship with the good god Rang by making sacrifices to him, and could placate the irascible Bau Rang with more victims. The most important sacrifice was the buffalo or, in mountain areas, the mithun. Today most Wancho are Christian and the only vestiges of their aggressive period are local weaving in bright colors and attractive patterns and the production of headdresses adorned with colored feathers and tusks.

154 center right Relationships between the Wancho are governed by a four-caste system with the chiefs and servants at either end. The system is not derived from the Hindu equivalent.

155 Today the Wancho are Christian but they earned their fame as savages during British rule, even if they were tame in comparison to their cousins the Naga Nocte, of whom they were often victims.

Bondo

INDIA [ORISSA]

156-157, 156 bottom left and 157 top. Bondo women use beads almost in place of cloth to make head coverings that they wear over a shaved head. Their necklaces are so large that they are almost an item of clothing. Another typical female ornament is the heavy metal rings they wear around their necks.

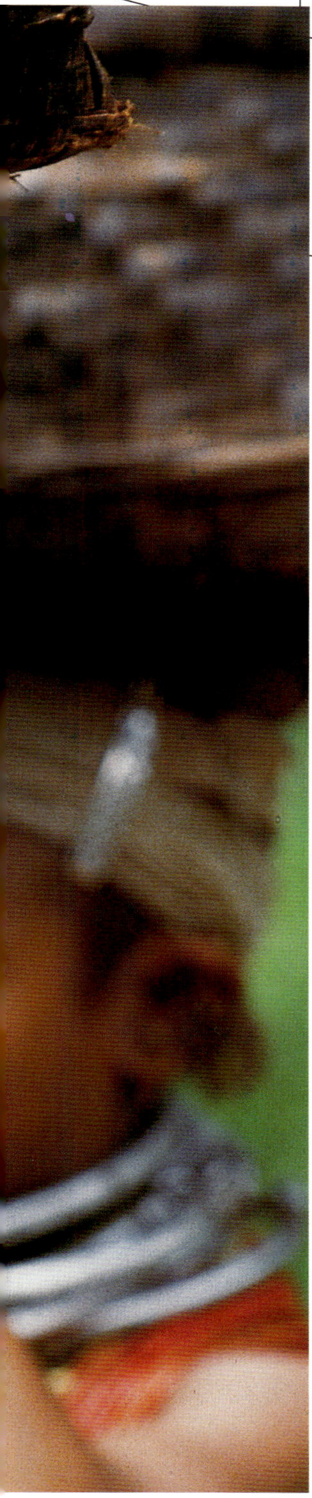

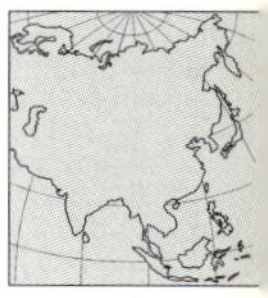

The Bondo are a community of just 5,000 or so that live in the wild hills of the district of Malkangiri in the south of the state of 0Orissa. Known as the 'pygmies of Orissa', they are an ethnic group that speaks an Austro-Asian language, but their isolation in this part of India has meant that they are incomprehensible to other tribes belonging to the same linguistic family. If it were not for the markets, where they can purchase iron and plastic tools from Indian merchants, the Bondo would still be technologically in the Stone Age. Their religious and funerary monuments are, in fact, megalithic: when a relation dies, they erect a menhir near the village and, three years after the death, they build a dolmen to his memory along the path that leads away from the habitation. Although they are divided into subtribes and clans, the village is the only exogamous social unit. A wife can therefore be a member of any clan but must come from another village. The most curious aspect of their social life is that a marriage can be made between an adult woman and a young boy; in this way, the wife increases her probability of being maintained by her husband into late life without risking widowhood. A consequence of this is undoubtedly incest as a de facto consequence is that the bride becomes the lover of her father-in-law.

Their religion requires a series of sacrifices to thank the gods and spirits of agriculture. A pig is sacrificed to the Goddess of the Earth at the start of spring each year, but the most solemn and exceptional sacrifice has a bull as its victim. Their gods and spirits all dwell beneath the earth with the exception of Singi-arke, the Sun-Moon God. Singi-arke is not offered sacrifices but prayers. The Bondo economy is exclusively agricultural as their uncontrolled hunting exterminated all the local wildlife, but the poor results of their primitive slash-and-burn technique mean that this tribe is the poorest tribal population in India. To produce extra income, the women make good quality brooms from sorghum that they sell in the market, but these find few buyers as the Bondo are renowned as witches. On this note it is odd to note how, even among the Bondo, the broom is considered to have the power of flight.

156 bottom right The Bondo use bamboo to build their huts, of which there are usually four or five in each village. Technologically backward, this people has only a few basic tools.

157 center and bottom The only 'accessory' in the limited clothing of the Bondo is a cotton blanket that they wear during the coldest hours of the night and early morning.

Sherpa

NEPAL

The Sherpa are a Mongoloid people that speak a Sino-Tibetan language. They mostly live at an altitude of 13,000-14,500 feet close to Mount Everest in the regions of Khumbu, Pharak and Solu in eastern Nepal. Although in Tibetan *sharpa* means 'man from the east', it is certain that this people originally came from Kham, i.e., the easternmost region in the Autonomous Province of Tibet, to the northeast of the valleys where they currently reside. They most probably migrated there at the start of the sixteenth century.

The land they inhabit is so devoid of means of sustenance that the Sherpa have always had to depend on semi-nomadic trading and seasonal grazing to survive. Between May and October, in the warmest period (a euphemism seeing that above 12,000 feet the temperature rarely exceeds freezing point and might only touch on 60°F on sunny days), the herdsmen take their yak up to the mountain pastures.

The Sherpa make the most of the 'summer' to grow potatoes, which, for the past couple of centuries, has been fundamental to their rather poor nourishment. As the pastures are eaten down and the season advances, the herds are driven up to higher pastures, which is why it is said that the Sherpa has three homes: the first in the village, the second the summer barn in the main summer meadows and the third a rough hut at the highest pastures used briefly during the warmest period of the year.

Sherpa villages have few houses that all face in the same direction. Surrounded by vegetable gardens and dry stone walls, the two-storey houses are made from plastered stone. The lower floor is used as a stall, while the upper one is one large room where the family eats, deals, works and sleeps, along with any guests they may have.

Besides livestock breeding and seasonal agriculture, traditionally Sherpa practiced caravan trading, taking iron to Tibet and importing rock salt into Nepal but the Chinese invasion of Tibet closed down this source of income when the borders were shut. To compensate the Sherpa turned to other activities, in particular offering services as porters and guides on the many hiking and climbing expeditions in the

158 Studied for decades, the prodigious capacity of the Sherpa to utilize to the maximum the little oxygen available at high altitude (37% less than at sea level) is a result of the greater concentration of hemoglobin in the blood and not of a greater volume of the thorax, which in fact is lesser at high altitude.

159 The Sherpa are commonly thought of simply as mountain porters but they have only been involved in this activity since the 1920s when Western climbers started to visit the Himalayas. Moreover, today most of the porters are from other Himalayan tribes.

highest mountains of the Himalayas. Their physical resistance to high altitude, their knowledge of the mountain environment and their capacity to carry heavy loads (by balancing the packs carried on their backs with a strap passed across their foreheads) have made them famous around the world. This is enhanced by the fact that the porters and especially their *sirdar* (leaders) are considered almost totally reliable.

The Sherpa are divided into 18 main clans, and this fact imposes a requirement for marriage within the tribe though this infringes the universal canons of Buddhism. The endogamous rule is a strict one, but this cannot be said of their sexual lives, and parents turn a blind eye to the pre-nuptial behavior of adolescents. If a baby should result, this does not upset family life or represent a hindrance to marriage with another partner. Marriage is a contract between equals and signifies the union of the goods of the two families involved.

This equality of the sexes is extended to the fields of work, the village assembly and the economic decisions made within a family. Generally the Sherpa are monogamous but both polyandry and polygamy are possible (and practiced) in Sherpa society.

Buddhists of the Nyngmapa faith use *gompa* (monasteries) as a place of pilgrimage and as a setting for assemblies, festivals and trade between villages. In addition to the official religion (Buddhism), there is a fairly strong and tolerated existence of the region's original shamanism (*Nyngma*) with aspects of Bon-po. The roles of the shaman are as a healer, an exorcist and, in collaboration with a Buddhist monk, a psychopomp, i.e., as a guide for the souls of the deceased to reach the kingdom of the dead.

160 top left and right More open and visible in public life than the women in other zones of Nepal, Sherpa women (or Sherpani) have the same responsibilities and tasks as the men; consequently, it is not uncommon to see girls carrying improbably heavy loads and men caring for the children.

160 bottom The Sherpa venerate the mountains, which they consider the abode of the gods, and frequently criticize foreign climbers for their lack of respect.

160-161 Foods (in this case the curdled milk of ghee) are cooked in small earthenware ovens that provide the only source of warmth in Sherpa houses. The traditional fuel – yak dung – has been replaced by wood in recent decades to content tourists, with the result that the mountains have been severely deforested.

161 bottom Older children are responsible for looking after their younger siblings and collecting wood and dung, however, it is not uncommon for the youngest also to be porters.

Sherpa

ASIA

162 top left It is probable that this young Sherpa boy weighs less than the basket he is carrying. An average load is about 65 pounds but often porters accept double that to increase their earnings. Work conditions have improved in the last few years but modern equipment is still too expensive, so that most of the tools that they use, like baskets and walking sticks, are made out of bamboo.

162 center left and bottom The growth rates of Sherpa children reflect adaptation to the almost constant cold and lack of oxygen at high altitude: in early infancy they are taller and heavier than their plains' compatriots or even the Tibetans, and this and greater vascularization of the muscles helps them to conserve their body heat with great efficiency.

162 top right Wool is produced by hand on large looms and is one of the Sherpa's most important resources. Textile products are exported to the capital, where trade with foreign buyers brings good profits, and abroad, especially to North America. In the Tibeto-Himalayan region, the spinning and weaving of coarse wool have probably existed since the eleventh century. The wool today is a top quality product, if not unique, as the animals that produce the fleece are among the few not to have been crossbred.

163 Until a few years ago the child mortality rate in the Himalayan mountains was one of the highest in the world owing to lung and intestinal diseases. The improvement in hygiene, the introduction of water purification equipment (pollution was one of the major causes of death amongst children), the availability of health services (which until the 1960s did not exist at all) and the increase in education levels have together drastically changed what were some of the world's hardest living conditions.

Tibetans

AUTONOMOUS REGION OF TIBET, CHINA

The name 'Tibet' is a Hindi word. The Tibetans call their land 'Bhod' and themselves 'Bhotia', but this second designation is more cultural than ethnic. In fact 'Tibetans' are an amalgam of various peoples that have mixed over time. The earliest tribe known to us, and the one that can boast being the 'purest' Tibetans was the Khampa clan of Mongols, which began to populate the Himalayan arc from the eighth century BC probably after they were forced to take refuge in the mountains by some other warlike Mongol people.

We do not know if during their migration southwest this group encountered any peoples already inhabiting the area, even if some archaeological finds suggest that the region around Tingri (south of the Tsangpo River, which becomes the Brahmaputra in India) was inhabited in the early Paleolithic period. Whatever the situation was, over the centuries other tribal groups came into contact with the Khampa of which 18 are known, including the Na-khi, Moso, Lolo, Wassu, Nashi and Ngolok peoples. Scythian-Parthian and Tungus tribes also entered Tibet from the west. Leaving aside the already mentioned 18 smaller peoples, the three dominant groups in Tibet from the seventh century AD were the mixed Scythian-Kham tribe, the mixed Tunguso-Kham tribe and the 'pure' Khampa people. Though professing different faiths – from Nestorian Christianity to Mongol shamanism – these peoples had a unifying element in the Bön religion. Fundamentally shamanic, Bön had an organized structure, almost ecclesiastic, that centered on certain figures of divine kings.

It was because of Bön that Tibet appeared a fairly homogeneous state by the seventh century, the period during which king Srong-btsan Sgam-po centralized the power of Tibetan tribal feudalism in his own hands and launched a policy of diplomatic and aggressive expansion.

In just a few years the king penetrated deeply into

164 A land of seemingly immutable traditions, Tibet is actually changing quickly, as this young girl from Lhasa, dressed in 'European' style, demonstrates.

165 top, 165 center and bottom left People from the plateau: burned by a sun that does not warm, the faces of Tibetans are often adorned with jewelry made from turquoise, fossil coral and amber or, as seen in the photograph of the girl in the center, by zhi onyx.

165 bottom right Babies are breastfed for up to three years in Tibet. The relative poverty of the diet and scanty refinement of the various foods makes a mother's milk very important in ensuring the health of children that grow in such an inhospitable environment.

166 top left A worshiper approaches a prayer wheel. Tibetans do not just express their prayers verbally but spin large or small cylinders like this one and fly colored prayer flags everywhere in Tibet and Nepal.

166 center and top right The monks, pilgrims and common people (mostly of advanced age) who complete the circumambulation (khora) *of Jokhang monastery in Lhasa perform an act of great ritual value. Their ritual takes them between colorful stalls that sell sacred articles and a multitude of everyday objects.*

166 center A traditional Tibetan offering is törma, *which are colored simulacra carved in butter.*

166 bottom Although the Dalai Lama – literally the 'Master of oceanic wisdom' – has not lived in the Potala Palace for many decades, to Tibetans his residence remains the most sacred place in the country.

167 The religiousness of Tibetans is fully demonstrated by the ciak *(prostration of the entire body). Usually a worshiper performs 108 but it is not infrequent for pilgrims to cover miles in this manner.*

China, even obliging the emperor to sue for peace. In the meantime Srong-btsan Sgam-po forced the king of Nepal to declare himself a Tibetan vassal and marry a daughter of each of the two foreign rulers. As both the Nepalese and Chinese princesses were Buddhist, Srong-btsan Sgam-po was induced to embrace the faith himself and impose it as a state religion. How successful this attempt was is hard to say, but what is certain is that the king was given a shamanic funeral. The resistance given by the followers of the traditional Bön religion to the imposition of Buddhism is well known, and Buddhism was only definitively installed in Tibet as a result of the visit to the country from India of Padmasambhava at the end of the eighth century.

Bön survived but was reformed to imitate the Buddhist monastic structure and was finally incorporated into Tibetan Tantric Buddhism. The bönpo that did not reform and refused to be assimilated remained a phenomenon at village level, and their faith was considered to lie somewhere between superstition and magic.

Tantric Buddhism had a prodigious unifying effect: above all it gave all these different peoples a uniform belief, but it also resulted in the creation of a Tibetan alphabet (derived from Sanskrit) so that the sacred texts of Indian Buddhism could be translated. This innovation led to the linguistic unification of the country and standardized education.

The exogamic and endogamic barriers of the tribal and clan structures began to fall with the introduction of Buddhism, and, perhaps the most surprising effect, the warlike and bloodthirsty people was transformed into what it is today peace-loving to the point of being defenseless. However, the isolation of some of the valleys led to the conservation of some tribal behavior, for example, until recently bandits still fell on caravans of yak and there still existed pockets of magical and shamanic cults.

Nonetheless, this has had no effect on the unity of the nation, as is made clear by the unanimity of the Tibetans who went into exile in neighboring Nepal and India after annexation of Tibet as an autonomous region by the People's Republic of China.

Tibetans

168-169 On important festivals like Losar (New Year), many monasteries produce a large tangka *containing a brightly colored representation of the Buddha.*

168 bottom left Chanting the prayers in a deep voice, Tibetan lamas fill the rooms of the monasteries with loud echoes, which to the ear of the unaccustomed can sound menacing.

168 bottom right Under the portrait of the 14th Dalai Lama, an old monk reads the sutra *(literally 'threads'), which are ritual and philosophical aphorisms.*

169 top Monasticism is also practiced by women, though they are in a minority. Historically, entering a monastery in Tibet was a means to avoid the uncertainties of pastoral life, although the life of a monk was anything but easy.

169 center Tibetan monasteries are slowly being refilled. They are places of worship and study that trapa *(novices) enter at the age of six. It takes 12 or so years of service to graduate to being a full monk.*

169 bottom left A young monk studies in the quiet of the Tantric college where he learns the more 'esoteric' aspect of Vajtayana Buddhism, also known as 'Lamaism', which was introduced to Tibet in the eighth century.

169 bottom right The large shamanic drum is beaten rhythmically by the monk to provide the rhythm of the mantras. These are sacred formulas whose recitation with other items of the Buddhist doctrine leads to enlightenment.

170-171 When on the move, the smallest children ride on the folded up ger *(tent) on the baggage. Many Mongols are resistant to the idea of a sedentary life and view the idea of owning a 'house' with disdain.*

170 bottom A group of nomadic herdsmen load their camels in the steppes of Mongolia. Livestock breeding is enabled by the vastness of the land (not by the quality of the grass) and is the foundation of the Mongolian economy.

Mongols

MONGOLIA AND CHINA

There are so many Mongol peoples that they have spread to all corners of Eurasia over the millennia: the Kalmyk on the Volga, the Buryat in Siberia, the Oirat, Dörbet and Torgut in Chinese Sinkiang and the Moguls of India were all Mongol tribes that raided and conquered their way across Asia. And then there are the Turks, who are such close cousins that in many periods the two have been confused. To get a clear idea, it is necessary to identify the Mongols as a single tribe, the Khalkha, which was the main one and the one ruled by Genghis Khan. We know little of the Khalkha (also called Tartars) except that from remote times they were nomadic herdsmen in the taiga and sub-Siberian sand deserts. The tribe was formed by the union on a patriarchal basis of a certain number of families; a wider association of tribes linked by blood ties was called an *aimaq*. This simple structure became more complicated during the era of conquests when the tribes were transformed into a purely military organization under the command of myriarchs, chiliarchs, centurions and decurions.

Like the ancient Turks, the Khalkha worshiped Tengri, who was a heaven-dwelling god to whom horses were sacrificed. All the other gods and spirits that filled the atmosphere and Earth were consulted and controlled by the shamans. Only Tengri remained unreachable, as pure and infinite as the taiga. Breeders of livestock – principally horses, reindeer and yak – it is probable that the Khalkha came into contact with the Scythians and Shaka of the steppes and may have interbred with them. Perhaps the Tokhari people was the result of these encounters, whose perfectly preserved mummies reveal individuals with Mongoloid features lying next to others with Caucasian characteristics: however, they are all dressed in the same colorful felt clothes.

The Khalkha entered history with Genghis Khan. We know that the authority of the Khans was controlled by the shamans, whose power and marvels gave the tribe a

171 top *Camels, horses and sheep are the most commonly bred animals but they also raise reindeer, which, in northern Asia, were domesticated in remote history.*

171 center and bottom *It is said that the immensity of the Mongolian landscape, one of the barest in the world, would probably be intolerable to those not born there; consequently, the Mongols have it all to themselves.*

172 top *A broad face, flat nose and 'almond-shaped' eyes are some of the facial features that have made the Mongols eponymous with the east Asian peoples that inhabit the region between Siberia and Indonesia. More correctly, however, this people is descended from the Tungus people of central Asia.*

superstitious sacred charisma. In order to take supreme power over all the Khalkha clans, Genghis restored the worship of Tengri, who was out of the reach of the shamans and an eminently imperial cult. Later, the Khalkha Mongols embraced Tantric Buddhism in its most erotic and macabre form, thereby becoming the cultural vassals of the Tibetan civilization. Skilful riders and nomads at heart, the Khalkha were unbeatable warriors armed with short, highly effective bows that had a longer range than any other fired weapon during the Middle Ages. Rapid in maneuvers, cruel and almost invulnerable, the Khalkha were believed to be devils that had flown out of Tartarus (a synonym for Hades), and thus were called Tartars by Christians.

Their traditional dwelling is the *ger*, which is a round tent made of skins or felt and supported at the center by a pole that had a cosmological symbolism as an *axis mundi*. It is lined with furs and felt to resist the cold of a sub-Siberian winter. To resist the low temperatures the Tartars were great meat-eaters and drinkers of alcohol.

Despite the passing of the centuries, their life has not changed much. Even Buddhism, which elsewhere, especially in Tibet, has greatly contributed to the pacification of the people, has not succeeded much in mellowing their behavior.

The horse may have been substituted by the motorcycle, and the bow by the rifle, but they still live in tents and have a low opinion of those who live in towns. In addition, after the fall of the philo-Soviet regime, the traditional curse of banditry broke out once more.

The women are generally very beautiful and participate in life on an equal basis with men in a manner that sometimes surprises Westerners, as they demonstrate their desires without embarrassment. For this reason, marriage is a social contract without any religious or moral connotations; it is just a simple transaction to create an economic alliance and does not preclude children conceived out of wedlock.

The fall of Communism led to the reopening of various Buddhist monasteries and the reawakening of shamanism. However, it is important to distinguish between the real thing and the version produced by the era of New Age thinking.

172-173 *Hawking (here with a golden eagle) has a long history in the steppes of Asia. As Marco Polo narrated, these birds of prey were one of the passions of Kublai, the grandson of Genghis Khan and ruler of the Mongol tribes and China in the thirteenth century.*

173 right *A young Oroqen boy wearing a fur hat with twisted horns and ears. Though there currently exist only a few thousand the population of this minority in Inner Mongolia and Heilongjiang (the northwest tip of China) is increasing.*

175 top The condition of Mongol children varies from area to area. For example, in China they have to attend a school where their language is not taught, unlike what occurs in the areas under Russian influence.

175 center and bottom left The ger is the result of centuries of experience and is enormously efficient. Although the roof alone is made up of 250 poles, the average time to put it up and take it down is no more than an hour.

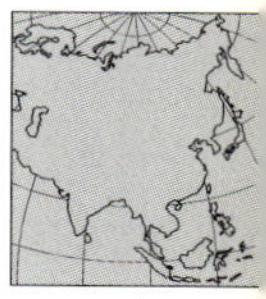

174-175 The tent of the Mongolian nomads is spacious and comfortable. The space is not partitioned by lengths of material, as occurs among the nomads of west Asia, and is divided into areas of responsibility: men and women respectively reside to the left and right of the entrance, which faces south.

174 bottom Near Xilinhot, in the heart of Inner Mongolia, a woman cooks in a trench dug in the turf. The fuel for the fire is argol *(dried dung), very rarely wood.*

175 bottom right A pastoral economy generally leaves the diet of nomadic peoples low in vitamins. In Mongolia, this lack is made up for somewhat by mares' milk, from which the alcoholic kumys *or* aïrak *is made. The liquid is rich in essential elements like vitamins A, B and C, and nourishing and easily digestible ammonic acids, fats and sugars.*

ASIA

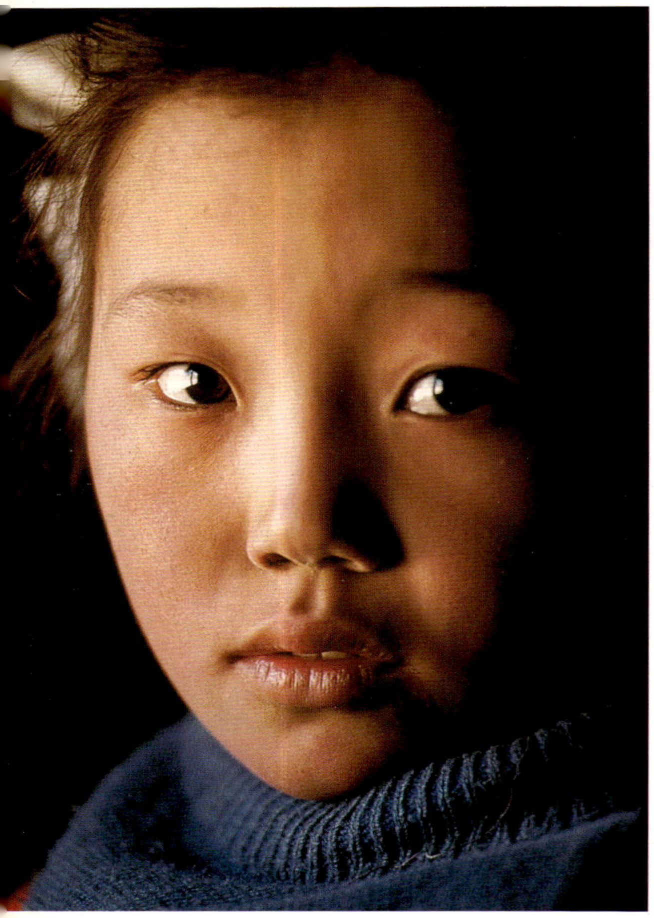

176 'The cities must be razed to the ground so that the world is a steppe in which mothers can suckle free and happy children'. Summing up the spirit of freedom, this is the future Genghis Khan hoped for his people.

176-177 This boy is sharing a bed-bench with the family sheep. Houses, mostly in cities, have only one floor and windows are repaired with sheets of paper.

178 top Grasping only the jacket of their adversary, these Mongol wrestlers have to throw their opponent using a variety of trips. Victory in this harmless demonstration of strength, popular with the young, separates the men from the boys.

178 center It is thought that Mongol saddles, uncomfortable by western standards, were the first to have stirrups. The close relationship between Mongols and their horses was one of the decisive factors in the foundation of the Khans' empire.

178 bottom A group of stockmen set off at the gallop at the foot of the Gurban Bogdo mountain range. This is the first chain in the mountainous area in northwest Mongolia. The Mongol horse is often called a pony, and it is in fact very small and stocky, with a large and heavy head. Less attractive than other horses throughout the world, it is extremely sturdy and reliable. Mongols learn to ride very young and children just five years of age are able to gallop for miles. Another ability that has made this people famous is sleeping in the saddle so that they can cover huge distances in a single day. It is said Temujin dreamed up this way of riding so that Mongols could ride 60 miles a day.

Mongols

178-179 *With a long pole that ends in the whip, a traditional tool of Mongolian stockmen, a horseman watches over the horses grazing on the prairie in Inner Mongolia.*

179 bottom *The Nandam ('play') festival is an assortment of traditional Mongolian competitions: horse races, archery (children also take part) and traditional songs and dances.*

180 top In traditional festivals the inhabitants of the villages dance to the music of five-stringed instruments. Other instruments used are drums and jew's harps.

180 center Inau *votive staffs covered with wood shavings are some of the Ainu's most important ceremonial objects. They are placed in the enclosures of houses or along hunting paths.*

180 bottom Traditional Ainu clothing is an embroidered jacket down to the ankles for women, and down to the calf for men. The material used is called attush *and comes from the inner fibers of elm bark.*

181 Ainu men wear a sort of cap that projects at the front and neck. The Ainu typically have a flat face, hollow eyes, square eye-sockets, a sloping forehead and a broad nose with a marked indentation.

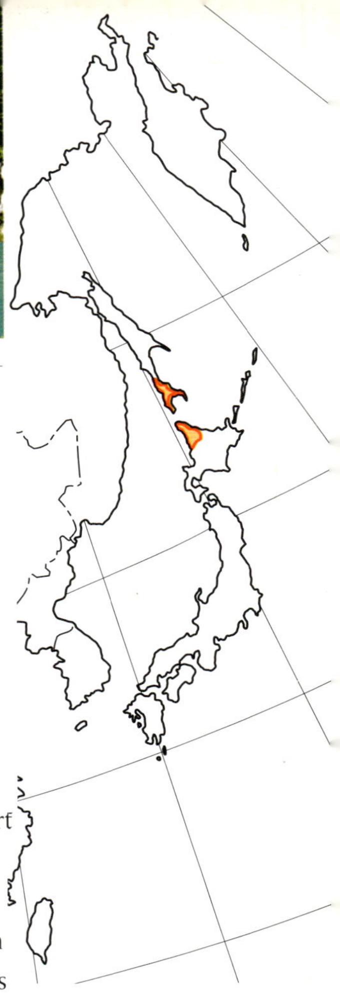

ASIA

Ainu

JAPAN AND CIS

The term Ainu means 'human being' or 'male' and is used to define an indigenous people in the Japanese province of Hokkaido and the neighboring islands. The Ainu are considered to be a homogeneous group. In fact, from a historical standpoint, there are a number of different and distinct ethnic groups. Generally the Ainu are connected with the Emishi or Ezo people, cited in historical Japanese documents, but their identification with the forebears of the Ainu is not certain. Nowadays, most of the Ainu live in Hokkaido but a few hundred inhabit the southern part of the Sakhalin Peninsula in what is today the Commonwealth of Independent States (CIS). Considered by the Japanese as a foreign ethnic group, since the start of the twentieth century the Ainu population has been drastically reduced by sickness and a very low birthrate.

The Ainu have often been called Caucasoid or Australoid but this classification is based only on infrequent though notable similarities, such as facial features, the fullness of their beards and the generally hairiness of their bodies. Recent systematic studies have shown closer links with some neighboring peoples like the Tungus, Altaic peoples and, above all, the Uralic peoples of Siberia. One of their most typical characteristics was, in the past, a tattoo in the shape of a moustache around the mouths of the women. This was begun at puberty and completed before marriage and symbolized the girl's entry into womanhood. Net-pattern tattoos were applied to the arms up to the elbows and on the back of the hands.

Towards the start of the Meiji period (1868), the Ainu progressively adopted a Japanese lifestyle, in terms of their houses, clothing and eating habits; they kept their traditional customs and religious objects for ceremonial occasions. The traditional Ainu house was rectangular, supported on poles and had a main room and a smaller room that served as an entrance. The walls and roof were made from bamboo leaves or miscanthus. A covered outlet in the center of the roof let the smoke escape from the hearth that was set in the center of the large room. The entrance door was protected by an animal skin or a drape. On the east side of the house was a window used for ceremonial purposes. The Ainu fished for salmon and trout in dugout canoes and hunted with bows and arrows. The animals most commonly hunted were bear, deer, rabbit and weasel. While the men were busy hunting or fishing, the women collected seeds, wild plants, tubers and edible roots. Today hunting, river fishing and gathering have been replaced by the cultivation of rice and other plants and by professional sea fishing. The most unusual feature of Ainu society is the dual system of family descent: the males are part of a patrilineal system, symbolized by coats-of-arms of animals (*itokpa*) and the females of a matrilineal system, symbolized by hereditary chastity belts (*ponkut* or *upsor*). Each *kotan* (village) numbers about 20 houses built along riverbanks or near hunting grounds.

The relationship between the Ainu language and other languages of Hokkaido has not yet been defined clearly. Its phonemic and agglutinate structures are similar to those in the early Asiatic languages of northwest Siberia, but the vocabulary and various grammatical functions resemble those of the languages of Southeast Asia and Oceania. Although the Ainu have no written language, their oral tradition is rich in *yukar* (epic poems) and stories in both prose and poetry with recurring formal qualities. The process of assimilation and the advent of compulsory schooling mean that the young Ainu generally speak Japanese rather than their traditional language.

182-183 Miao girls work in the fields wearing traditional dark blue clothes with decorations on the sleeves. Using a crescent-shaped tool, they harvest the rice one plant at a time.

182 bottom Daily life in Miao villages is lived according to simple, traditional rhythms with the use of tools derived mostly from nature. This old woman is carrying hencoops made from plant fiber with the balancing system used right across east Asia for thousands of years.

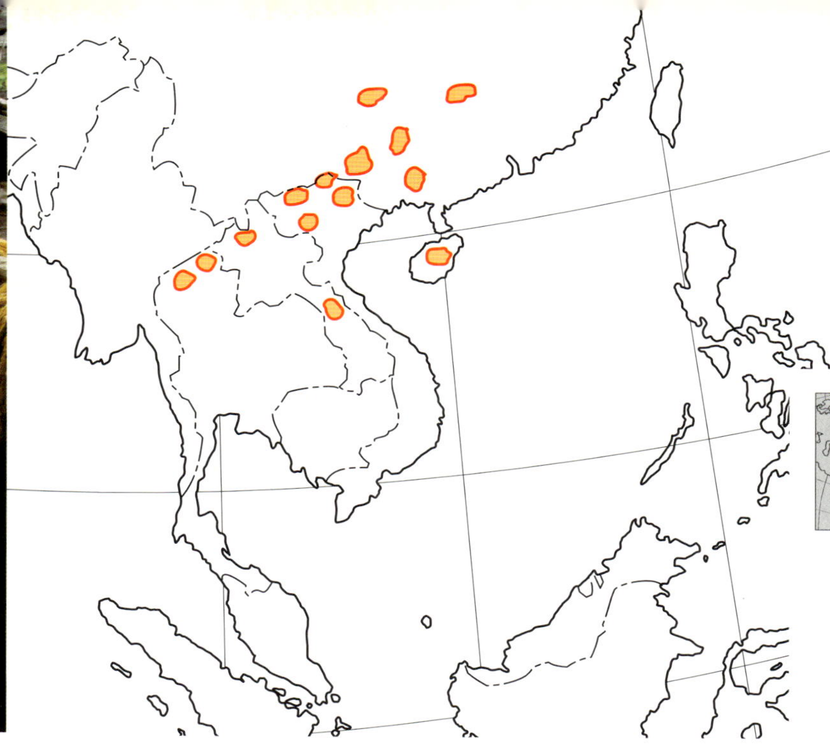

ASIA

Miao

CHINA, THAILAND, VIETNAM AND LAOS

The Miao, also known as the Hmong, are one of the most numerous ethnic minorities in China. It is calculated that there are 80 or so of their communities spread across the provinces of Guizhou, Hunan, Sichuan, Yunnan and the autonomous region of Guangxi. In addition, a small group live on the island of Hainan in the province of Guangdong and in the southwest of the province of Hubei. However, the largest communities are found in Thailand, Laos and Vietnam. Most of the Miao live in very closed groups, particularly so in societies inhabited mostly by other ethnic groups. The zones they choose have many watercourses, natural resources, a mild climate and plenty of rain, which they use to carry out successful and surprisingly varied farming.

The spread of the groups across such a huge territory is the result of migrations over the centuries. According to Chinese sources, the forebears of the Miao lived in western Hunan and eastern Guizhou in the third century BC, after which they began to migrate west towards northwest Guizhou and along the river Wujiang in south Sichuan. In the fifth century some groups moved to east Sichuan and west Guizhou, then, 400 years later, other groups were taken prisoner and deported to Yunnan. Finally, in the sixteenth century, a number of Miao settled on the island of Hainan. The wide distribution of the people has led to a profound difference in customs, dress and dialect. Their language belongs to the Sino-Tibetan group and has three dialects in China; in the other areas in which the Miao live, the languages of other ethnic groups have been adopted.

Their traditional dress varies from community to community. The first distinction exists between everyday clothes and those for special occasions. In both cases the age, civil status, sex and provenance of the wearer are further reasons for differentiation. Clothes vary in their style, patterns, color, ornamentation and accessories so that, according to some experts, between 23 and 80 local styles might exist.

183 top Meat in the traditional Miao diet comes exclusively from domestic animals or fowl that they raise themselves.

183 center During the transplantation of the rice, the women wear new clothes to show their respect to the Cereal God. Ancient legend says that rice can only be transplanted in odd numbers and not before the whole village has paid tribute to the god during a ceremony held between April 19 and 21.

183 bottom After the harvesting of the rice, the large sheaves are taken to the village to be laid in the sun to dry. Currently, this type of rice culture is only practiced by the Miao in Guizhou.

Long-Horned

ASIA

184-185 The Chiangjaio Miao ('Long-Horned' Miao) live in mountains at a height of 6,600 feet. Their 12 neighboring villages in total accommodate 4,000 people.

185 Women in the Long-Horned Miao group bind their hair up on the top of their heads in a knot and hold it in place with a piece of cotton. Their unusual name comes from the custom of adding a cow's horn to their hair for decorative purposes.

186 top Given its complexity, the striking hairdo of the Small Flowers requires external help.

186-187 The Gha-Mu are also known as the Xiaohua Miao ('Small Flowers' Miao) and live in the counties of Shuicheng, Nayong and Hezhang in northwest Guizhou. This subgroup, one of the largest, currently numbers about 80,000 people.

187 *The lovely jackets worn by the 'Small Flowers' women in the province of Guizhou are made from satin and decorated with cross-stitch patterns. Embroidery is one of the most characteristic crafts of this people.*

Small Flowers

This extreme variety in clothing has led in China to the classification of the communities on the basis of the color and style of clothes, hairstyle and presence of certain accessories. The result is that there exist Red, Long-Horned, Silver, Black, Flowered, Long-Skirt and many other types of Miao.

Given the abundance of building wood in most of the zones inhabited by the Miao, their houses are usually made from wood with roofs made from fir bark, tiles or straw, whereas in central and western Guizhou they are covered with stone slabs. Their houses can vary notably in style: in the mountain areas they are generally built on slopes and rest on platforms, beneath which the domestic animals find shelter. In the zone of Zhaotong in Yunnan and on the island of Hainan, the Miao mostly live in straw huts or what are called 'branch houses'. These are made from woven branches and strips of bamboo and lined with mud.

The Miao are rigidly monogamous and their families are never particularly numerous. Weddings are usually arranged but men and women of marriageable age are free to court, and this is particularly what happens at popular festivals when youngsters from different villages gather to sing love-songs in counterpoint. Until a few decades ago in Chuxiong in the province of Yunnan, 'courting houses' used to be organized. Here, after a day's work, the young would gather to sing, dance and court others of the same age. If two people are mutually attracted, they exchange a love token but marriage requires parental permission. A practice that is often followed is called the 'abduction of the bride', which is in fact organized by the young couple with the help of friends and the family of the young man. After long negotiations conducted by the elders of the respective villages and the offer of valuable wedding presents, the parents of the girl generally yield and give their consent to the wedding. If they do not, the woman may return to her family without problem as the wedding will not have been consummated.

There are 15 or so popular festivals that in many cases coincide with festivals in the Chinese lunar calendar, yet the dates and related ceremonies may be very different from their Chinese counterparts and even between communities. One of the most important is the Miao New Year, which is celebrated in the county of Rongshui in southeast Guizhou and Guangxi on the 'day of the rabbit' or 'day of the ox' in the lunar calendar. Other typical festivities are the festivals of the Sisters, of the Cows, of the Mountain Flowers (May 5) and the Tasting of the New Rice (June or July).

Some – like the Festival of the Dragon-Boats, of the Pure Light, and of Mid-Autumn – are Chinese in origin but, among the Miao, are celebrated in a particularly impressive way. The people sing and dance to the sounds of the drums and *lusheng* (a reed flute) and there are bullfights and horse races. In the zone of Guiyang on April 8 the people dress up and assemble around the largest fountain in the city to play the *lusheng* and a simple pipe in exaltation of the legendary

188 left The extreme variety of the different Miao groups explains the custom (not accepted everywhere) of differentiating between them by the most apparent aspects of their dress.

188-189 and 188 bottom 'Small Flowers' girls dressed in traditional costume and red turbans take part in a popular festival in Nankai.

189 top During the ceremony, Xioahua Miao men from Guizhou wear hats with pheasant feathers.

189 bottom The Miao carry their children on their shoulders using specially fashioned and richly decorated seats.

Miao hero Yanu. In Yunnan, a very popular festival is 'Trampling the Mountain Flowers' in which childless couples repeat their marriage vows to the god of fertility. Unmarried youngsters are offered wine in bottles that hang from a pine tree, beneath which they sing and dance.

When a new love affair blossoms as a result of this ceremony, it is considered auspicious for those couples that are already married but childless.

Large sums of money are lavished on magic and superstitious festivals and rituals: in western Hunan and northeast Guizhou, for instance, prayers asking for a woman to get pregnant or a sickness to be cured must be accompanied by the sacrifice of two oxen, and these rituals are followed by celebrations that may last between three and five days.

190-191 As the Miao have no written records, their clothing is the best source for studying the rich culture of this peaceful and clever people who love festivals and color.

190 bottom left During a festival, a line of women wears the hats that give their group the name 'Pointed Hats'. Celebrations of this kind often coincide with events in the Chinese lunar calendar.

190 bottom right A group of musicians plays the lusheng *(a long bamboo flute), which is the most common traditional instrument in Miao culture. The Miao repertoire of traditional songs includes compositions with thousands of verses.*

Pointed Hat

191 The traditional costume of the 'Pointed Hats' is also worn by the children on ceremonial occasions. The fertility of the soil in the area where this group lives also provides plants that can be used in weaving: the fibers of ramie (Boehmeria nivea) *are ideal for producing gauzy fabrics.*

Song and dance are at the cultural center of all Miao communities.

Traditional literature is of equal importance and highly developed, with easy unrhymed songs of lengths that may vary from a few verses to tens of thousands. The Miao use many types of musical instruments: the most common is the *lusheng*, then there is the flute, copper drums, the mouth organ, *xiao* (bamboo pipes) and horns. Popular dances include the dance of the *lusheng*, the dance of the drum and the dance of the bench.

Local crafts are generally highly colored and include such as cross-stitch embroidery, weaving, paper cutting and the extremely old tradition of batik. In recent years, technological development has allowed the Miao to produce more sophisticated batik and this has now become one of their principal exports.

Silver

192 top left Near Anshun in the province of Guizhou there is a village of Hua Miao ('Flowered Miao') where more than 30 families live. Whether large or small groups, the communities of the Miao are generally inward-looking.

192 top right The silver ornaments worn by Miao women, which sometimes tower as seen in this photograph, include necklaces, collars, armbands, tiaras, brooches, combs, rings

192 bottom Silver is a symbol of wealth and beauty and is the Miao's favorite metal. The silver ornaments they make are usually shiny, symmetrically formed and finely worked in imaginative styles. The most common forms are inspired by nature.

192-193 The Miao in Kaili (capital town of the Autonomous Prefecture of Miao and Dong, of which 70% of the population is composed of ethnic minorities, the Silver Miao being the most numerous) clap their hands to the songs and dances during a festival. The many celebrations of the Miao include those derived from Chinese tradition but are given a more sumptuous treatment, as the children's costumes show.

Blacks

Outside of China the Miao (or Hmong as they call themselves) are numerous in Thailand, Vietnam and Laos. Cross-border migration seems to have begun in the eighteenth century when the Miao moved towards Tonkin and Annam and eventually reached Thailand at the end of the nineteenth century where they now represent two percent of the population.

It is said that most of the Miao entered Thailand after the Second World War but in fact they were nearly all already there in all the mountain ranges over 3,300 feet. Called Meo by the Thai (this is a pejorative term as it means 'barbarians'), the Miao have spread mostly into north Thailand and are generally classified in two subgroups: the Blues and Whites. In the area around Chiang Mai and to the west of the city, most of the villages are inhabited by the Blues, whereas those to the east are all White.

Blue Miao women wear their hair in a large chignon and their pleated skirts have red, blue and white horizontal stripes. They also wear black satin jackets with wide cuffs and collars embroidered in yellow and orange. Blue men wear baggy black trousers and jackets, similar to those of the women, which are closed by a button on the left shoulder.

White Miao women wear loose black trousers, held at the waist by a long blue sash that falls to their feet, and simple jackets with blue cuffs. Some groups wear a blue brimless hat.

The Vietnamese Miao, who are much more numerous, have settled in 13 provinces and are divided into several subgroups: these are referred to as the Whites, Greens, Blacks, Blues, Reds and Flowered (or Multicoloreds).

Most of these groups came from the provinces in southern China during three waves of migration. The first, which took them from Guizhou to Dong Van in the extreme north of Vietnam, occurred 300 years or so ago at the time of the struggle against the 'Land Reform and Ethnic

194 top The people in the district of Sapa are mostly Miao and live in small scattered communities that assemble to celebrate similar festivals to those in China, though less colorful and magnificent.

194 center and bottom The Miao are the eighth largest ethnic minority in Vietnam. The local subgroups include the Whites, Greens, Reds, Blacks and Flowered Miao. The young woman and child and the man with the silver necklace are from the Flowered subgroup.

194-195 and 195 bottom left The clothes of the Blacks are restrained and without decorations or embroidery except on the belts of the women. Generally the ornaments are made from silver.

195 bottom right With panniers on their shoulders, a group of Miao women in northern Vietnam return from the fields. The local rice paddies only provide one crop a year because of the high altitude.

ASIA

196 bottom left and 196-197
The Miao that spread into the northern areas of Vietnam were obliged to build their villages in the most difficult to reach areas – therefore uninhabited by indigenous peoples – in the provinces of Ha Gian and Lao Cai. They built terraces to grow rice and also used the traditional technique of slash-and-burn. The A-hmao are a subgroup that lives in the Chinese provinces of Yunnan and Guizhou and in Vietnam where they are also known as Multicolored or Flowered Miao for the assorted colors in the decorations and fabrics of their clothes.

Flowered

Rearrangement' policy of the Ming (1368-1644) and Qing (1644-1911) dynasties. The next wave took place about 200 years ago, during the era that the Miao in revolt were defeated in Guizhou (1776-1820). This dramatic episode forced refugees to cross the border north into Vietnam and then move northwest. Most of these emigrants came from Guizhou and nearby Yunnan.

The third and last migration was caused by another Miao rebellion, this time against the anti-Manchu movement of the Taiping Tianguo ('Kingdom of Heavenly Peace') between 1840 and 1868. This phase resulted in the largest group so far crossing the border. Having fled from Guizhou, Yunnan and Guangsi, the refugees settled in Ha Giang, Lao Cai and Yen Bai, all of which are in the extreme north of Vietnam. It is clear that the principal cause of these three waves was the constant conflict between the Miao and the central Chinese rulers.

Today the Miao groups in Vietnam live in mountain areas at altitudes between 2,600 and 5,000 feet. Due to the dearth of agricultural soil, they have to transport the earth from other zones to fill the gaps between rocks. The altitude means that rice can only be harvested once a year, which is hardly enough to satisfy the requirements of the Miao families for just six months. Irrigation is difficult despite the increasing use of modern techniques to irrigate, protect the soil against erosion and fertilize. In addition to agriculture, the Miao in Vietnam weave, produce tools and make handcrafts.

196 bottom right The Flowered Miao flock to the Sunday market in the village of Bac Ha in the Vietnamese province of Lao Cai to sell their wares, including a famous corn liquor.

197 The wearing of traditional dress is useful to the Flowered Miao for reasons of economic integration and as a tourist attraction. The life of Vietnamese Miao is generally more difficult than that of their Chinese counterparts. The altitude and the poverty of the soil of the places where they have settled make cultivation extremely hard despite attempts to modernize irrigation systems and improve the means of exploiting the land. Furthermore, their status as immigrants, who fled bloody revolts in China in the eighteenth and nineteenth centuries, does not favor integration. However, in the extreme north of the country, the tribal groups of Miao are often the largest communities.

ASIA

Padaung

MYANMAR

The Padaung are a subgroup of the Karen, and are also known as the Karen Padaung. The name Karen applies to various tribal peoples in southern Myanmar who speak languages in the Tibeto-Burmese family but which are influenced by the Austro-Thai group.

The Karen are not homogeneous ethnically and striking linguistic, religious and economic differences exist between groups. A general classification divides the Karen into White and Red Karen. The former include the Sgaw, Pa'o and Pwo tribes, and the latter the Bre, Yinbaw, Zayein and Padaung. They occupy the southeast zone of Myanmar along the lower stretch of the Salween River , zones that neighbor Thailand, the Pegu Yoma mountain range and the south Myanmar coast of the Irrawaddy Delta.

There are few Padaung in the plains except for the settlements near the Thai border. Although there are only roughly 7,000 Padaung, they have captured the interest of anthropologists and tourists for their practice of elongating the necks of their women with the use of a long brass coil. New rings are added during a woman's life until a maximum of 25 is reached.

Each time a new series of rings is added, the neck is elongated, the chin is pushed upwards and the cervical vertebrae are compressed. The first ring is positioned around the age of five or six in a ceremony at which the entire village participates. The date is chosen on the basis of calculations made by the village shaman. The neck of the girl is massaged for hours with liniment before the officiator winds the brass wire around her neck. To avoid grazes, padding is placed between the metal and the skin which is removed at a later date.

Each time new rings are added, the body requires several days to accustom itself to the increase in pressure and distortion, but before long the woman is able to restart normal daily life.

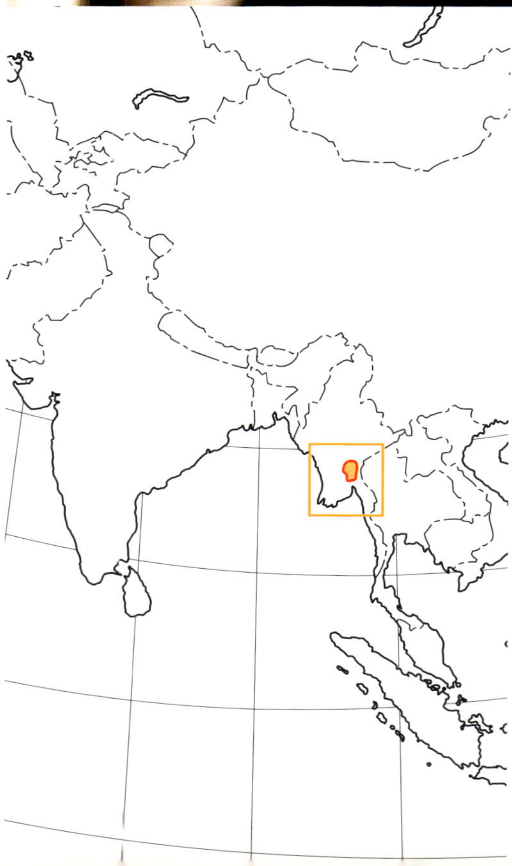

198 top In his 1934 novel Burmese Days, George Orwell (1903-50) wrote about beautiful women with giraffe-like necks. This was perhaps the first mention in a Western work of literature of Padaung women, whose practice of elongating the neck with brass rings has made them one of the main attractions in 'ethno-tourism' in Southeast Asia. However, the circumstances of the Padaung are very difficult both in Myanmar and Thailand; in the latter because tourist companies have seriously distorted the life of this peaceful people.

199 top and bottom right The greater the number of rings around the neck of Padaung women, the greater the prestige of their wearer. It is also a means for a family to demonstrate its wealth: 25 rings indicate a very high social position. Almost extinct 20 years ago, this practice is returning to fashion; now girls of just five years of age are made to wear them, so as to ensure a future income to their parents.

198-199 and 199 bottom left The first ring is applied to young girls before puberty. In the past, there were few women who wore this ornament, usually not more than one girl in each family, but for her the parents were able to ask a much larger payment from her future parents-in-law.

200 top There have been many attempts to explain the origin of the custom of the rings. An early interpretation was linked to the mythical origins of this people. According to legend, the Padaung were the children of a dragon and the wind, therefore, might the long neck of the women be a means of commemorating the long necks of their dragon ancestress?

200 bottom Other hypotheses are more concrete but no more convincing. To some, the rings protected the women from tigers, for others, they were a means of ensuring marital faithfulness, for, in the event of proven adultery, the rings would be removed and the guilty woman would be obliged to spend the rest of her life lying down or supporting her neck with her hands.

By the time girls have reached marriageable age, their necks may have been lengthened by 10 inches, and since the total weight of the rings is between 11 and 22 pounds, a number of adaptations need to be made to perform normal daily functions. For instance, more time and care is required in washing and dressing, and, during sleep, the neck must be rested on a high bamboo cushion to support the weight of the rings. Moreover, Padaung women are unable to look down so that they cannot see their babies during breast-feeding. If the rings were to be removed, the woman would suffocate as the neck muscles atrophy and become unable to support the weight of the head.

In addition to the neck coil, most Padaung women wear brass anklets and often silver bracelets. The women in other Red Karen tribes wear less adherent neck rings, and necklaces made of coins or moon-shaped pieces of metal or cowrie shells.

The traditional Padaung dwelling is a small square hut made from woven bamboo strips with a roof of palm leaves. A wide, open arcade stands in front of each hunt beneath which the women spin and weave while the men are working in the fields.

The traditional economy of the Padaung and of many other Karen tribes along the Myanmar-Thai border was based on the cultivation of cleared and burned portions of forest where they grew rice, vegetables and tobacco. The Padaung exchanged their crops or livestock for tools and industrial products in the markets of nearby towns. Occasionally, performed temporary paid work. At the end of the 1980s, during the war between the Myanmar army, groups of Karen rebels and drug barons, the inhabitants of many villages sought refuge in Thailand. Here, after centuries of the same peaceful and isolated existence, the Padaung found themselves catapulted into the twentieth century. Without resources or experience, they were exploited by the local tourist industry; after a period during which the refugees were treated practically as prisoners by unscrupulous tourist companies, which exhibited them to visitors in search of ethnic experiences, the Thai government stepped in and put an end to this embarrassing situation. A 'typical' Padaung village was built near Mae Hong Son which the Padaung were asked to run. It was not of course a real village but a group of pavilions in which the Padaung 'performed themselves' in a series of tableaux vivants, weaving, selling handmade goods to tourists and posing for photographs in traditional dress. Although for mercenary reasons, tourism has revived a dying tradition, even if the price paid has been the uprooting of a people.

200-201 and 201 bottom Recent development has increased the living standards of the Padaung but the high income that the women earn by allowing themselves to be photographed has convinced the men to abandon their traditional work in the fields and to depend exclusively on the women for income.

A S I A

202 top *The hairstyles of Balinese women are famous throughout the world for their elegance and complexity, but on a daily basis they use simple colored shawls called (tenguluk) to hold their hair in place.*

Bali-Aga

INDONESIA

[BALI]

Considered the indigenous inhabitants of the island, the Bali-Aga live in the mountain villages in the center of Bali. They are mostly farmers who work in cooperatives and cultivate rice on terraces of the mountain slopes. Each village is an autonomous community guided by an assembly of married men and presided over by a Council of Elders. The council is responsible for the affairs of the community and the cults associated with the village's three temples: the temple of the ancestors, which normally stands at the top of the village, the temple dedicated to the dead, built at the bottom, and the temple of the community where fertility rites are celebrated and the council meets.

Deeply rooted in daily life, Balinese beliefs combine Javanese Hinduism and Buddhism with ancient animistic traditions like the cult of the ancestors and the cult of the spirits of the emerged world (sun, land, water and mountains) and the underground world (spirits of evil and demons) in an attempt to balance out their contrasting influences. They perform rituals, offerings and sacrifices related to these beliefs in more than 20,000 temples across the island. The temples are sacred buildings believed to be resting places for gods visiting the Earth.

Of the many ceremonies, the most important is the *odalan* ('arrived' or 'apparition') that commemorates the day on which the divinity stopped in the temple for the first time. It is believed that on this anniversary – celebrated every 210 days – the gods come down from heaven to visit the temple, so the local congregation organizes a parade at the edge of the village to welcome the gods with dances and songs and escort them to the temple where offerings of flowers and food have been carefully prepared by the women. The simulacrum of the gods are carried in procession towards the sea or nearest river where they are submerged in the water and then taken back to

203 bottom left *A modern crop cultivated by the Balinese (who traditionally grow rice) is seaweed. This new product has opened new opportunities for the island.*

203 bottom right *The Balinese produce a wide variety of containers made from bamboo or rattan fibers completed with palm or banana leaves, like the baskets carried by this farmer.*

202 bottom *This Balinese breeder followed by a flock of ducks and ducklings wears a sarong, which is an item of clothing used by both men and women.*

202-203 *A group of women picks rice in the sun. The 'hat' visible on the right is in fact a* sok *(basket) of which the Balinese are expert manufacturers.*

204 top left *Traditional dances are one of the most interesting aspects of Balinese culture. The most fascinating is the legong, which is an elaborate series of steps, gestures and winks that have been precisely codified.*

204 top right *White, perfumed frangipane flowers adorn the crown of this* legong *dancer. No less complex than the choreography, the various parts of the costumes are defined in great detail.*

204 center left *At the start of the twentieth century, court theater and dances were in decline. This priceless legacy, however, has at least in part been saved by the growth in mass tourism.*

204 bottom left *No gesture is without significance in court dancing. In the past the dancers were the property of the prince, who chose the most graceful pre-adolescents to be found in the villages.*

204-205 *The musician and choreographer instructs two dancers. The girls train for five years, then have a fairly short career of just nine or 10 years as dancers.*

the temple. The celebration continues until dawn with food and dancing and with the theatrical performances that are a feature of all Balinese ceremonies.

Of the many performances, one that is very popular is that of the ritual struggle between two mythological figures: Rangda (an evil witch) and a Barong demon (that has the features of a dragon). The actors that wear the costumes and masks mime a drama but the plot remains incomplete: the witch retires unbeaten and the dragon dancers, who have gone into a trance, turn their destructive fury on themselves, pretending to stab themselves with their *kriss*, the sacred dagger with the wavy blade. The music that accompanies the show is performed by *gamelan* (musicians) on drums, gongs, bells, cymbals, xylophones, vibraphones, flutes and violins. Each village has such a group of musicians for its festivals and ceremonies.

Funerary ceremonies are also taken very seriously as the ancestors might get angry and visit sicknesses or misfortune on the family if a suitable service is not provided. The ceremony and its treatment generally reflect the caste or prestige of the deceased. The body is buried but later exhumed for cremation, which is done to liberate the soul. A festive parade in which the entire village participates accompanies the coffin (normally carved in the shape of a bull, cow or lion depending on the caste of the deceased) on its journey to the pyre where it is burned with personal belongings of the deceased. Then the ashes are scattered on the sea.

The Hindu caste system is represented by *wangsa* (hereditary titles) that establish the rank of each person. Social distinctions are also respected in the use of language of which three forms exist – high, middle and low – depending on the rank of the speaker. An unusual activity on the island is cock fighting, on which a great deal of care is expended. This cruel sport is interesting from an anthropological viewpoint as the fights are governed by rules handwritten on palm leaves and passed down from generation to generation in a custom that denotes the Balinese desire to conserve and hand down their millenary cultural heritage.

205 top During the odalan *(the splendid ceremony that commemorates the settling of a god in a temple) a procession of costumed women carry* gebogan *(offerings of fruit and sweets) on their heads.*

205 bottom During the celebrations the practice of adorning their heads with elaborate headdresses or simple floral compositions is not a question of coquetry but a sign of respect and homage.

peoples of the World

OCEANIA

List of peoples

Written by Mirella Ferrera

206 left The Asmat people in Irian Jaya remained isolated from the rest of the world until the middle of the last century. The name they give themselves means 'real people' and also 'tree people'.

206 right The didgeridoo is a traditional instrument of the Australian Aboriginals. It is a simple wooden cylinder but the technique to play it is complex and requires sophisticated breath control.

207 Discovered only about 50 years ago, the Chimbu and other groups on the highlands of Papua New Guinea were involved in a state of 'perpetual war' that had become traditional.

208-209 The disquieting war masks of the Gururumba in Papua New Guinea are in fact helmets made from gray clay and applied objects, like the teeth and ears. The name of this people means 'wild men' but they are more commonly known as 'mudmen' as they cover their bodies with the clay from which they make their masks.

Introduction

In the broadest and most widespread meaning of the term, Oceania covers Australia, New Guinea, New Zealand and the myriad of smaller islands, archipelagos and atolls scattered across the immensity of the Pacific Ocean that go by the names of Melanesia, Micronesia and Polynesia.

The human settlement of this vast area began around 40,000 years ago and occurred in migratory waves of groups coming from Southeast Asia. Colonization was gradual and began with the occupation of New Guinea and Australia. The extreme variety in physique, language and culture of the peoples of Oceania is explained by the mixing of groups who arrived at different times and/or from different origins, combined with the isolation of certain ethnic groups and the adaptation to local environments such as the Australian desert, the highlands of New Guinea, and the volcanic islands and coral atolls of the Pacific. This differentiation is generally simplified into the 'cultural areas' of the Australian Aboriginals, the peoples of Melanesia (including the groups in Papua New Guinea), Micronesia and Polynesia.

From archaeological finds that reveal human settlement from about 20,000 years ago, experts believe that Australia was populated by small groups that arrived in primitive boats having used the long chain of Indonesian islands like stepping stones, settling first in New Guinea, and then crossing the Torres Strait to reach the Cape York Peninsula. The enormous deserts prompted the dispersion of the groups and this in turn resulted in a fragmentation of languages (there are more than 600 languages and dialects spoken by the Australian Aboriginals) and a subsistence based on hunting and gathering. The consequence of isolation was the conservation of peculiar physical and linguistic characteristics that are not assimilable to other groups in Oceania.

The cultural area of Melanesia (which literally means 'islands of blacks') includes New Guinea, the Solomon Islands, the New Hebrides and New Caledonia. The oldest local settlement, which has been found in New Guinea, dates to 2,500 years ago and was settled by Negroid peoples, probably groups of 'negritos' from Southeast Asia. The means of livelihood used by the Melanesians was predominantly itinerant agriculture in the forest, supported by fishing along the coastal areas and on the islands.

The geographical separation of the groups as a result of natural barriers like the highlands of New Guinea and the distance between the smaller islands corresponds to linguistic variations. It has been calculated that there are about a thousand spoken languages, which are divided in two groups: roughly 750 in New Guinea (these make up the Papua group, which for the most part are unrelated and not descended from any linguistic family) and 250 in the smaller islands that belong to the Malayo-Polynesian and Austronesian group (this stretches from Madagascar to Polynesia through Southeast Asia) and were probably introduced 4,000 years ago.

Colonization of Micronesia ('small islands') and Polynesia ('many islands') occurred more recently. The Micronesian cultural area covers the Mariana, Caroline, Marshall and Gilbert Islands and was colonized between 3000 and 2000 BC by peoples from the Philippines and Indonesia, who are therefore genetically related to the Melanesian groups. Polynesia consists of many Pacific islands and archipelagos: the Hawaiian, Society, Phoenix, Ellice, Cook and Marquesas islands, Tokelau, Uvea, Samoa, Tonga, Fiji, Easter Island, Tuamotu, Tubuai, Mangarewa, Pitcairn Island and, in purely ethnological terms, New Zealand.

The Polynesian population has genetic variations compared to the other groups in Oceania but is remarkably consistent linguistically and culturally. It seems that, in certain cases, the initial wave of colonization was followed by a second wave of groups that had remained isolated long enough to have developed their own genetic and cultural characteristics. These were probably peoples of the Lapita culture from New Guinea and other islands who spread across the thousands of islands in the area, starting from the Tonga Archipelago around 1600 BC and moving towards the Cook Islands, Solomon Islands, New Zealand and Easter Island, which they reached before 500 AD. Some islanders in Samoa and the Ellice Islands were to return west, landing in Micronesia and creating the outlying cultural centers of Nukuoro, Kapingamarangi and the Melanesian islands of

Ontong Java, Rennell, Bellona, Rotuma and Tikopia. The fascinating hypothesis that colonization took place from the coasts of South America remains to be proven.

The slow European 'discovery' of Oceania began in the sixteenth century with New Guinea but flowered fully by the eighteenth century when the entire area was being criss-crossed by explorers in search of the fabulous continent of the south, the famous *Terra australis incognita*, on behalf of the European maritime powers that wished to expand commercially in the Pacific.

Contact with the colonizers soon gave rise to new languages, known as pidgin, that were largely used between indigenes and colonists and mostly composed of words of European derivation. In 1788, when Australia became a British penal colony, the number of Australian Aboriginals was roughly 300,000 fragmented in, 300 tribal groups, each of which had its own territory and existed by hunting and gathering. During this same period, Melanesian islanders used a system of exchange based on the redistribution of wealth by means of which the different peoples established alliances that supported and maintained commercial relationships.

The spread of Catholicism and Protestantism by missionaries did not prevent certain aspects of traditional beliefs being retained, for instance, the cult of the ancestors, which included the veneration of their skulls. As symbols filled with supernatural power, skulls were kept in the 'men's house', which was a ceremonial place reserved for the male members of the community.

This form of exclusion illustrates an aspect of Melanesian culture that is still current: the male control of social and ceremonial life. This is expressed through the rigid separation of work responsibilities, social and ceremonial roles, and living areas between the sexes. The culture of Papuan groups revolves around male rituals that extol male fertility and, in consequence, the power of the group. Male prestige is recognized by the number of pigs exchanged and sacrificed, and the size of (phallic shaped) tubers; they also display themselves in spectacular dances featuring large masks, body painting and feathered headdresses.

In contrast, in Micronesia there is no division between the sexes and women take part in both the group's social and ceremonial lives. On some islands society was organized in matrilineal clans all descended from a single mythical forebearer. Micronesians lived on cultivation and fishing (still fundamental to their existence) but trading with distant archipelagos by means of outrigger canoes was also frequent.

At the time of the European exploration of Pacific routes, Polynesian societies were already fairly evolved and mostly structured in two classes: the nobility and the commoners; in some cases there were even monarchies. Their local culture was generally very rich, as is demonstrated by the complexity of the languages of Hawaii, which includes a highly flexible system of pronouns, and Easter Island, which has a script that has not yet been deciphered.

Many environmental and historical factors have contributed to transforming the Oceanic peoples; though often lumped together in the Western imagination as similar inhabitants of an insular Eden, they are in fact very different to one another. Their adaptation to foreign ways of life and the economic and strategic importance of Oceania as a whole have done away with part of their cultures and traditions in such a way that only the impenetrability of islands like New Guinea has permitted the survival (even if partial) of an authentic culture. As happens elsewhere and with increasing frequency, however, the peoples of Oceania – first and foremost the Maori – have had the strength to achieve recognition of part of their culture which, until a few years ago, risked disappearing forever.

210 Archaeology suggests that the Maori custom of ta moko *(face tattoos) originated in eastern Polynesia, however, New Zealand is only considered Polynesian in ethnological terms.*

211 Like other tribal populations in the interior of New Guinea, the Foré people have officially abandoned cannibalism, the practice of which is purely ritual.

212-213 An enclosure of tree trunks surrounds a traditional Dani village on the slopes of the Baliem River. The purpose of the enclosure is to defend the village against incursions by other tribes and stands in the center of a large clearing.

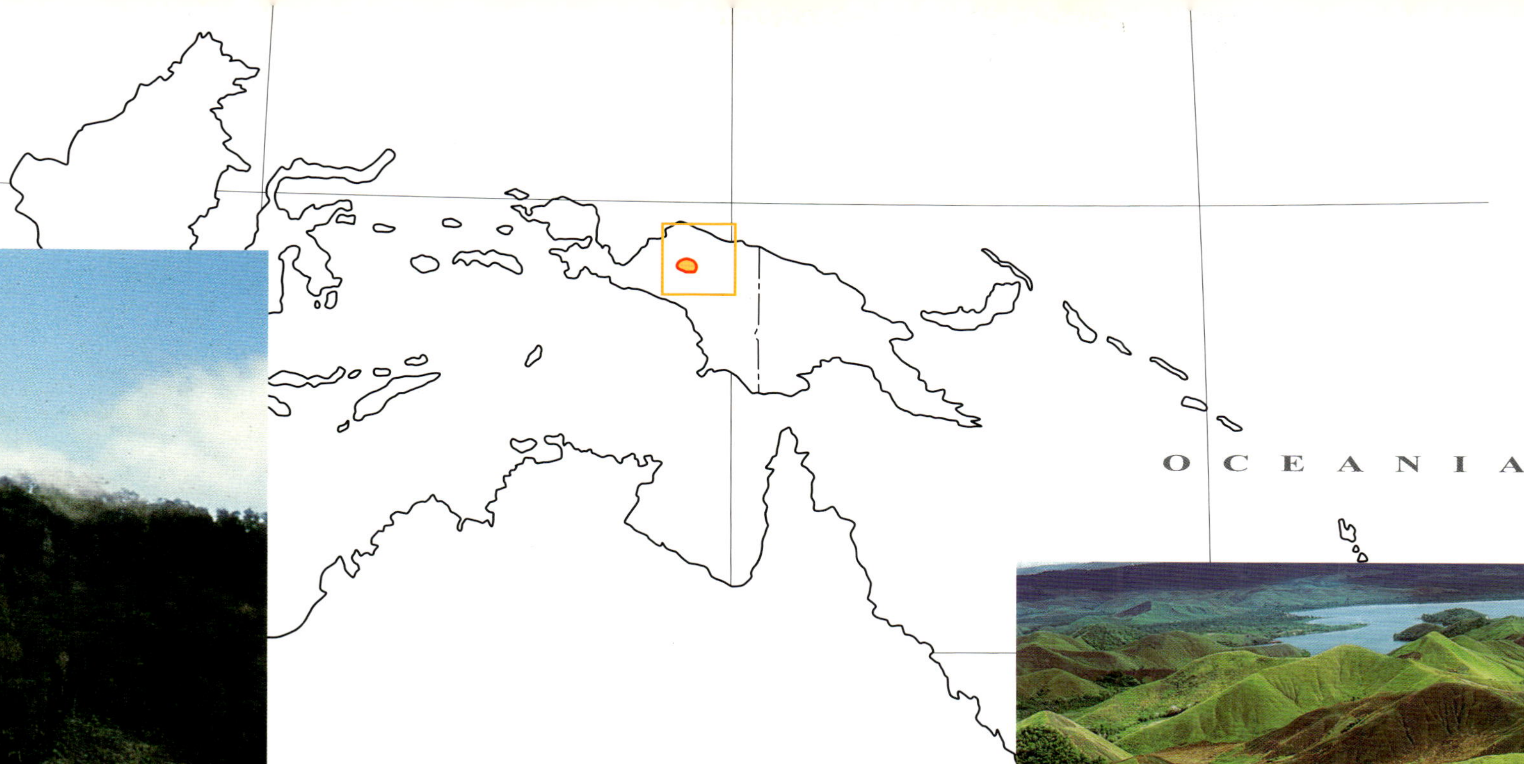

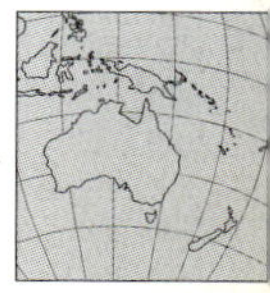

Dani

NEW GUINEA

[IRIAN JAYA]

There are an estimated 100,000 Dani to the north of the watershed of the Maoke Mountains in Irian Jaya at the western end of New Guinea. The various communities live in scattered communities on the mountain slopes, subsisting on hunting and the cultivation of taro, sweet potatoes and bananas. They also breed pigs, which they use in trading and ritual sacrifices.

As is seen among other Melanesian groups, traditional villages center on the 'men's house', but a particular Dani characteristic is a lookout built to monitor possible attacks by enemy groups as war is traditionally one of the main activities of this and other peoples on the island. First the Dutch and then the Indonesian government attempted to stem this endemic state by launching a series of peace-making campaigns.

Until the recent past, the clashes – which the men prepared for by smearing their bodies with fat and wearing headdresses – were frequent though often in the form of a ritual battle: this took place in the open with hand-to-hand fighting and the use of bows and arrows but the number of men hurt was limited. However, there also existed surprise attacks that led to the destruction of entire villages and indiscriminate massacre when deaths could reach the hundreds.

The belief was widespread that the ghosts of those killed in battle demanded vengeance, and this was what lay at the bottom of the cycle of almost continuous conflict. The only interruptions occurred with the arrangement of periodic alliances between leaders of those groups in conflict. These were celebrated ritually with dignified 'festivals of the pigs' in which the alliances were endorsed by the exchange of material goods like pigs, shells, the feathers of birds of paradise and even marriages.

The peace agreement was sealed by the sacrifice of hundreds of animals.

212 bottom left Seen from above, the cultivated plots along a series of channels fed by the river seem well-organized. Agriculture principally provides tubers from which the Dani make a nourishing flour.

212 bottom right An ingenious suspension bridge over the Baliem River. Though fragmented and often hostile, certain tribes in New Guinea have developed complex techniques to transform their territory.

213 top Villages on the shores of Lake Sentani are known for their traditional art, for example, painted tree bark and cups carved from sago palm.

213 center and bottom Honai (Dani huts) are covered with layers of fronds to make them waterproof. The men live separately from the women, children and animals.

214 top Ritual feasts of pig meat are important in the life of the Dani. The men wear their warrior costumes even though the feasts often represent temporary reconciliation between tribes at war.

214-215 Village women surround the fire separate from the men. Sexual segregation is common to most of the peoples in Irian Jaya and Papua New Guinea.

214 bottom Despite intermixing with other ethnic groups, the Dani still have markedly Australoid features, like the other Melanesian tribal peoples; for instance, they are medium-tall and long-limbed. The islands of the Indonesian chain were used as stepping stones by migrating peoples around 20,000 years ago and served as a bridge to the Australian continent.

Other elements peculiar to the cultural traditions of the Dani are sexual abstinence for a period of up to six years by the parents after the birth of a son, and the male form of costume of a long sheath worn over the phallus and tied around the chest by plant fibers; (this symbolizes fertility and offers protection when fighting). Female clothing is limited to skirts made from plant fibers.

Cremation, followed by the burial of the ashes outside the village, is the standard form of funerary ritual. Fear of the dead is an important element in the Dani culture and, to placate the ghosts of the dead, who are considered potentially dangerous and a cause of misfortune and sickness, animals often need to be sacrificed.

Today Christianity is fairly widespread among the Dani following the arrival of missionaries in the 1950s. Islam has made little headway owing to the importance to the Dani of the cult of the pig, which is actually common to all Melanesian cultures.

215 top The face of this woman is covered with yellowish clay to signify that she is in mourning. The Dani cremate the body of the deceased, then bury the ashes. The spirits of the dead are greatly feared, particularly those of enemies killed in battle. Even the specters of relatives are held in respect to prevent reprisals.

215 center Women circle a companion who is either sick or in disfavor, trying to cure her with lamentations or by shaking herbs. The patient is covered by the bag that the Dani use to gather plants and other products such as salt.

215 bottom Generally speaking, men's duties are related to the use of arms, such as intertribal wars, hunting and feuds within the clans. Today they are mostly Christian and a little closer to at least partial integration in society in Irian Jaya. Sometimes they travel to the coasts for work or to study.

Yali

NEW GUINEA [IRIAN JAYA]

216 top Yali villages are built at medium height, often around 6,600 feet. Women are essentially responsible for the crops and gathering, as occurs among the Dani, their neighbors with whom they share their language.

216-217 The aim of war for the Yali is not territorial conquest but to repay the offences suffered in past clashes. They are conducted by small groups of men who attack suddenly with bows, arrows and spears.

217 The fertility of the soil provides the Yali with materials useful for combating the climate: pandan leaves, offer shelter from the rain, which can be as much as 200 inches annually.

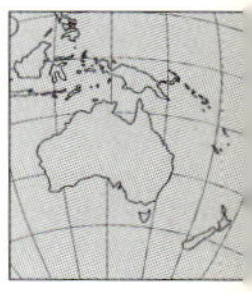

The roughly 30,000 representatives of the Yali tribe live in villages on the mountains to the south and north of the Jayawijàya range and to the southeast of the Dani, with whom they share their language. Their subsistence economy is based on itinerant agriculture, hunting and gathering and the breeding of pigs.

In common with other groups in New Guinea, the division of roles means that Yali men are responsible for war, hunting, tilling and deforesting cultivatable land and building houses. The women look after the children, cultivate vegetables, harvest the crops, collect wood and gather forest fruits.

Consequently, male children grow up in a female environment until their initiation into the adult male community, when they are allowed to enter the 'men's house'. Experts claim that this separation of educational roles between the sexes, plus the lack of a centralized authority, would explain the unrest that is endemic to the Yali, who are constantly engaged in intertribal and intratribal war. As we have seen for the Dani, war is not for the purpose of territorial conquest but created by the need for retribution for offences suffered (adultery, theft, murder, unpaid debts, etc.). It includes blood feuds and the ritual cannibalism of the bodies of killed enemies.

Combat is waged by small groups in the form of 'strike and flee' tactics in which the attackers rapidly approach and unexpectedly rain down arrows on their adversaries, then chase the survivors. Defensive clothing is composed of the *sebiàp* (reed armor worn around the waist), a mesh headdress and a protection worn over the phallus.

Periods of conflict alternate with periods of ceasefire: after long negotiations, which may last years, the two parties are reconciled during peace ceremonies accompanied by ritual exchanges, dances and the sacrifice of pigs.

218-219 and 218 bottom A group of Una pygmies makes stone tools from basalt in the midst of the sturdy, cylindrical huts of a village. Manufacture of these tools is entrusted exclusively to a clan numbering just a few hundred individuals in this small tribe. Discovered in the 1970s, the Una were immediately described as the last people of the Stone Age and, in fact, their refined techniques have much in common with those used in the Paleolithic period. Finished stones are the most precious objects of this people, who attribute a direct divine origin to stone.

219 top No less bellicose than other groups on the island, the Una and the other pygmoid tribes are all short in size, perhaps because of adaptation to the cold and remote living conditions in the highlands. One theory is that they are of African origin, given that the only other groups of pygmies in the world also inhabit wet sub-equatorial forests.

219 center An Una pygmy shows how he killed an enemy. Although cannibalism has almost been abandoned by the Una, intertribal clashes are still a feature of the less controllable areas of the island.

219 bottom The Una collect basalt rocks along a dry river bed in a steep valley. The first task in working the blocks is to split them using fire.

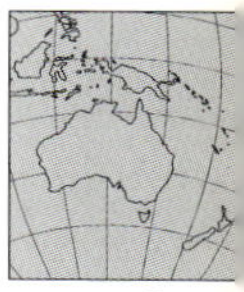

Una Pygmies

NEW GUINEA

[IRIAN JAYA]

Various Pygmoid peoples live to the east of the territory of the Yali in the highlands of Irian Jaya. Their average height is about 4'4" as a result of genetic mutations associated with their isolation and adaptation to adverse environmental conditions. One of these groups is the Una people who inhabit the valleys of the tributaries of the Steenboom River ; the estimated 4,600 Una (calculated in the early 1990s) are settled in a mountainous region with a cold and damp climate. For the most part gatherers and vegetable growers, they also breed pigs and hunt with the help of dogs. Like other peoples on the island, the Una practiced ritual cannibalism until a few years ago.

Their villages stand on mountain or cultivated slopes and number a few dozen round huts covered with conical roofs made of pandan leaves. Standing at the center of each village is the 'men's house' where the males who have undergone initiation rites can meet.

The Una Pygmies are distinguished from other groups by their manufacture of stone tools, which they make from blocks of volcanic basalt found along the course of the Heime River inside their territory. These blocks are worked by members of a particular clan to form thin, flat slivers that, when rubbed down, are turned into blades about eight inches long. These are used for cutting down trees, removing roots, etc., but are also used as goods for exchange. They may be bartered with neighboring groups for the feathers of birds of paradise, plant fibers for making mats or baskets, or other materials; they are also useful for consolidating social alliances and paying the 'bride price'. These blades also have a mythical and religious meaning as the Una attribute a mythic origin to stones; according to the Una, stones were born from the womb of Alim Yongnum, the bride of the cultural hero Alim Berekwa of the Balyo clan, i.e., the clan to which the Una stone-workers belong. Possession of traditional stone blades brings great social and economic prestige.

OCEANIA

Korowai

NEW GUINEA

[IRIAN JAYA]

This Melanesian people lives in the rainforest south of the large mountain chain in the center of Irian Jaya, which lies between the tributaries of the Digùl and Eilànden rivers. The Korowai subsist on hunting, fishing, growing vegetables and gathering plants. Like other groups in the area, they build *khaim* (houses) in trees at a height of about 60-70 feet from the ground to protect them from insects, snakes, enemy attack, evil spirits and, above all, the frequent floods. The houses are made of wood and accommodate from one to five nuclear families. They are divided into sections for the men and women separated by wooden partitions.

Similar to other peoples in New Guinea, the Korowai are in perpetual conflict with their neighboring tribal groups.

The fighting is in part nourished by the belief in *lalèoalin* (evil spirits), which are believed to take the form of people not belonging to the Korowai territorial clans. The negative influence of these spirits may be opposed with magic although, according to local beliefs, there also exist individuals with *khakhua* (magic powers) used for harmful purposes. Wizards and witches of this sort can cause epidemics, famines, floods and disease by firing invisible arrows into the hearts of their victims.

When cosmic harmony – which is necessary for the continuity of life – is threatened by negative influences of this sort, the Korowai organize a feast to placate the spirits and re-establish the order upset by black magic. The feast is used as an occasion to hold weddings, which are celebrated with singing and dancing, and the religious leaders perform propitiatory rites accompanied by the sacrifice of pigs and the ritual consumption of beetle larvae.

The larvae grow in the trunks of palms (which the Korowai hold to be symbols of fertility and eternal life) that supply sago, the flour that is used throughout the Indonesian chain of islands.

220 top *Flooding in the wet, low altitude forests prompts the Korowai and nearby peoples to build houses 'in the clouds'. Climbing the poles to reach them is difficult but this offers protection against animals and attacks by other groups.*

220 center The tree-houses of the Korowai are so solid that they can accommodate several families, but they are divided into sections to separate the sexes. Children grow up with the women until, still young, they are considered ready for instruction reserved for males. After 10 or so years of this, they undergo initiation rites.

220 bottom and 221 bottom The Korowai are hunter-gatherers and mostly use tools made from stone and bone. Body ornaments are made from the bones of pigs and flying foxes.

220-221 As often occurs in New Guinean tribal groups, construction of khaim *is a job for the men, but the Korowai must be talented engineers to build safe houses. The wood of many equatorial trees is extremely hard and this supplies the materials for the structure, whereas lianas are used to secure the wood.*

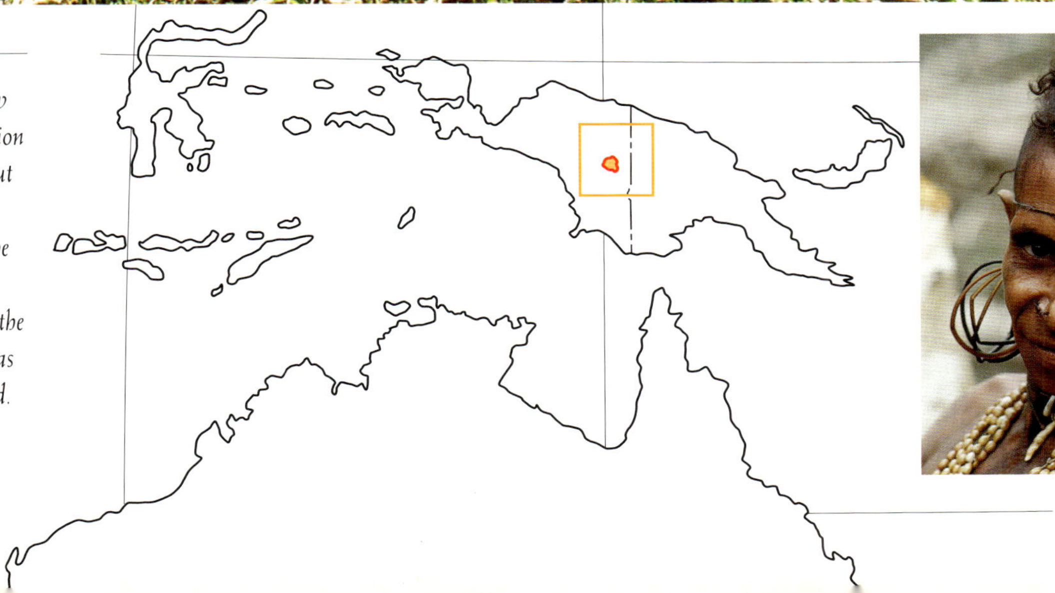

Arapesh

PAPUA NEW GUINEA

The Arapesh are a Melanesian people numbering just a few hundred individuals that lives in a part of the swampy Sepik Valley in Papua New Guinea. Their subsistence is traditionally based on the cultivation of tubers (igname and taro) and bananas, fishing and pig breeding. The possession of pigs is a symbol of a high social status and is useful in ceremonial exchanges between and within tribes in all the various Melanesian cultures. At one time exchanges of this kind were the foundation of temporary alliances between neighboring groups that were often on a war footing with one another.

Generally built on high ground, all Arapesh villages have a 'men's house', called a *housetambaran* in local pidgin, which serves as the community's social and religious center but which women are not allowed to enter.

As is the case among other Melanesian groups, male dominance in social and ritual life prevents the tribe's

222 top A group of Arapesh display their traditional costumes and headdresses, adorned with flowers, beetle wings, butterflies and the feathers of birds of paradise. The feathers are also used as items of value in exchanges and peace making.

222 bottom Ritual scarification (scarring) is a feature of Arapesh culture and an important part of the preparation for life. The patterns are created by inserting ash into incisions to slow the healing of the skin.

222-223 The dream of every Arapesh male is to become a 'big man': this figure is of proven courage in battle and has qualities like generosity, which confer him with great prestige. It is the big men who fight and negotiate peace terms with their rivals and therefore who govern the most important social relationships.

223 top right and bottom left Face painting, elaborate hairstyles with totemic symbols and bone ornaments are deliberately conspicuous and reflect a very close and harmonious relationship with various aspects of existence: society, nature and the supernatural. The dead – whether enemies killed in battle, relations or ancestors of the clan – are still part of the life of the clan and are exhumed so their 'vital fluid' can be acquired.

women from taking part in the most important ceremonies, such as male initiation rites.

With regard to community decisions, the Arapesh are subordinate to a 'big man' who is recognized on the basis of the influence he exercises, his skill in battle and the generosity he shows in ceremonial offerings. Great care is devoted to the cult of the ancestors, whose spirits, if offended by infractions of the rituals, may cause sickness in the community, but adversity may also be the result of witchcraft.

Wizards and shamans act as intermediaries between the Arapesh and the world of the spirits. According to traditional beliefs, after death the *mishin* (soul) survives as a spiritual entity and flies toward the sea. The dead are buried, but the bones of particularly important individuals are dug up and, if the deceased was a man, used for magical purposes in order to acquire his special qualities.

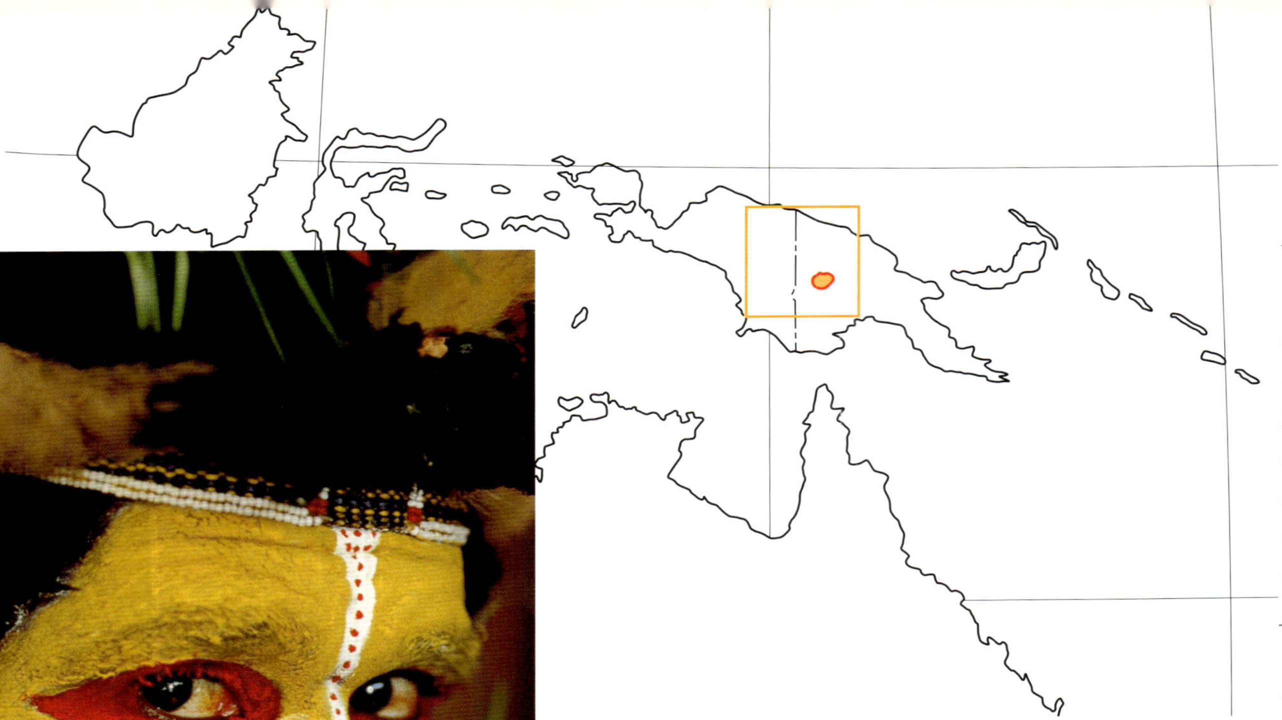

224 left *The Huli are distinguishable from other peoples in New Guinea by their face painting on a chrome yellow background. They are also known as 'wigmen' because of the imposing hairpieces that every warrior begins to create from his own hair during the years of preparation for adult life.*

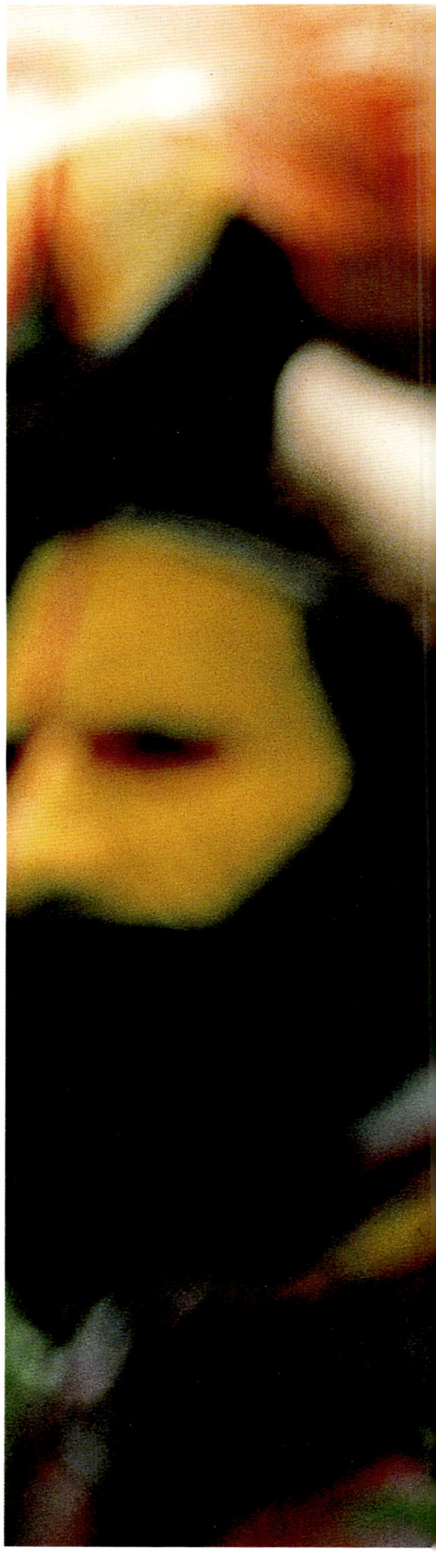

Huli

PAPUA NEW GUINEA

The Huli live in the highlands of eastern New Guinea (Papua New Guinea) just south of the watershed that divides the island lengthways and roughly 125 miles east of the border with Irian Jaya. As with other populations in the area, they have a subsistence economy based on itinerant agriculture, pig breeding, hunting and the gathering of forest products like pandan nuts, which are rich in protein.

In keeping with the customs of other Melanesian tribes, the Huli also practice the separation of male and female living quarters and the division of roles and work tasks. Women look after the children and vegetable gardens, and are helped by their daughters in raising the pigs.

Male children leave the maternal home around nine or 10 years of age to live with their father and the male community. From that moment they no longer eat food cooked by the women and are instructed by their fathers to cultivate, hunt, fight in battle and to respect and obey their elders. During *haroli* (the period of male 'apprenticeship'), the young boys live apart from the community in the forest where they are taught by a *daloali* (male unmarried elder) about the tribe's mythology, war, survival strategies in the forest and how to protect themselves from the negative influence of the spirits and women.

The Huli believe in many spirits – the *damia* – that inhabit the sky, rivers, forest and mountains and which exercise control over the land, climate, fertility of the soil and livestock. These spirits can cause sickness and troubles but their influence can be placated and their powers taken advantage of.

The Huli also believe that women have a certain power, called *tomia*, that can cause sickness or death. Their negative force is especially present in menstrual blood and has a powerful effect over men, who are obliged to teach ritual formulas and techniques to defend themselves.

224-225 Not unlike African peoples such as the Bororo and Surma, Huli men spend a great deal of time decorating their bodies. In general, the Huli are more given to traditional activities than war; many, in fact, have received a modern education and speak English, but very few leave the highlands.

225 top This man has a snakeskin across his forehead and earrings lined with opossum fur; he is wearing the hairpiece he made during haroli*, the long initiation period in which the young boys, separated from the rest of the community, are taught by an unmarried elder to defend themselves from the negative influence of women.*

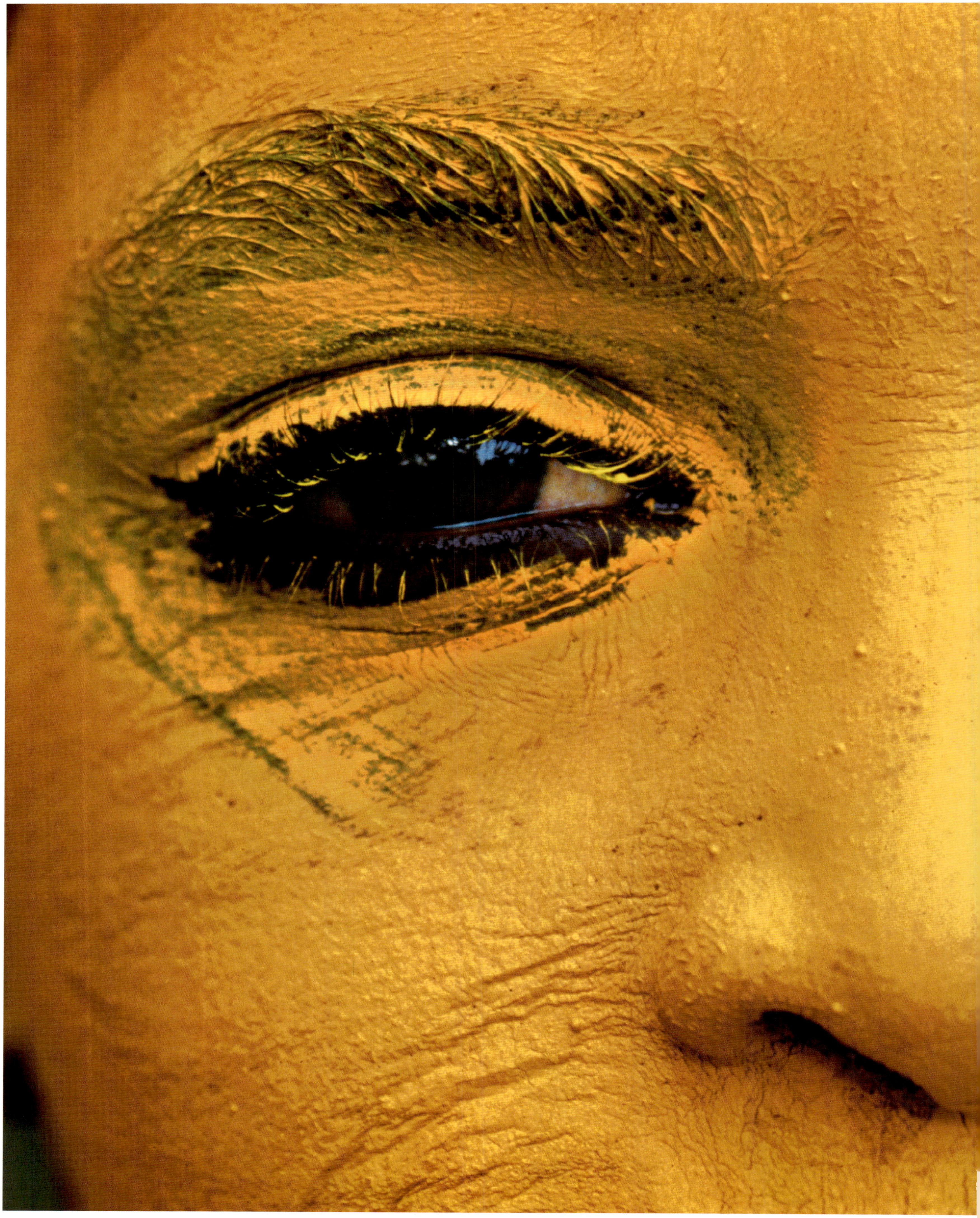

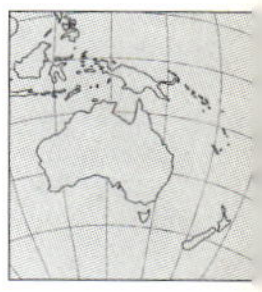

OCEANIA

226-227 *In the past, yellow colorant was obtained from a clay called* ambwa, *but today it has been substituted by commercial colorants. Other colors were also obtained from red and vermilion clays, and the wigs were tinted with smokeblack.*

The Huli do not inherit social roles so individual status depends on innate ability or talents acquired such as producing a yield from a vegetable garden, being a skilful warrior or knowing ritual formulas.

228-229 The bark taken by these two youngsters from the Arnhem Land aboriginal reserve will become 'pages' on which the creation myths will be drawn in ocher.

228 bottom left Depending on geographic location, around 20% of Aboriginals' diet is made up of fish, in particular, a species of bream.

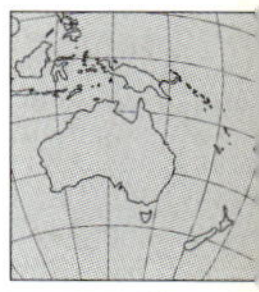

OCEANIA

Aboriginals

AUSTRALIA

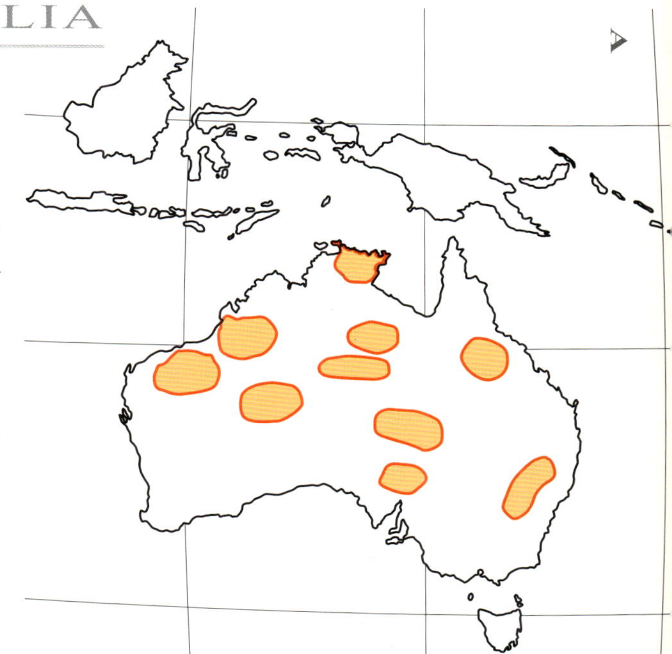

When Europeans began to settle in Australia at the end of the eighteenth century and founded a penal colony, the Aboriginals were divided in many tribal groups and organized in nomadic, hunter-gatherer bands across the continent. This was the only form of subsistence practiced by the groups who inhabited the arid interior, whereas those on the coasts were able also to fish and gather mollusks; on the other hand, they were exposed to contact with Europeans. Those living in Tasmania, for example, were exterminated by the colonists by the end of the nineteenth century.

The following are just some of the many Aboriginal tribes who between them speak about 250 related languages: the Aranda, Murngin and Walbiri of Northern Territory, the Kariera, Karadjeri and Pitjantjara of Western Australia, the Dieri and Kamilaroi of South Australia, the Kurnai of Victoria, the Wongaibon of New South Wales, the Lardil of Queensland and the extinct Tasmanians. Each tribal group was further divided into totemic clans, i.e., in groups whose members had a common ancestor. This aspect meant that marriage could not take place between members of the same clan (clan exogamy). The ancestor was thought of as a supernatural being and recognized with a totem in the form of an animal, plant, stone or other kind of natural phenomenon.

The creation myths of the Aboriginals was centered on the Dreamtime, which was a primordial epoch in which the totemic ancestors crossed the continent singing out the names of everything they encountered along their way (animals, plants, rivers, rocks, mountains, etc.) and thereby giving origin to the world. On his or her journey through the territory, each ancestor left a wake of words and musical notes known as the 'Tracks of the Ancestors' or 'Songlines'. These paths have remained on Earth as lines of communication between the various tribes and are still used by the Aboriginals during migration, when they listen once more to the songs of the Ancestors. Even the ownership of land was regulated by the Songlines: each Aboriginal inherited a strip of land over which the song of his Ancestor

228 bottom right For Aboriginal children who do not live in cities, and who therefore only receive partial education, traditional instruction continues to be a feature of life.

229 top There are two types of boomerang: the more famous hunting version that returns to the thrower, and the heavier war boomerang designed to lodge itself in the body of the enemy.

229 bottom An Aboriginal from Arnhem Land returns from the hunt. When hunting birds, Aboriginals tie large nets made from plant fiber between the trees.

230 The totemic decorations of Aboriginals identify for men (top) and for women (bottom) the ritual progress of the individual through the phases of life from initiation (center).

231 Fishing is often a job for the men, who might use boomerangs, spears or traps. Fishermen in the interior use bark boats on the rivers.

passed, and the verses of the songs were like title deeds that could be lent or exchanged during *corroboree*. These are ceremonies in which different totemic clans conceded each other the right of passage through their territories, exchanged sacred objects, arranged marriages and entered into alliances. The elders were the depositaries of the group's mythology that was passed onto the new generations during initiation rituals. Initiates were subjected to ordeals such as circumcision and sub-incision for males, and ritual defloration for females. This allowed the young to enter the community fully and take on their responsibilities as members of the group. Initiates were shown and given the *tjurunga*, which are sacred tablets covered with inscriptions that represented the paths of the totemic ancestors of each owner. The creation myths were renewed in different artistic and ritual means, for example, in music (poetic songs), dance or painting (rock paintings or decorations on ritual objects placed in particular sacred sites) or body painting. To qualify as sacred, a place had to show signs of the passage of the Ancestors (a rock, pool, eucalyptus, etc.). Accompanied by songs and dances, ceremonies were celebrated to evoke fertility rites and the myths of the origin of the human people so as to guarantee the life of the totemic species and the human species. Access to sacred places was only allowed to those related to members of the clan and trespassing was severely punished. This system of 'preservation' has been rendered valueless by the establishment of farms and mines and the construction of railways, creating conflict within Aboriginal groups for control of and access to sacred sites. Recently there have even been legal battles over claims of property rights over the Ancestors' lands. Today the Aboriginal people are sedentary but only represent two percent of the population of Australia. Little remains of their traditional culture or their lands, over which great effort has been made to have their rights recognized, even though in recent years the federal government has implemented policies to support and develop their cultural assimilation.

232 top *Unlike other Polynesian peoples, the Maori have developed extensive wood and bone carving handcrafts. Their best-known objects are tiki, which in the past were connected with the memory of the ancestors and today are handed down through the generations as a sign of good luck.*

232 bottom and 232-233 *For traditional Maori, tattoos were aesthetic and also ritual in the sense that they recorded rites of passage and certain important events in the life of an individual. Today this type of extreme body decoration has also become an affirmation of cultural identity.*

Maori

NEW ZEALAND

Originally from Polynesia, the Maori probably emigrated from the southeastern region of the Pacific Ocean (perhaps from the Society Islands) to New Zealand around the ninth or tenth century AD. Local legends tell of a 'Great Migration' around 1350 from an island named 'Hawaiki' in the direction of Aotearoa ('The Land of the Great White Cloud', the Polynesian name for New Zealand), though these tales may refer to a second migratory wave. The Maori suggest that Hawaiki was one of the islands in the Hawaiian archipelago, but, whatever the reality of the situation, the ancestors of the Maori were organized in *hapu* (tribal divisions) formed by *whaanau* (extended families) and led by an *ariki* (supreme chief) whose power was controlled by the elders of each family group.

Each village was governed by relations of the tribal chief. Society was divided into ranks: below the chiefs and the priests of the noble class were the common people; slaves, the bottom rank, were the descendants of prisoners of war. The Maori developed a warlike society in the belief that war reinforced the power and spiritual prestige (*manu*) of the tribe and that the cannibalism of one's enemies imbued the eater with the vital force of the deceased. Each tribe had its own *haka* (war dance and war song) that was performed before battle and which has become known across the world. Like that of other Polynesian groups, traditional religion was based on the belief in a supreme being (who was reserved to the chiefs and priests) and minor gods (for the common people) but the cult of the ancestors and spirits was also of great importance. Elaborate ceremonies accompanied by animal sacrifices were officiated by priests in *marae* (a special sacred place in each village) that lay in front of the house where community assemblies were held.

The ruling classes used to adorn their faces and bodies with intricate *ta moko* (tattoos). On women tattoos were limited to the cheeks but men of importance could decorate their entire bodies.

233 bottom left The traditional technique of tracing tattoos required the use of bone chisels. The size of the earliest chisels suggests that the patterns were originally composed of straight lines.

233 bottom right The hongi *(traditional greeting) requires people to touch heads. To the first Europeans who landed with Captain Cook, this welcome seemed more like a threat.*

234 bottom left *A Maori salutes the dawn with the sound of the* pukaea, *a wind instrument made of decorated wood that can be heard at a great distance.*

234 right *The* waka taua *is propelled by two dozen paddlers who sing to create a rhythm. Today they are commonly seen again in New Zealand waters for various occasions, from ritual celebrations to sporting events.*

235 *Maori bring ashore a war canoe that carries an important person (seen at the back dressed in a grass cloak). The bow and stern are decorated with figureheads in human form.*

234 top left *The Maori still remember the names of the canoes and their captains that first landed in New Zealand. Matahorua and Tahirirangi left on their journey of discovery in 925 AD under the command of Kupe and Ngake.*

234 center left *Having almost disappeared, the tradition of the canoe had a resurgence in 1990 when a number of northern tribes fitted out a fleet of new* waka taua *(war canoes).*

With the arrival of Europeans, New Zealand became a destination for whalers, missionaries and adventurers in search of fortune. Soon the occupation of the land by *pakeha* (colonists) provoked violent clashes with the Maori but the indigenous people was cut down by firearms and the diseases brought by the whites. Those Maori that survived had no choice but to move to more isolated areas of the country from where their descendants only emerged after the Second World War, enticed by the possibilities offered by the economic boom. Despite assimilation into the urban culture of New Zealand, in the late 1960s the traditional Maori culture began a resurgence, driven by the desire to establish their identity and territory, which led to an increase in interest of New Zealand society in the Maori language, arts and traditions. The Maori language, like many other Polynesian languages, is now taught in schools along with English.

The Maori are attempting to consolidate their ethnic and cultural heritage by transmitting their ancestral traditions to the younger generations. To this end, urban *marae (stone enclosures)* have been created for ceremonial assemblies where the ancient language is spoken and ritual songs and struggles of the ancestors are evoked. These events and these places are symbolic of the renewal and confirmation of Maori culture.

The New Zealand rugby team, the All Blacks, begin their matches with a performance of the ancient *haka* (war dance and war song). And cultural identity is further strengthened by tattoos and the recently won back right to have access to family lands where the Maori want to be buried so as to be welcomed to the land of the ancestors. Today the Maori represent 15% of the population of New Zealand, which may make them a minority but not a community without influence in terms of integration or culture. Until a few years ago they were a defeated people, but these ancient warriors have won the most difficult battle of their history.

236 top *The warrior qualities of the Maori were recognized by the British straightaway. In the front row, a man holds up a stone that symbolizes* mana, *i.e. the fame and dignity of the tribe.*

236 center *The* haka *(dance) has become famous in its warrior version. The practically invincible New Zealand rugby team begins all its matches in this manner, charging itself with energy with this form of physical discipline.*

236 bottom *A team of gunners in the New Zealand navy perform the* haka *with fearsome shouts and aggressive gestures.* Ka mate! Ka ora! *'It's death! It's life!' are the first verses of the song, the power of which is based on the strain placed on the diaphragm, on the contraction of the muscles and on vocalization.*

236-237 You have to be fit to perform the haka. *Not unlike other martial arts, the* haka *unleashes emotional and physical energy in such quantities that the body is put under substantial stress and is placed very quickly in conditions of hypoxia (i.e., the blood is starved of oxygen), which may be dangerous for those unaccustomed to it.*

237 bottom Maori prepared for the art of war from infancy, when the future warrior trained physically and mentally to enter the phase of proper martial instruction. Certain moves used in fighting with the taiaha *(war club) were inspired by the natural world, for example, by the behavior of birds.*

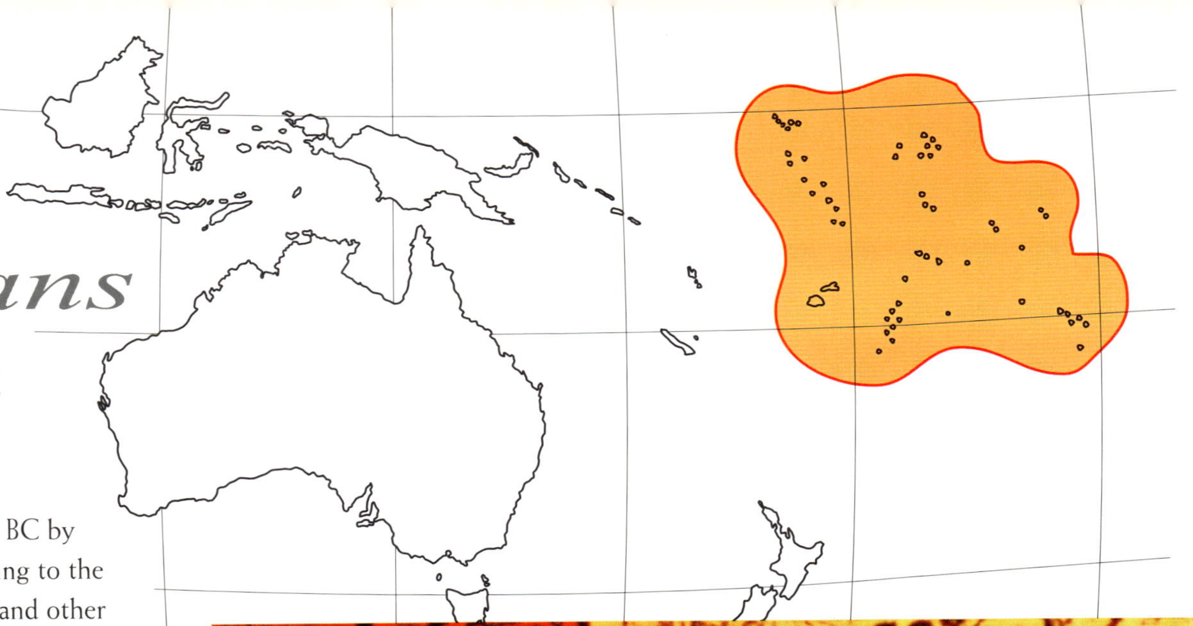

Polynesians

POLYNESIA

The islands of Polynesia were colonized from around 1600 BC by ocean-going peoples belonging to the Lapita culture. They came from New Guinea and other islands in Oceania and are considered to have been the ancestors of modern Polynesians.

When Europeans arrived, Polynesian society was divided into classes: there were the *ariki* (chiefs), the aristocratic families of landowners and priests, the administrative class and the commoners whose job it was to cultivate the lands of the upper classes. Endogamy was strictly practiced among the nobility in order to preserve their superior rank and related privileges. Rank was the basis for the structure of the hierarchies of supreme chiefs, the village and the family, for marriages between families on different islands and for governing the set of behavioral and alimentary taboos. Social and ritual activities in villages took place in *marae*, which were stone enclosures where assemblies were held and priests officiated over religious ceremonies, offerings and animal sacrifices.

Subsistence depended on agriculture, the raising of chickens and pigs and fishing in the lagoons and open sea in outrigger canoes carved from a single tree trunk. Large double canoes were used on longer voyages for trading

between islands or military expeditions.

Traditional culture has survived contact with Europeans and the spread of Christianity and is still practiced today on some islands in west Polynesia, however, in the central and eastern areas (Hawaii, Samoa and New Zealand) assimilation into Western lifestyle is more marked. In west Polynesia, tradition exists alongside the transformations engendered by modernity without great contrast, for example, in some villages the dug-out canoes and wooden hooks of the fishermen coexist with small boats that unload Western goods and tourists. Similarly, the islands are governed by modern politicians and the respected royal and noble figures of tradition.

238 *One of the most typical and authentic expressions of Polynesian culture is the tattoo. The patterns are traced by making deep cuts in the skin, which are filled with a colorant obtained by burning grubs or from a gummy substance taken from cowries.*

238-239 *The light filters through* pareo *hung out to dry at a dye works in Tahiti. These light fabrics, cut into pieces measuring 3'3" by 6'6", are the traditional and versatile dress in Polynesia and are worn by indigenes on formal occasions.*

239 top *Rings of fire that each dancer creates by swinging two torches light up the night during the* tamure *(drum dance). This was opposed by missionaries but came back into popularity in the 1950s.*

239 bottom *The features of Polynesians have their origin in southern Asia but, according to another theory, the area may have been colonized from the West, i.e., from the coasts of South America.*

Even the ritual of *kava* has remained: *kava* is a drink that brings a sense of well being and was at one time reserved for ceremonial occasions, but today it is drunk at village meetings, weddings, funerals, concerts and youth assemblies.

The cult of the ancient kings is relived every year on Easter Island or Rapa Nui ('the large island'), which has been made famous by the *moai* (large anthropomorphic stone heads). On the anniversary of the death of King Hotu Matua, the young men of the island challenge one another in tests of courage on which the honor of the entire community depends, not to mention the respect and favors of the young women.

In keeping with tradition, the participants prepare by smearing their bodies with clay, coloring themselves with war paintings and wearing no more than a loincloth made of banana leaves.

After the competition a nightime ceremony is held on the beach at which all the inhabitants of the island gather round the old women who tell stories of the past in their ancient tongue.

This is an event of great importance to the Easter Islanders as, through these tales, the historical memory of the group is passed orally to the younger generations, exactly as happened in the past.

THE AMERICAS

List of peoples

Written by Mirella Ferrera

240 left This Quiché woman in Chichicastenango market is wearing a tzute *on her head; this traditional, brightly colored cloth is also worn as a cloak.*

240 right Pisac is a town of just a few hundred souls, but on market day it fills with people from the surrounding Urubamba Valley, where Machu Picchu lies.

241 For the Cuna people in the Panamanian archipelago of San Blas, the gold ring they wear through their noses offers protection against evil spirits.

Introduction

The American continent was populated by groups of Paleoarctic hunters that, at different times over the millennia, crossed the bridge of ice and shallows that linked the two sides of the Bering Strait. In this fairly continuous movement of peoples, it is possible to discern three principal groups: in order of arrival they are the Amerinds, the Na-Dené and the Eskimo-Aleuts. No archaeological remains have been found in the Americas that indicate the presence of hominids earlier than the presence of modern *Homo sapiens*, and this suggests that, before the arrival of the Amerinds, the Americas were uninhabited.

Genetic and linguistic studies reveal three main groupings of the Amerinds that populated South America: they inhabit the Andes, Amazonia and the southern plateau of Patagonia and Tierra del Fuego.

The groups in the Na-Dené linguistic family of North America completed their colonization of the continent around 15,000 years ago. These embrace the peoples of the northwest Pacific coast (Tlingit, Kwakiutl, etc.), the Athabaska language groups of the Canadian plains (Chippewan and Yellowknives) and those of the desert highlands in Arizona (Apache and Navajo). More recent immigrants to North America are the Eskimo-Aleuts, which, around 10,000 years ago, settled on the Arctic coasts. The Asian origin of most of the American peoples is partly confirmed (in addition to the genetic evidence) by the survival throughout the continent of a Paleosiberian derived shamanic religion that the first hunters brought with them from northeast Asia. Although they developed differently historically, the cultures of all the American groups are characterized by a form of shamanism deeply rooted in their religious and social systems.

The shaman was a figure of great importance in their societies because he was able to have direct contact with the spirits of nature and the supernatural forces on which the survival of the individual or community depended. To communicate with the supernatural world, the shaman had to go into a trance, which was induced by the taking of hallucinogenic plants or by subjecting his body to tests of physical endurance. The shaman was also a priest, soothsayer and healer able to cure the human spirit and body, however, he was also able to use his power in a negative fashion.

Trances were not just the prerogative of the shaman. All members of the community attributed great importance to dreams and hallucinatory visions, which they considered fundamental to the attainment of knowledge and understanding.

In this book, the peoples chosen to represent the many traditional cultures of the Americas have been grouped in four cultural areas. Those in North America are the Amish (a German-speaking community originally from northern Europe that emigrated to North America in the eighteenth century) and the Native Americans, once improperly referred to as Redskins Indians owing to Christopher Columbus' mistaken identification of the land he 'discovered' in 1492. Differentiated from one another by the manner of their subsistence – hunting, gathering, livestock breeding and agriculture depending on the resources available to them – and fragmented linguistically, the native peoples of North America were similar from a religious standpoint, in that they shared a belief in a supernatural being to whom they made offerings so that order and continuity in the group would be maintained. Individually they also attempted to attain visions in order to get closer to their guardian spirit, generally an animal, that was thought to protect them from birth.

This form of totemic religion (known as nagualism or tonalism) was also common to the peoples of Mesoamerica. The term *tona* in the ancient Nahuatl language referred to the guardian animals that corresponded to the days of the ritual calendar. Even today the day of a child's birth is used to determine the animal with which he will be associated for the rest of his life. This custom reflects the intimate relationship that exists between man and nature, and from infancy children are taught both to respect and communicate with the natural world that surrounds them.

In rural zones of Mesoamerica, indigenous village communities assemble in civic or religious centers where the image of a patron saint is celebrated annually with festivities. The subsistence economy of these communities is based on

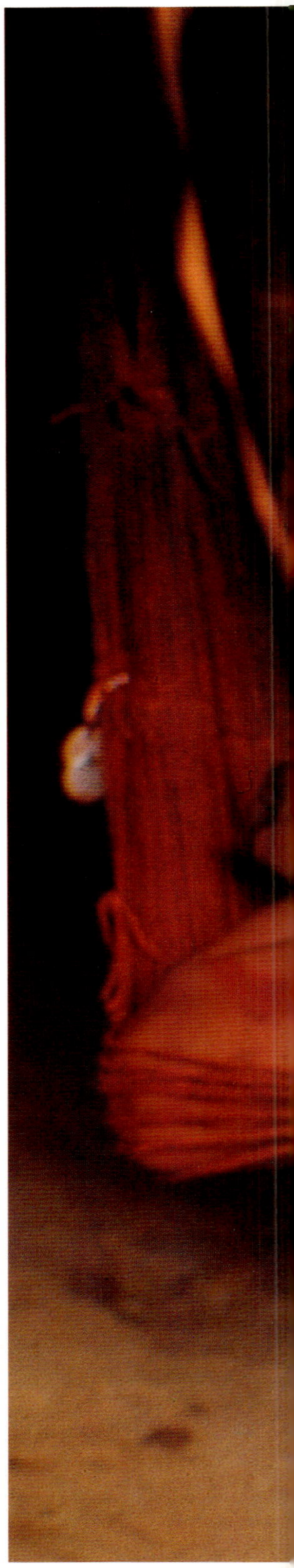

242-243 *The Yanomani live in what has been called the 'Green Hell' – the Amazonian forest. If it were not for the threat posed by the modern world, the material life of this people would be much less difficult that one might think. The work required to maintain a village takes only a couple of hours a day, with the result that the Yanomani are free to spend most of the time with their families and community.*

agriculture with the most important crops being maize, beans and squash. The communities are administered by local authorities with political and religious responsibilities (*principales mayordomos*). Present in almost all these communities is the social institution known as *compadrazgo*, which unites godparents and parents in a relationship based on mutual collaboration and support.

The rural communities in Mesoamerica and South America described in this book are descended from Pre Columbian peoples (Maya, Aztec and Inca) but have been heavily influenced by the Spanish colonization. In addition to the use of Spanish (and Portuguese) and the social and political institutions of the various countries, the Iberian cultural legacy is most evident in the Roman Catholic faith. The main religious festivities of the indigenous peoples are based on the Christian calendar but are overlain with Pre Columbian practices.

Catholicism has been absorbed by the indigenes but has been integrated with traditional beliefs that have resulted in interesting syncretic cults that, for example, identify Christian saints with indigenous ancestors and the Virgin Mary with the Earth Mother, thus making Mary a symbol of fertility and a source of sustenance for the agricultural peoples of the two regions.

Whereas the Mesoamerican and South American groups have maintained their traditional culture and adapted it to the Hispanic-Christian model, the isolation of the tribal groups in Amazonia has resulted in the fairly intact conservation of many facets of their culture. Amazonian indios are generally organized in nomadic bands of hunter-gatherers who survive on fishing and itinerant agriculture. They live in villages consisting of *malocas* (large common huts), and the 'men's house', which is a ceremonial place and sleeping area for unmarried men. With subtle differences between tribes, the various groups paint their bodies and wear crowns of feathers for ornamentation. Another widespread custom is the application of objects of different sizes to the nose, ears or mouth (lip disks). The shamanic cults in Amazonia are also accompanied by the taking of hallucinogenic plant substances.

Despite their common Paleosiberian ancestry, the languages of the American peoples are significantly diverse. This can probably be explained by the fact that the groups coming from Asia dispersed through the Americas in successive waves, taking their autonomous languages with them.

The linguistic separation is increased by the isolation of the peoples and internal migrations that brought further modifications. In consequence, the various American languages have been classified with extreme difficulty and some degree of contrivance, but in this forum it is enough to cite the linguistic groups of the peoples discussed. In North America, the Eskimo-Aleut family belongs to the American Arctic group: though isolated, the Tlingit and Haida languages are part of the Na-Dené family; the Algonkian language represents an entire family on its own; the Siouan, Iroquoian, and Caddoan families fall within the Macro-Siouan line; and the Hopi and Shoshoni languages belong to the Mexican Aztec-Tanoan family.

In Mesoamerica, the Mayan languages stand alone, the language of the Huichol belongs to the Uto-Aztecan group, and that of the Cuna is classified in the Chibchan family. The Aymara and Andean Peruvians of South America speak Quechuan, which is part of the Andean-Equatorial group, whereas the language of the Yanomani in Amazonia is isolated.

244 The unusual headdresses worn by many Native American tribes are seen in the Great Prairies during pow wows, the traditional assemblies that they organize with increasing frequency.

245 Persecution in Europe for their religious ideas, which include a refusal to handle any kind of weapon, led the Amish to emigrate to North America from the eighteenth century where today their communities are mostly dedicated to agriculture.

246-247 *A Tlingit sculptor poses before a large totem. A totem is the 'coat of arms' of the group and is often decorated with the forms of animals – such as foxes, wolves, eagles, etc. – linked to the destinies of individuals and the community.*

246 bottom *The tablelands of Arizona dominate the homeland of the Navajo; this tribe was the heir of the peaceful, agricultural and crafty' peoples that lived in the Southwest before the arrival of the white man.*

247 top left *In New Mexico's Narrow Canyon, a woman cooks bread in a beaten earth oven. Nomadic hunter-gatherers, a thousand years or so ago the natives of the Southwest copied farming techniques from the Mexican culture that were efficient enough to allow tribes such as the Anasazi, Navajo and Zuñi to change over to the cultivation of cereals and the construction of permanent villages.*

Native Americans

CANADA, UNITED STATES

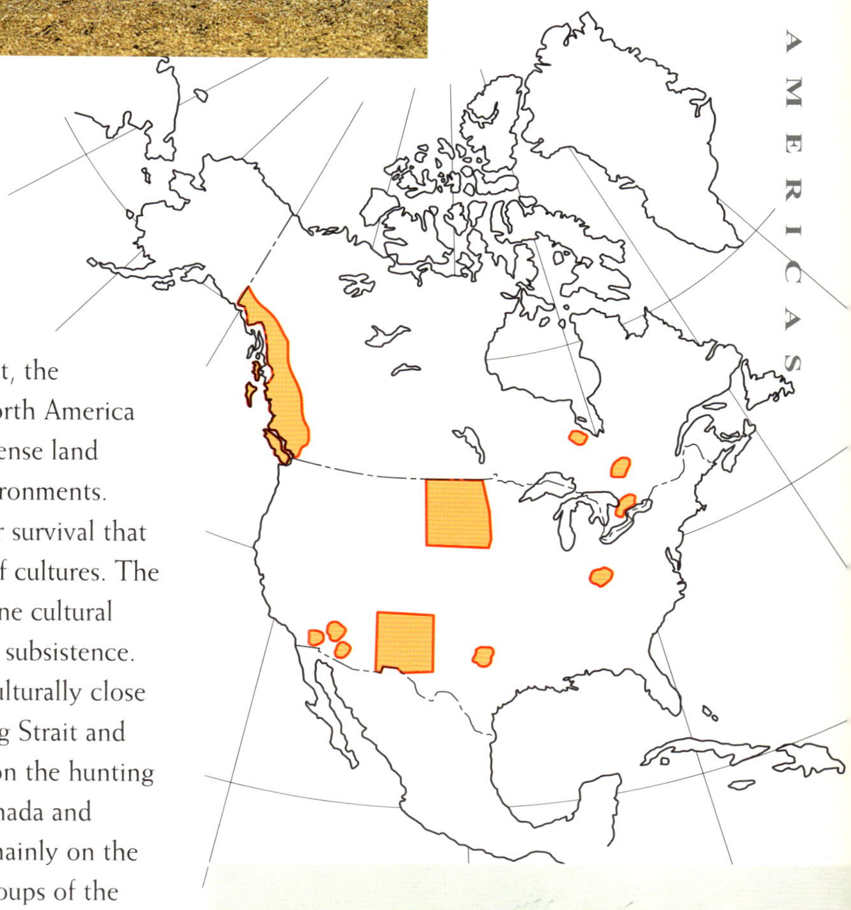

After crossing the Bering Strait, the autochthonous groups of North America found themselves in an immense land marked by extremely varied climates and environments. They adopted equally diversified strategies for survival that today are reflected in an exceptional variety of cultures. The Native American peoples are classified into nine cultural areas by their area of settlement and means of subsistence. The Arctic peoples – known as Aleuts – are culturally close to the Inuit and distributed between the Bering Strait and northern Quebec. Their subsistence is based on the hunting of sea mammals. In the sub Arctic zone in Canada and Alaska, the Ojibwa and Cree tribes survived mainly on the hunting of moose and caribou. The coastal groups of the northwest – Tlingit, Haida and Kwakiutl – fished for salmon and cod, hunted sea lion and traded with the peoples that lived inland. Similarly, around the Great Lakes, the tribes of the northeast – including the Algonquin, Mohicans and Iroquois – practiced a mixed economy of hunting, gathering, fishing and trading amongst themselves. Generally speaking, the villages of these settled peoples were formed by bark-lined huts and a large common building (the 'big house'), which was used for religious purposes and assemblies. In the Plains and Prairie areas, following the introduction of horses by Europeans, the Blackfeet, Sioux, Cheyenne, Arapaho and Comanche peoples developed an economy based almost exclusively on the hunting of bison. Bison provided food, hides for tents, leather for clothes and moccasins and bones for making tools. Their villages were therefore mobile settlements of conical or dome-shaped teepees.

In the Southwest – the desert plateaus and immense canyons in what are today New Mexico, Arizona and northern Mexico – the Hopi, Pima, Apache, Navajo and Tarahumara tribes grew maize and raised sheep. Sheep provided them with wool that they used to weave blankets

247 top right and bottom Integration into Western life of the new generations of Native Americans increased notably during the last 50 years. However, the reassertion of native cultural identity (which began with varying degrees of protests and struggle) has struck a particular chord with the young. Thanks to the efforts of their elders, today young Native Americans grow up conscious of the value of their traditional culture.

248 top The ecstatic expression on the face of this young man reveals one characteristic shared by the many Native American tribes, which are otherwise culturally fragmented. Shamanism and the importance placed on visions are the legacy of the original Paleoarctic hunters that peopled the Americas, and remain at the base of the religious practices of all Amerind peoples.

248 bottom Despite his youth, this child at a tribal gathering is wearing warrior dress and has a painted face. As is customary among tribal populations, each element of traditional dress has a precise symbolism and identifies the status and achievements of the wearer.

and rugs. Living mostly in canyons, where the climate was more favorable, these groups developed the characteristic architectures of the pueblos (communities in high-walled canyons) and plains settlements (built of stone, wood and mudbrick).

The semi-nomadic 'small tribes' of California, though fishers and hunters, were generally more hostile than their neighbors and survived by raiding and plundering.

The area of the southeast (now Alabama, Georgia, Tennessee and Florida) was inhabited by tribes of hunters like the Seminole, Caddo and Cherokee tribes, while the groups in the Plateau area bounded by the Rocky Mountains depended on salmon fishing and hunting. The 'Digger Indians' in the Great Basin, such as the Salish, Shoshoni and Paiute tribes, survived on the gathering of plants and plant roots; they were semi-nomadic and moved around with large herds of horses.

Although broadly similar in terms of economy (determined directly by the resources available to them), the Amerinds of the north were, and are, extremely differentiated by their languages, to the extent that the tribes of the Great Plains created a *lingua franca* based purely on gestures.

One element that many groups of Native Americans had in common was inherited from the shamanic culture brought from Siberia, in which great importance was attributed to dreams and hallucinatory visions. These phenomena were considered fundamental means of attaining knowledge. 'Vision quests' were induced by the ingestion of natural drugs or subjection of the body to physical endurance tests such as fasting, enforced sweating, torture, etc., in order to bring the individual's guardian spirit closer. Their ceremonies invoked the spirits present in all elements of the universe – associated in particular with animals and plants, but above all with the cosmic power that generates life (*wakanda, manitu, orenda*) – so that the tribe would be blessed with well being and continuity.

The several hundreds of thousands of descendants of the early Amerinds today live integrated in the modern Western societies of the United States and Canada, but they are often active in the attempt to reawaken political and tribal awareness of their ancient cultures.

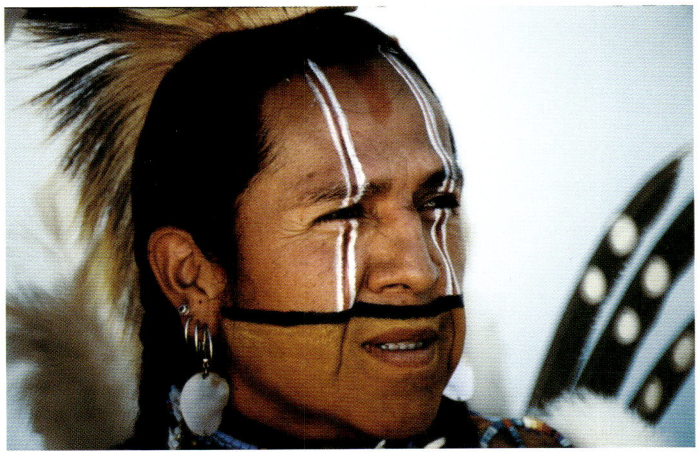

248-249 A profusion of feathers, skins, tails and bone and bead ornaments form the striking costume of this Native American at a pow wow. Intertribal assemblies have today become frequent, popular gatherings; in the nineteenth century powwows were the only form of assembly permitted by the authorities and were thus an important occasion for the tribes to conserve their traditions.

249 bottom Celebrations held regularly by Native Americans center on singing and dancing and are still marked by a degree of competitiveness that today is manifested in the prolific care dedicated to clothing and facial decoration.

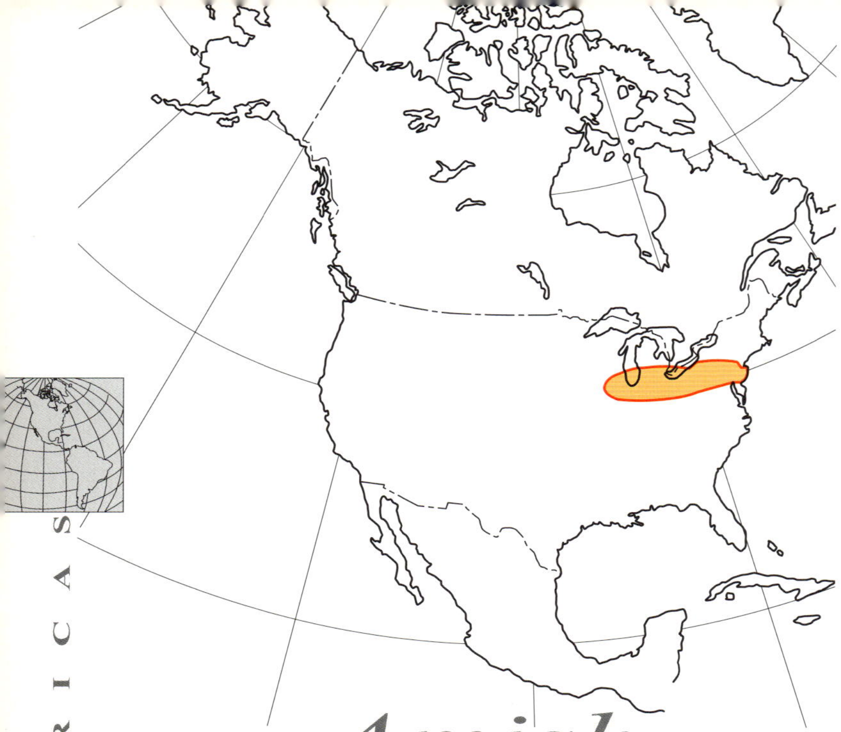

Amish

UNITED STATES

250 top *In the county of Lancaster (Pennsylvania), the Amish work in the fields with the help of harrows and mules. Dogged champions of the purity of tradition, they do not use any tool that has a motor.*

250 bottom *Having emigrated to North America from Switzerland and other European countries, the Amish have conserved their forefathers' language, known as 'Pennsylvania Dutch', but in the community's schools they are also taught English.*

The Amish are members of a religious community that adopted the Anabaptist thinking of the Mennonites. Until the seventeenth century they lived in communities in Switzerland, France, Holland and Germany, but, persecuted for their religious philosophy (one element of which was the refusal to handle weapons) in the early eighteenth century some of the German-speaking groups belonging to the Old Order Amish Mennonite Church – which was set up in 1693 following a split within the Mennonite movement – emigrated to North America where they founded a number of colonies. The first main wave (1727-90) headed for Pennsylvania but the second (1815-65) spread into Ohio, New York, Indiana and Illinois.

Currently about 130,000 Amish live in the United States in religious communities that they keep independent and isolated from the rest of American society because their religious principles forbid them from participating in worldly life (as occurred in the Anabaptist movement) or from sharing the values of the outside world. Consequently, the Amish marry within their group and live in rural areas. Their livelihood is based on agriculture but they shun the use of modern tools or technologies such as electricity. Even their clothing eschews modernity and their dress reflects the styles in vogue in Europe at the time they began their migration.

Endogamous marriage and parental links strengthen the social structure of the Amish community, which is based on the family. The ideal of farming as a way of life encourages small family-based companies and the community helps young couples to create their own traditional company within the community by offering various forms of assistance, including financial. Farms are family-run units in which all members of the family cooperate.

Endogamy has resulted in the genetic isolation of the Amish community, and this has caused various hereditary diseases and physical anomalies such as muscular dystrophy, hemophilia and dwarfism. Evidence that marriages have taken place almost exclusively within the group over the past two centuries is the diffusion of the same surname among family groups.

The presence of the outside world has undermined the desire for isolation of Amish groups and forced them to face reality. Consequently, members of the congregation today accept working outside of the community and participate as normal citizens in the social life of the various states in

250-251 *Agriculture provides the principal means of livelihood for the Amish, who work on large family-run farms. The young are encouraged to remain within the community even after marriage and to start their own farms, thereby perpetuating the traditional isolation of the Order.*

251 bottom left *The Amish men wear untrimmed beards but shave their moustaches because of their secular association with military life.*

251 bottom right *Solidarity and cooperation are fundamental values in the communal life of the Amish.*

252 top left The broad-brimmed hat made of straw or black felt is the traditional headgear of Amish men.

252 center left Amish women dress as was the custom two centuries ago. They wear ankle-length dresses, aprons and bonnets. During community prayers, unmarried girls wear black and married women white.

252 bottom left Even the children's games seem to belong to the past, though not such a distant one. Until the 1950s, rural America was not accustomed to 'luxury'.

252 right The buggy is the Amish means of transport. Sometimes accused of 'primitiveness', the Amish are in fact very caring of the natural environment and refuse to use chemical products.

253 The severe face with the hint of a smile of this old Amish man suggests his gaze is an ironic one. Persecuted in Europe, the Old Order Amish (the most orthodox order) has kept itself separate from the outside world. American society finds it difficult to accept the Amish refusal to provide military service or to send their children to state school, although, in fact, the Amish traditions provide a lifelong moral education.

Amish

which they live: they pay taxes and accept their right to vote. Nonetheless, the internal rules of the Order still prohibit their members from serving in the military, entering politics or accepting any form of government subsidy.

In the 1970s, several communities ran into legal trouble with the authorities over their refusal to send their children to secondary school. The issue prompted the Amish to found their own schools with syllabuses that reflect the traditions of the religious community.

The congregations in the Old Order Amish Mennonite Church are formed by 20 to 30 nuclear families within a district, each with its own church. The church-communities (called Gemeinde) do not have a centralized authority but sometimes the districts also operate as governmental entities under three elected key figures: the deacon, the preacher and the bishop. The first is in charge of the distribution of offerings, the second celebrates Mass and gives the sermon, while the third celebrates baptisms and marriages.

The behavioral standards of the Amish are founded on their interpretation of the Scriptures. If a member breaks their moral or religious codes, the community can decide to ban him from the group, which is an extremely serious sentence. While the ban remains in place, no member of the community can have social relations with the transgressor.

254-255 This Huichol weaver is wearing bead ornaments, typical local handcrafts, around her neck. The most well-known local product is the nierika, *which is a piece of cloth decorated with shamanic motifs. The role of the shaman is important to this people, who have created a rich creation mythology and an extensive pantheon of gods.*

254 bottom and 255 top The Huichol wear palm-fiber sombreros decorated with pendants on the brim and eagle feathers on the crown.

255 center The people in a Nayarit village gather around the marakaame *(shaman) who is exercising his powers as a* curandero *(healer). In his left hand he holds the staff that symbolizes his authority.*

255 bottom The Huichol diet is based on squash, beans and, above all, maize. Maize is associated with various divine figures.

Huichol

MEXICO

In the Cora-Huichol language, belonging to the Uto-Aztecan linguistic family, the Huichol people refer to themselves as 'Wirrarika'. They live in villages they call *rancherias* in the western Sierra Madre, a mountainous region composed of valleys and highlands. The inhabitants of a village are related and their dwellings are huts built of stone and sun-baked clay brick. Agriculture is the principal form of livelihood, and they grow maize, beans and squash on small plots of communal land worked by various families. There are five Huichol communities, each of which functions as a political, social and ceremonial entity, and is run by a hierarchy of functionaries. The various responsibilities are assigned after a 'dream session' in which the gods indicate the candidates. A Council of Elders (*cahuiteros*) has the task of selecting the political and religious authorities (*mayordomos*) entrusted with the guarding of the Catholic-derived idols. The Huichol religious ceremonies are strongly syncretic, with the worship of Catholic saints during Holy Week mixed with that of Pre Columbian gods ('familiarized' personifications of nature, like Tatewari, 'Our Grandfather Fire', and Tamatsey Kayumari, 'Our Brother Deer'), shamanic visions and rural ceremonies.

The religious mythology of the Wirrarika is of equal complexity. They have many creation myths relating to the world, sun, fire, divine ancestors (Kakaûyari) and the gods of maize and peyote. Evocation of these myths, or Sacred History, is 'sung' by the wise man of the group (*cantador*) on ceremonial occasions. The shaman (*marakaame*), who also sings during ritual ceremonies, is an important figure in Huichol culture and his functions include those of a priest, healer (*curandero*) and soothsayer. One of the most important ceremonies is the annual pilgrimage to Wirikuta (Real de Catorce) in the Zacatecas Desert where the sacred peyotl cactus (*Lophophora williamsi*) grows. This powerful hallucinogen is identified with the Deer God and, when taken in small doses, it erases hunger and thirst and alleviates fatigue. In larger quantities it triggers visions that allow the Huichol to communicate with supernatural beings. The pilgrimage takes three weeks of walking to arrive Wirikuta, but, today, pilgrims only walk for a few days, taking the bus or riding on trucks for the remainder of the journey, and stopping to make offerings at sacred places along the way. For the harvest to be good, before leaving on the pilgrimage tribute must be paid to the gods and the individual must purify himself by means of strict sexual and dietary restrictions and confess all his sins as he sits around the fire on the eve of departure. Although the pilgrimage is only for men, the women at home are charged with looking after the 'sacred fire', which must be kept alight until the pilgrims return. Their return is celebrated with the *Xicury Néyrra* ('let's go and dance the peyote') when everyone eats the cactus. Ritual eating of peyote also occurs during the ceremonies held for the sowing and harvest of maize, which, for the Wirrarika, is a sacred being and used as an offering and ceremonial food in all rites in addition to being celebrated in various festivals. At the end of the harvest, each head of the family sets aside five types of maize for the next cycle, thereby ensuring the reproduction of this indigenous plant.

Common to the agricultural cultures of Mesoamerica is a profound religious relationship with the Earth Mother, the divine source of fertility and regeneration. Man, who is her child, cannot own his mother, therefore the land is the collective property of the community.

Maya

MEXICO, GUATEMALA AND HONDURAS

The descendants of the Maya in the Mesoamerican region are divided into a number of groups that reside in Chiapas (Chamulan, Lacandon and Tzotzil), Honduras (Chortí) and the highlands of Guatemala (Quiché, Cakchiquel, Ixil, Kekchí, Uspantec and Yacaltec). On the whole, they are small village-communities composed of extended families. Their subsistence economy rests upon cultivating of maize and beans, breeding pigs, chickens and goats, fishing, hunting and gathering whatever vegetables and fruits they can find.

The farm work, in which the entire community participates, is carried out on family-owned and communal plots. This is bolstered by working as farm-laborers on the coffee and sugarcane plantations of the estate owners (with seasonal migration towards the coast) or by selling farm products or handcrafts in the cities.

The government of the communities, both politically and religiously, is the responsibility of *principales* (local authorities). Ancient religious beliefs coexist with Catholicism, which the locals consider an equally valid and easily integrated means of expressing one's spirituality. When faced with a sickness, for example, the family of the invalid will turn to *curanderos* (indigenous healers) as well as reciting the rosary.

The fusion of Mayan and Christian religions have resulted in syncretic gods, for instance, Catholic saints represent the ancestors, the Earth Mother is identified with the Virgin Mary and the Sun God with Jesus. Ceremonial offerings of food and cans of drink are therefore made to the saints as well as to the ancestral spirits and indigenous gods. Aspects of the ancient cults that have been conserved are propitiatory agrarian rites and shamanic trances, which are induced by the ingestion of hallucinogenic plants.

256 and 257 top left This young Quiché woman from Chajul in Guatemala (top left) wears a huipil decorated with stylized zoomorphic and floral patterns.

257 top right An essential element in male dress is the moral, the shoulder bag worn by this boy.

257 bottom A Chajul woman cooks a staple of Mayan food: tortillas made from maize flour.

258-259 In general the Maya are rather reserved in their personal relations, and sometimes the markets are surprisingly quiet.

260-261 *The Maya inherited the craft of weaving from their Pre Columbian ancestors, and the backstrap loom is one of the most common tools they use. It is fixed to a tree or a column, then fastened to the hips of the weaver so that she can control the tension of the yarn.*

260 bottom *The style, colors and embroidery on traditional costumes differ from zone to zone. The men in Todos Santos, for example, wear bright red striped trousers and shirts with embroidered collars.*

A Council of Elders elects the people who will be responsible for the many *mayordomos* (saints' days) that provide a welcome interruption to the work routine.

Mayan culture is intimately linked to nature, and this bond is expressed in nagualism and the religious closeness to the land. The dialog with nature begins from birth, as the day on which a child is born determines the baby's *nagual*; the *nagual* is a sort of natural guardian spirit associated with a person throughout his or her life.

The land provides the main source of livelihood for these peoples, who refer to themselves as 'maize people', according to the Guatemalan Rigoberta Menchú, the most important representative of the liberation movement of the indios. Maize forms the basis of the Mayan diet and is used in foods (tortillas) and drinks (coffee and corn brandy). Maize is also considered a god.

The cycle of the agricultural year is marked by ritual ceremonies. The Earth Mother (a goddess) is beseeched for permission to cultivate her in a ceremony at which *copale* incense is burned and candles are lit in the home of each family. Then seeds are chosen and blessed and offerings are made to the gods so that the harvests will be good.

The ripening of the crops is also commemorated with ceremonies and festivities, the most important of which is dedicated to the harvest and celebrated with a collective thanksgiving ceremony to the Earth Mother. This approach to the use of the land may help in explaining the desperation of the appeals made to the authorities by the indigenous people for the restitution of the lands of their ancestors, which have been usurped by the colonizers.

Another element in Mayan tradition is the handcrafts produced by the women. These are mainly made for the tourist market and so the characteristics of the pottery and cotton and woven wool products are dictated by what will appeal to the buyer. Examples are the handcrafts (mats, belts, dolls, shawls and sandals) produced by Chamula women for sale at the crowded monumental sites built by their ancestors.

The traditional dress of the Mayan women is a *huipil*

261 top The cut of the men's clothing is clearly based on Spanish models but the Maya, who tenaciously hold on to the past, find ways to conserve various elements of Pre Columbian dress, like the ponchitos *(black aprons) that they wear over their trousers.*

261 bottom This brightly dressed woman from Chichicastenango wears a tzute *on her head. This is a square piece of cotton that was originally used to make it easier to carry objects on the head. Today it is often used simply as a colorful head covering or mantle.*

(loose jacket), a skirt, an apron and a shawl. Young girls receive a *huipil* at the age of 10 to mark their coming of age as an adolescent, an event that brings a sense of responsibility. This woven garment expresses the artistic nature of Mayan women: the patterns, colors and symbols record the history of the wearer, her age, social condition and her link with her ancestors.

262 top In the harsh mountain district near San Francisco El Alto, New Year is celebrated with ancient rites, the roots of which are lost in the remote past of Guatemala.

262 center and bottom During the celebration, sacrifices over the fire relive the practices of the ancient Maya. The victims of these sacrifices are chickens, which are thrown on the embers. The symbol of the cross (bottom) is present as the Maya consider Christianity a means for perpetuating ancestral rites.

262-263 Participants in the celebration go down from the high altar to the bottom of the Nueve Sillas ravine where rites are held around other fires and new offerings made. The man with the staff near the altar is leading the ceremony.

263 bottom The Maya have used the Nueve Sillas Ravine for ceremonial purposes for centuries, as the color of the rocks testifies. They have been blackened by the smoke of innumerable ritual fires.

264-265 Dozens of people in the church of San Andrés de Sajcabajá pray around the offerings of incense and flowers during a ceremony for the dead.

264 bottom The face of this man praying during the Good Friday Mass shows the emotional involvement of the Maya in religious ceremonies. Just as their ancestors did, modern Maya believe in the omnipresence of God and the constancy of the individual's relationship with Him.

265 top The smoke from copale incense is always present in religious ceremonies and expresses the desire to satisfy the needs of the dead and to merge the souls of the living with those of the dead.

265 center and bottom On Good Friday, shackles, whips and thorns are the customary means used by penitents who are part of the Hispanic culture. However, self-flagellation was a common practice among the ancient Maya, who used agave thorns for the purpose. This sort of blood offering, like a human sacrifice, was thought to be essential for keeping the gods alive.

266-267 and 266 bottom left The production of a mola (the typical blouse worn by Cuna women) requires differently colored pieces of fabric to be sewn together. It is a complicated job and takes dozens of hours of work.

266 bottom right The San Blas Archipelago is composed of 365 small islands. Despite the lack of freshwater, the environment is much healthier than on the mainland coastline, which was mostly abandoned by the Cuna in the mid-nineteenth century after an epidemic.

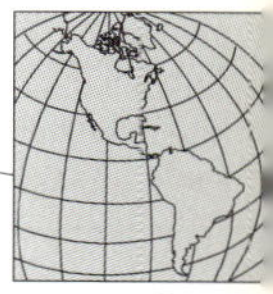

Cuna

PANAMA

The Cuna or Kuna indios have been settled in the San Blas Archipelago off the northeast coast of Panama since the nineteenth century. The archipelago, known as Cuna Yale in the local language, numbers 365 islands, only 50 of which are inhabited, and is bounded to the east by a coral reef. 'Cuna' was a term introduced by the Spanish but the indios of the San Blas islands prefer to call themselves Tule or Tulemala. Their language, Tule Kaya, belongs the Chibchan linguistic family.

There are roughly 40,000 Cuna, 25,000 of which live on the islands and the rest on the mainland coast. Only a few hundred still live in their original homeland, the Cordigliera Centrale that runs between Panama and Colombia.

The Cuna have peculiar physical features: a short stature, a highly developed chest and a hawk nose. Another characteristic of the Cuna is the traditional costume worn by the women, which is a brightly colored *pareo* of printed cotton, a *mola* (a short shirt made up of several layers of embroidered cotton), a red cotton scarf worn on the head, ornaments worn on the face and around the neck, strings of red, black and yellow beads worn on the legs and arms and, finally, the *olo*, which is a gold ring worn through the nose.

The Cuna on the mainland live in settlements that stand near watercourses where they fish using dams and poisons taken from plants.

The island Cuna also fish but support this with the itinerant cultivation of rice, maize, yucca and sugarcane. They also have plantations of coconuts and bananas, which are sent for export.

They use nets, spears and dugout canoes to fish but they also use motorboats. They hunt tapirs, monkeys and various types of birds using traps, blowpipes, bows and arrows, rifles and dogs.

267 top The 40 or so Cuna settlements on the San Blas Islands are made up of spacious houses built with a solid wooden structure and windowless bamboo walls.

267 bottom The last touches are put to a young girl's dress with the help of a friend. The long necklaces made of beads, seeds and animals' teeth are wrapped around the neck several times.

The island Cuna have to import wood and fresh water, the latter, in particular, being absent in the archipelago with the exception of Pines Island, which is covered by jungle. The villages consist of rectangular huts with walls made from wood and sugarcane, a roof made from straw and a floor of beaten earth. They sleep in hammocks fixed to the walls.

In the center of the village stands the 'ceremonial house' where the communal activities are held, such as the *congreso* (assembly) presided over by the *saila* (village chief). The *saila* is responsible for maintaining order in the community and contact with the national authorities.

Cuna society is matriarchal. After a couple marries, they go to live with the family of the bride (i.e., in the matrilocal residence), and this tradition means that extended families living in the same house are linked through female relations.

Rites of passage that mark the phases of life are first and foremost associated with the female component of the Cuna population. During the *ikko inna* ceremony, the nose of the young girls is pirced with a gold ring. Called an *olo* which is thought to offer protection against evil spirits. In the *inna suit* initiation rite, the bodies of young girls are painted with vegetable dye, after which the girls put on traditional costume and have their hair cut in a helmet style. Then, the girls are given a new name and officially enter a new life as women ready for marriage. The ceremony ends with a big party, with drinking and dancing put on by the families of the initiated girls.

Cuna ceremonies always feature singing and dancing, from those that celebrate the birth of a baby, to female initiation rites and funerals. Healing ceremonies are accompanied by the singing of the *nele* (shaman) in an attempt to persuade the guardian spirits to free the various *purba* (souls) of the sufferer from evil. During funerals, the song sung by the master of ceremonies accompanies the soul of the deceased on its journey while the dead body is buried in its hammock. It is traditional to build a small house above the grave where objects of daily life can be placed.

268 top Cuna society is matrilocal, i.e., a newly wed couple go to live in the house of the bride's family. The males live under the authority of the oldest man and his wife performs the same role for the female component of the family.

268 bottom and 269 The female rites of passage are of crucial importance, first and foremost the initiation ceremony. This rite represents a rebirth of the individual; at the end of the ceremony the young initiate is given a new name and begins a new life as a woman.

270 and 271 bottom Close examination reveals the technique used to make a mola: it is in fact a patchwork of oddments arranged in layers and sewn onto an underlying piece of cloth. The patterns are inspired by geometric and animal forms and religious themes.

271 top Traditional women's dress includes a shawl used to cover the head. It is always bright red in color.

271 center The use of tailor's scissors and industrially dyed fabrics has made the manufacture of molas much easier and broadened the range of patterns and symbols used. The result is that the Cuna are now able to export their products. It is thought that this handcraft had its origin in painted clothes, which were in turn derived from the custom of body painting.

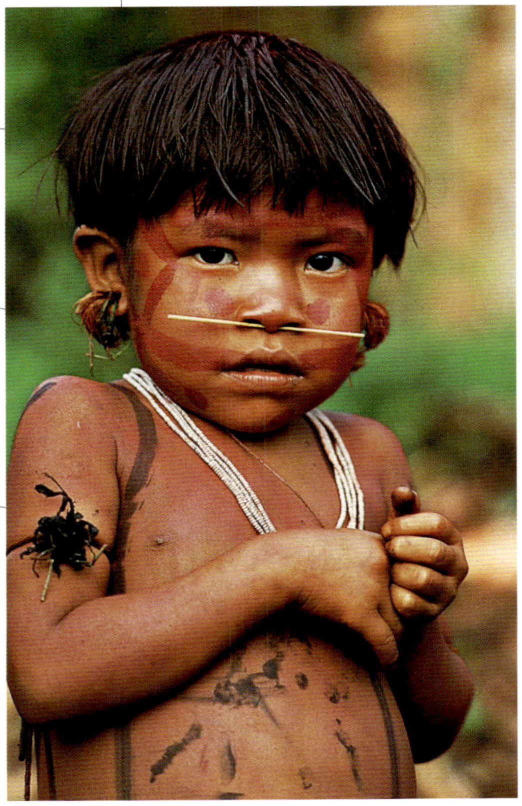

Yanomani

BRAZIL, VENEZUELA

272 top left This Yanomani girl is wearing grass earrings and a tuft of tobacco on her arm to dry.

272 top right Highly prized ornamental feathers are provided by the colorful birds of the forest, in particular the red macaw.

272 bottom and 273 Face paints are red and black in color and are used in all celebrations, from birth to death and from war to the welcoming of guests. In general, red is associated with life and black with the transition between one phase of life and the next.

The Yanomani indios inhabit the region on the Brazilian-Venezuelan border covered by equatorial forest. It lies between the basins of the Orinoco Delta and the Amazon River.

Their subsistence activities are independent of the market economy, being based on hunting, gathering, fishing using plant poisons and slash-and-burn agriculture of bananas, maize, manioca and tobacco. They usually chew rolled up leaves of the tobacco plant, which releases alkaloid substances that help to resist fatigue and hunger.

Every two or three years, the group abandons the fields and village they have created. The villages are built hidden in the forest and on high places to avoid flooding and render attack by enemies more difficult. A typical Yanomani house is the *sapono* (communal house), which is a large round hut up to 330 feet in diameter in which different families live.

The forest provides all the food types and materials the Yanomani require: the bones, teeth and skins of animals are used to make blades, arrowheads and containers; plant fibers are used to make huts, roofs, bags and hammocks; plants also provide dyes used in body painting, poisons in fishing and herbal medicines and powerful hallucinogens used by the shamans when healing or visiting the *hékura* (world of the spirits).

The Yanomani believe themselves to be the 'moon people' because, according to the myth with which they explain their origins, they were created when the blood of the moon dripped onto the earth. They are a warrior-like people that often indulge in raids on nearby groups with which, during peacetime, they create alliances with by exchanging gifts and women. To prepare themselves for battle, the men paint their bodies black, the color of war.

Great importance is placed on body ornamentation: men adorn themselves by painting their bodies and decorating themselves with feathers, leaves and flowers, whereas the

274 top A woman shows what she has caught using poisons taken from plant roots. The abundance of plant species offers the Yanomani not just poisons but also powerful natural medicines, which are today being studied with great scientific interest.

274 center A group of women heads off to the conuco *(the community's cultivated area) where wheat, cotton, bananas, yuccas and tubers are grown. The men's role in agriculture is mainly limited to clearing the plots of forest.*

274 bottom left A canoe carrying hunters slips through the water of a tributary of the Orinoco. There are two types of hunt: the heniyomou *(to provide food for feasts and celebrations) and* rami *(for everyday survival).*

274-275 Fishing is of fundamental importance to the Yanomani. All the members of the group have a role to play: the women catch the fish by hand, choosing the rivers with placid waters and using natural substances that contain enough alkaloids to stun the fish; the men use a bow and arrow or sticks. The use of toxic substances in hunting and fishing does not pollute the environment because the quantities used are minimal. The most serious risk to the rivers and peoples of Amazonia is posed by the mercury-based techniques used by garimpeiros *in cleaning gold, which can lead to neurological damage.*

274 bottom right The group all lives in a single conical structure that accommodates between 40 and 300 people.

women insert thin sticks through their nose, cheeks and chin to call up the spirit of the jaguar.

Initiation rites for girls begin at their first menstruation when they are obliged to remain isolated for a certain amount of time and respect particular restrictions on their diet and behavior. When this period ends, they are moved away from the group and their hair is cut. This marks their entry into womanhood and their readiness for marriage. They then make their triumphal entry into the village accompanied by the women in the group.

The Yanomani's funerary ritual is equally complex and is based on cremation. This takes place in front of the deceased's house when his or her personal objects are burned along with the corpse. The bones are collected after the cremation and placed in a basket, they are then ground down and mixed with crushed bananas so that they can be eaten by the nearest kin and the rest of the community. The purpose is for the living to enter into communion with the deceased and the world of the dead.

The discovery of gold deposits in Yanomani territory during the 1970s led to an invasion by *garimpeiros* (gold diggers), laborers and the military who together furiously cut down the forest. The consequences for the indios were fatal: malaria, tuberculosis and alcoholism spread, the rivers were poisoned by the discharge of mercury used in the gold-working process and many of the Yanomani were shot on sight or given poisoned food. The word 'genocide' might be suitable in this circumstance. Today the Yanomani are growing in number again. It is calculated that there are around 21,000 and are therefore one of the most numerous peoples in Amazonia.

Since 1988 the new democratic regime in Brazil has formally recognized the rights of the indios to the ownership of their lands, however, the state organization charged with setting out the boundaries is constantly being impeded by the interests of various groups such as animal breeders and logging companies and mining companies.

276 top left A man in the large communal building prepares fibers to make baskets and other containers, like the large plates used for yucca flour.

276 top right Hammocks made from plant fibers are used by the Yanomani to sleep in.

276 bottom The red and purple body dyes are made from the seeds of the anatto tree, which is common in the Amazon forest. It contains a resinous violet dye with a pleasant smell.

276-277 Epena is a natural hallucinogen reserved for the men that induces a sense of euphoria but is not habit-forming. By blowing down a long bamboo stem, the men help each other to inhale the substance, which immediately enters the blood circulation through the mucous layer. The use of epena is strictly ritual and implicates the Yanomani's beliefs in the role of the shaman to restore harmony to the group during internal crises.

277 right The plants gathered in the forest and placed in baskets are carried by the women as the men must be ready to protect the group in the event of danger.

Yanomani

278 top left *The coca plant has been traditionally used in Peru since the period of the Inca Empire when it was used exclusively by the nobility and priests for ceremonial purposes. Today the consumption and trade in this stimulant has spread to one and all.*

278 top right *Brightly colored cloths are typical of Peru, where weaving has been practiced for thousands of years.*

278 center and bottom *The difficult conditions of life in the Andean highlands place children under great physiological strain, owing to the altitude, cold and dryness of the air.*

279 *With a long history of cultivation at high altitude, the Peruvians grow potatoes, cabbages, carrots and varieties of chenopods, which they use for medicinal purposes.*

Peruvians

PERU

The Andes Cordigliera is one of the Earth's highest mountain chains and stretches for over 3,000 miles from Venezuela to central Chile. On the eastern and western sides of the peaks, there are high plateaus of varying width that are most extensive in the mountainous region between Peru and Chile where they measure 500 miles east to west.

This high altitude environment is inhabited by indigenous peoples that have conserved various cultural aspects of their predecessors, including the language: Peruvian indigenes speak both Spanish and Quechua, which was the *lingua franca* of the Inca Empire. As is seen among Himalayan and Tibetan populations, the mountain dwellers of Peru have developed genetic and physical characteristics to help them survive at high altitude as the lack of oxygen in the air makes physical work extremely tiring. Also their subsistence activities – mostly agriculture and livestock breeding – have had to adapt to the mountain environment.

Potatoes (the name of which is derived from the Quechua word *pata*) and coca are able to withstand the cold Andean climate. Similarly, the physical systems of the alpaca and llama, not unlike those of the humans, have adapted to exploit to the utmost the little oxygen available. Since they were domesticated around 4,500 years ago, these animals in the camel family have been two important pillars in the Andean economy.

Over the centuries, the local cultivators have selected roughly 400 varieties of potato. Those that grow at high altitude are more bitter; they are dried in the intense cold and then their excess moisture is squeezed out to create *chuño* (potato flour), which can easily be conserved and transported.

IU
IU

280-281 The vibrant patterns of the clothes vary from zone to zone: this young Quechua boy comes from the Cordigliera di Vilcanota to the east of Cuzco, one of the highest and barest habitats in Peru.

281 right Children live in close contact with their parents until they marry, providing mutual help in combating the difficulties of high altitude life. Schooling in the Peruvian countryside is a problem for several reasons, including the difficulty of finding teachers willing to settle in remote villages.

282 and 283 top left As the Maya have done, so the Quechua have adapted Christian rituals to their ancient religion, which they relive in ceremonies of great emotional involvement. These photographs illustrate the annual celebration of Corpus Christi at the church in Qoyllur Rit'i in the Cordigliera di Vilcanota. There is a chapel but many prefer to remain outside, praying before the lighted candles placed in front of sacred rocks that have been worshiped since antiquity.

283 top right Celebrations in Qoyllur Rit'i (Quechuan for 'star of the snow') include songs and flute music. Together with ocarinas and drums, flutes are traditional Andean instruments.

283 center and bottom Pilgrims on their way to Qoyllur Rit'i come from various Andean communities, each one represented by figures in elaborate costume. The groups are distinguished by their different traditional clothes and by the flute music played. This young man's cumbersome head covering identifies him as Capa Chuncho, a 'mountain warrior', and there are also costumes that poke fun at the Conquistadores.

284-285 *The Ukuku are intermediaries between the Apu (mountain gods) and the faithful. They carry a cross adorned with offerings and pieces of cloth up to the Colquepunku Glacier at an altitude of 16,000 feet.*

284 bottom *After the cross has been placed and Mass celebrated, the pilgrims return to the chapel of Qoyllur Rit'i carrying snow, which, once it has melted, provides drinking water that is considered miraculous.*

Llamas can carry heavy loads for long stretches on the mountain paths, and alpacas provide good quality wool used to make cloth and woven fabrics. The dung of these animals is used both as a fertilizer and a fuel for fires.

The highland indios chew coca leaves for the stimulating and invigorating properties that enable them to withstand the cold, physical fatigue and hunger. According to the indios, the coca plant also has prophetic properties: soothsayers are able, for example, to make predictions about the future, health and the crops depending on how the coca leaves fall.

At one time the members of traditional Andean communities, known as *ayllu*, were families dispersed throughout the mountains that shared a common ancestor. They helped one another mainly through trading agricultural products: cereals (barley, quinoa and maize) and vegetables that were grown in the valleys and exchanged for potatoes and coca leaves, which are grown in the *puna* (mountains). Under the Inca Empire, all the land was owned exclusively by the Inca (emperor) himself so that private property did not exist. With the arrival of the Spanish, the conditions for the indigenous people worsened drastically: the creation of *haciendas* (large farming estates) forced the indios off their lands and put an end to the economic institution of the *ayllu*, which led to the destruction of an agrarian and social system that had been created, perfected and consolidated over 3,500 years.

The conquistadors brought with them the Catholic religion, which today coexists in perfect syncretism with the traditional Pre Columbian beliefs and is recognized by 90% of the Peruvian population. The celebrations in the Christian calendar coincide with the ancient agricultural festivals in the Inca calendar based on the cycle of the seasons, and it is through these religious celebrations, so popular with the Peruvian indios, that the rich cultural heritage of the Andes is freely celebrated and perpetuated.

285 top left Respected and held in awe, the Ukuku have to leave during the night to reach the site in the morning. The procession is illuminated by candlelight alone.

285 top right and bottom The faith of the Peruvian peoples is also evident in the great difficulties they tackle for ritual purposes: it is only by sacrificing oneself that one receives the benevolence of the Apu and heaven.

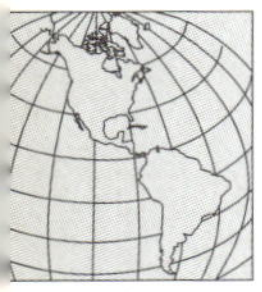

Aymara

PERU, BOLIVIA

Until the fifteenth century the Aymara inhabited a large area between Cuzco and the coast to the south of the city, but the rise of the Inca Empire forced them to move to the southern shores of Lake Titicaca. With the arrival of the Spanish conquistadors, the name Aymara was extended to all the indigenous groups that lived on the lake's south shore and in the highlands between Peru and Bolivia.

The subsistence economy of the Aymara communities is based on the cultivation of potatoes, barley and maize (from which they make *chicha* beer) and on the breeding of sheep,

alpacas and llamas. Those living on Lake Titicaca fish using large nets and small boats made from balsawood and *totora* reeds, a plant that grows in abundance along the shoreline. This material is employed for different purposes: in addition to boats, for which the reeds are tied into bundles, it is used above the houses in the form of roofing and beneath them as floating platforms on the lake that are anchored to the lake bed with stones. Each artificial island can support two or three nuclear families.

According to legend, the son of the Sun God, Viracocha – the cultural hero of Aymara myths – was born near Lake Titicaca. Catholicism, introduced by the Spaniards, was absorbed by the indigenous communities but is overlaid with traditional religious beliefs and practices to create interesting syncretic cults in which the Christian God is identified with the Sun God Inti and the Virgin Mary corresponds to Pachamama, the Earth Mother. The traditional ceremonies follow the Christian calendar. Pilgrimages dedicated to the image of Mary and celebrations of the patron saints bring together the different communities, which, during the rest of the year, are dispersed in celebrations that can last several days. Team dances are held in the main square of each town or city in front of the church. The organization of the celebration is passed in turn between members of the community who support the costs with contributions of money, food, fruit, beer, alcoholic drinks, coca leaves, etc., made by the local participants.

Aymara men wear an ankle-length poncho with Western-style clothes beneath, and on their feet they wear sandals made from leather or tire rubber.

286 top right *The Andean peoples were great builders, as these terraces on the mountainside show. Some experts believe that the Aymara are the descendants of the builders of Tiahuanaco, the megalithic religious center not far from Lake Titicaca.*

286 bottom left *On the Island of the Sun – one of the 41 small islands that emerge from the waters of Lake Titicaca – an Aymaran woman carries her baby in her multicolored* aguayo, *which is also used to carry vegetables and cereals. The important archaeological remains of the 'Temple of the Sun', built during the Inca period, can be seen in the background.*

286-287 *The bowler hats worn by these women (who are visiting the Bolivian national festival at Copacabana) are typical of Aymaran women's dress, though not traditional; they were introduced by the British engineers that worked on the Andean railway.*

On their heads they wear a conical, ear-flapped knit wool hat. Women's traditional dress is a *pollera* (a pleated skirt narrow at the waist), a coarse cotton blouse, a wool blanket wrapped twice around the shoulders and held in front by a brooch and an *aguayo*, which is a knotted, colored cotton shawl that forms a sort of bag that they use to carry babies or things to sell in the market place.

The women also wear a felt bowler hat, which was introduced in the twentieth century by the British engineers that built the railway.

287 top *The Aymara festivals feature dances derived from Pre Columbian times and thus little influenced by Hispanic culture.*

287 center right and bottom *Estimated at 800,000, the Aymara are one of the most numerous Andean peoples. Like the Quechua, they practice a religion that has merged Christianity with their ancient beliefs.*

288 top and center Uros fishermen live on the Peruvian side of Lake Titicaca. They use boats made entirely from totora *reeds that are tightly bound into bundles. They generally catch catfish and two species of fundulus, but in the last century trout were also successfully introduced into these mineral in the rich waters.*

288 bottom Potatoes are the most traditional crop on the Andean Plateau. It is thought that the Aymara were the first to domesticate them and invent techniques to dehydrate them.

288-289 Totora *grows abundantly in the shallows and shores of Lake Titicaca. It is a strong material that, when dried, is used in the construction of houses and to line the exterior of boats whose structure is made from balsawood.*

289 bottom In these clothes drying in the sun, we see the aguayo *shawl, top and pleated* pollera *skirt worn by Aymara women.*

Aymara

ARCTIC

List of peoples

Written by Mirella Ferrera

290 left The nomadic Saami have bred reindeer for perhaps 500 years, and all their requirements were provided by this animal until the mid-twentieth century.

290 right On the endless icy plain on the Melville Peninsula in northern Canada, an Inuit finishes off the igloo that will give him shelter during the hunting season.

291 Thick bearskins and sealskins have protected the Inuit from the Arctic cold for millennia (in winter the temperature can drop to -22°F) and even today have only been in part replaced by modern fabrics.

Introduction

The word 'Arctic' is derived from the astronomic term used by the ancient Greeks to indicate the trajectory of the Great Bear constellation (*arctos* is bear in Greek) around the Pole Star. It was only later used to refer to the geographical band (Arctic Circle) that lies between the North Pole and the extreme north of the American and Eurasiatic continents. The Arctic region stretches lengthways for about 4,000 miles from the northern regions of Scandinavia, across Siberia to the Bering Strait, and from Alaska to Greenland. The winters are long and very cold, with temperatures dropping to -22°F and snow remaining on the ground for 6-7 months, melting only in spring. Summers are short and mild. The tundra (the circumpolar ecosystem) is a damp, boggy expanse short on resources and almost uninhabited. The few peoples that halted in this inhospitable terrain reached it in various waves of migration over the millennia.

The Paleosiberian peoples originally from Asia first occupied the Eurasian tundra about 15,000 years ago, before it was colonized by Mongolids. Meanwhile, about 10,000 years ago, Mongolid groups, including the Eskimo-Aleuts, crossed the Bering Strait that lies between Asia and North America and occupied the coast of Alaska. Although there was a great deal of movement up and down both the Asian and American coasts of the strait, the picture was not uniform: the current Siberian peoples (Chukchi, Koryak and Itelmen) and the Eskimos have hybrid genetic and physical characteristics resulting from the continual mixing of Paleosiberian and Mongolid groups.

In more recent epochs, Eurasiatic groups like the Saami reached the Arctic. Various finds of weapons and tools prove their presence in Sweden around 4,000 years ago and, in southern Finland, perhaps 1,000 years ago. The Saami of northern Scandinavia differ genetically to other groups being descended from Uralic stock, i.e., the areas surrounding the mountain range that crosses Eurasia from the shores of the Kara Sea in Siberia to the Turgay Terrace north of the Aral Sea. It is therefore possible to distinguish three linguistic families for the populations of the Arctic: Paleoasiatic, spoken by Paleosiberian groups; Eskimo-Aleut, spoken by the Inuit; and Ural-Altaic, spoken by the Lapps.

Despite their linguistic differences, the similarity of their habitat means these groups share many cultural characteristics. The Arctic environment has obliged them to specialize for their survival hunting by land animals (for instance, polar bears)and sea mammals, fishing and, further inland, breeding of reindeer, the practice of which began to spread through the Eurasian Arctic in the second millennium BC.

The extreme winter cold and seasonal variability of the few resources available have obliged the Arctic groups to be nomadic, thereby preventing any permanent social or institutional structures from developing. The communities that they formed were fairly flexible, being composed of small groups of extended families that came together or separated in order to carry out economic activities, and which were united by the equal division of resources and cooperation they offered one another in the performance of work tasks.

Common to all groups is the use of particular materials to withstand the climate. In general, animal skins were used to make clothes, cover tents and provide the lining of boats. The *kayak,* a typical Arctic form of transport, is lined entirely with seal skin except for a small round hole that fits snugly around the waist of the user, who sits with his legs stretched out before him. The narrow, tapered shape of the light and easily transported kayak is perfectly suited to hunting and fishing in the waters of the Arctic Ocean. For large whale-hunting expeditions or for seasonal migration, the groups use the *umiak.* These large, open boats are about 30 feet in length, lined with sealskin and fitted with rowlocks and wooden crosspieces on which to sit. On land, the means of transport are skis and sleds, the latter used to carry goods and people.

Another important cultural element common to all Arctic groups is shamanism, which spread with the human migration from Siberia to northeast Europe (Lapland) and the American coast. The rationale of shamanism lay in hunters' cultural horizon and their vision of the world dominated by animals and the spirits of nature. The myths

292-293 *An Inuit fisherman glides across the water in his single-seat* kayak *off Qaanaaq in northeast Greenland. Another traditional boat in the circumpolar region is the* umiak, *the long, open hull of which is lined with the skins of seals or sea lions. An* umiak *is generally used when hunting large animals as the efforts of several men are required.*

of the Arctic peoples are also shamanic in origin. Oral traditions describe the supernatural powers of animals-shamans and guardian spirits like the polar bear; different myths lay down prescriptions on how hunting should be carried out, above all on the taboos regarding the protection of certain species of prey, or on the manner in which the remains of killed animals are to be treated. A creature's bones are considered the magical parts of a body, from which the animal can separate and return to its place of origin, and rebirth of the bones is a recurrent shamanic theme.

This idea of death and rebirth as a necessary shamanistic rite of passage can be traced back to ancient hunting rituals in which the bones of the animals were recomposed so that the animal might be resurrected. Pre-hunt ceremonies among hunting peoples were of fundamental importance, as were the cult of the polar bear and the propitiatory rites that followed a bear's death among all Arctic peoples.

The first accounts of Arctic peoples reached Europe at the start of the sixteenth century, written by explorers, travelers and mapmakers, though in fact the earliest knowledge of the ancient Eskimos dates to the discovery of Greenland by the Icelandic Vikings in the tenth century. In later centuries, the circumpolar regions were crossed by fur-traders, whalers and the occasional group of colonists. After the end of the Second World War, countries interested in exploiting the mineral and hydroelectric resources of the Arctic accelerated their industrial development of the area through the militarization and urbanization of particular zones, with the result that the local populations were transformed into 'ethnic minorities' within political and national boundaries.

Today the Inuit (or Eskimos) are distributed along the northern borders of Russia, the United States, Canada and Greenland (Denmark). The Saami (Lapps) inhabit the northern areas of Norway, Sweden, Finland and Russia. The Siberian Arctic is home to a number of different groups, including the Nenets (Samoyeds), Khanti and Mansi, the Evenk (Tungus), Chukchi and Koryaks. This section of the book will dwell on the traditional culture of the Inuit, with discussions of the modern daily life of these peoples, who are now familiar with computers and satellite technology.

The Chukchi will be taken as representatives of the Siberian groups, the language of whom has certain affinities with the ancient Eskimo tongue. Such similarities reflect the continuous interchange between the Chukchi and Asiatic Eskimos, both of which live in the Chukchi national district.

As the only European representative of the Arctic populations, the Saami had to be included; they too are traditionally fishermen and hunters but have integrated the breeding of reindeer into their economy in more recent times.

Over the last years, the authorities in the American Arctic have attempted to introduce livestock breeding among the Eskimo groups in Alaska so as to provide them with an alternative to the hunting of endangered species of whales.

294 These days Scandinavian Saami have abandoned the traditional life that centered on nomadic camps but they take every opportunity to wear their traditional brightly colored clothes embroidered with vivid patterns.

295 A Chukchi child peeps through the window of a brick house in Siberia. The pelt-covered tent (yaranga) *used by his forefathers is today only used by the* chavcu *(nomadic herders) who live inland.*

Saami

NORWAY, FINLAND AND SWEDEN

The Saami are also known as Lapps, but this is a term that they find offensive. They inhabit the area of the Arctic Circle that lies in Norway, Sweden, Finland and the Kola Peninsula in Russia.

The origin of the Saami is uncertain. Some experts claim that they migrated from central Europe, while others consider them a Paleosiberian people. Whatever the case, their language belongs to the Finno-Ugric group in the Uralic family.

Long established as hunters and fishermen, a few centuries ago they became nomadic reindeer herders. At that time the Saami were organized in bands of co-operating families that moved seasonally, and each controlled a set plot of grazing land. The life of the Saami herders followed the seasonal cycle of the reindeer: the periods of the shedding of the horns, mating and birthing were the calendar around which the survival of the tribe revolved.

Of the 40-50,000 Saami registered in Norway in the 1980s (to which can be added 15,000 in Sweden, 4,000 in Finland and 7,000 in Russia), only a few thousand still practice reindeer breeding as their principal livelihood, and not for subsistence but for commerce, as the meat of these creatures is a luxury item that is sold in Nordic countries through chains of butcher's shops.

Seasonal grazing has today replaced the traditional nomadic practice. Only herders move with the herds today, while their families remain in fixed settlements. Furthermore, the use of modern equipment, such as motorized sleds, has brought practical and productive benefits like the reduction of time spent moving from place to place. Despite the social changes prompted by industrialization, grazing has remained the central element around which Saami traditions revolve.

296 top Easter is an important festival for the Saami. They gather in large groups when links are retied, baptisms and marriages celebrated and races and competitions held. In Hætta in Finland, the Easter fair includes a skiing competition in which the entrants are dragged by impetuous, galloping reindeer.

296 bottom Gákti, *the Saami's traditional clothing, and their native language are the two major elements that mark this people's pride in their heritage. Wearing them is a deliberate confirmation of their cultural identity.*

296-297 The red hats worn by guests at a wedding brighten the snowy landscape of Kautokeino in the Norwegian country of Finnmark. This town is mostly inhabited by Saami.

297 bottom The decorative strips that the Saami use to mend tears in their clothes are made on small rectangular looms just eight inches wide. The term Lapp, from which 'Laplanders' is derived, is thought by some to mean 'darning patch' in reference to the appearance of their dress, but used in a pejorative manner.

298 top left A Saami family pose on reindeer skins in a simple but comfortable gamme, *the traditional wooden hut with turf roof.*

298 top right The traditional way to cook reindeer and fish is to smoke them over alder wood. This grills the meat and ensures it will keep.

Saami religious life is intimately bound up with their contact and deep knowledge of the Arctic tundra, which, they claim, is inhabited by guardian spirits associated with natural forces like the earth, wind and water. In *The Golden Bough* (1915), James Frazer describes the art of the Saami in propitiating the power of the winds.

Certain mountains and lakes are held as the sacred seats of the spirits of the ancestors and were once used as burial places. The Saami have a particular cult of sacred stones as these mark zones in which supernatural entities manifest themselves and are useful as landmarks during seasonal grazing migration. At one time, the cult of the stones – litholatry – was part of rituals and offerings in honor of the ancestors.

Derived from the ancient hunting economy of the Arctic Circle, the religious beliefs of the Saami are linked to shamanic cults, for instance, the elaborate ceremonies (common to all Arctic cultures) carried out before and after a polar bear hunt, as in Saami myths this creature is considered a guardian spirit with magical powers. Today, despite the Saami's adoption of Orthodox Christianity and Lutheranism since the eighteenth century, the memory of their ancient cults still remains, particularly among the older generations.

Another religious form found in some Saami communities, which came into being in the nineteenth century, is the syncretist Laestadianism practiced among autonomous evangelical congregations that professes individual asceticism and the public confession of sins.

298 bottom A reindeer herder surrounded by his large herd. Rationalized herding has become a costly livelihood and the number of 'private' herders has dropped. It is calculated that only 10% of Saami still practice reindeer herding.

298-299 Inhabiting all the Arctic, reindeer are bred by various peoples in different ways and for different purposes. The Saami use them to pull loads and in competitions harnessed to pulka *(traditional sleds).*

299 bottom Although motorized sleds have pretty much substituted traditional ones, reindeer herding still has to follow the cycles of nature. The grazing period is divided by the Saami into eight phases corresponding to the herds' movements in search of food.

Chukchi

RUSSIA

The Chukchi live in northeast Siberia between the Anadyr River and the Arctic Ocean. In their language, which belongs to the Paleoasiatic linguistic group, the term *'chukchi'* comes from *chavchu*, meaning 'herders'. Like other Siberian peoples, the Chukchi are split into two communities, each of which has its own means of subsistence: one hunts along the coasts of the Arctic Ocean and the Bering Strait, the other herds reindeer in the tundra. However, the two groups trade with one another and intermarry. The coastal group hunts marine mammals like walruses, seals and whales using both traditional methods (kayaks for transport and harpoons that they hurl by hand through cracks in the ice) and modern equipment (rifles and motor boats).

The herders follow the seasonal migrations of the reindeer. They take the herds to graze on the tundra during the summer and move back towards the coast during winter where the climate is milder and the temperature sufficiently high to allow mosses and lichens to grow. Reindeer provide them with all that they need: means of transport, milk, meat, skins for making clothes, shoes and roofing materials and tendons that they use as sewing thread. To withstand the winter cold, the Chukchi wear two heavy shirts made from reindeer and seal skins with sleeves and neck lined with wolf or fox fur, two pairs of trousers, mittens and leather boots.

The *yaranga* is the name of the traditional Chukchi dwelling; it is a large cylindrical tent with conical roof made from a wooden frame lined with reindeer pelts and anchored to the ground with thongs and stones. Hunters live in fixed villages of tents pitched half below ground; openings in the roof let the smoke out and are used as an entrance during winter.

Like other Siberian groups, the religious life of the Chukchi is linked to shamanism. Their mythology has

300 The physical features of the Chukchi are reminiscent of those of native Americans, which is unsurprising as they live in the northeast tip of Eurasia, close to the 'bridge' crossed for millennia by the groups of Paleosiberian nomadic hunters that populated the Americas.

301 This Chukchi fisherman is smoking a cigarette in a hand-carved pipe. Like the Inuit, the Chukchi carve whalebones and walrus tusks that are sold in Russia and, in particular, in Alaska, providing them with a good income.

302 and 303 top right In their maritime hunting, the Chukchi use harpoons and rifles to hunt whales. Banned in the 1980s, the Chukchi were once again given permission to practice this traditional activity in 1992.

303 left The huge prize is unloaded onto the beach where the women begin to cut it into sections. Nothing goes to waste: bones and tusks, for example, are used for traditional carvings of hunting scenes.

many tales and legends of animals and shamanic spirits. Various rites are celebrated to propitiate the *vairgit* (benevolent spirits), which are identified with the Pole Star, the sun, constellations, etc.) and the guardian spirits of the house, herds (Reindeer Beings) and hunt (Sea Beings). The latter used to be celebrated in a large autumn festival held by the maritime Chukchi during which sea creatures were sacrificed; the remains of the animals were restored to the sea in order that the creatures might return in greater numbers. Realistic hunting scenes carved in walrus tusks and whale bones are part of traditional Chukchi art.

The Chukchi were discovered in the seventeenth century by the Russians at the start of their colonization of Siberia. From that time, the territory inhabited by the Chukchi was constantly visited by traders and fur hunters from the European and American coasts, but they had a negative influence on the fragile economy of the native peoples.

In 1919 the Soviets took control of the territory and in 1930, with the creation of the Chukchi National District, a process of industrialization of the economic activities was begun in which the coastal groups were brought together in an association and the herders obliged to cooperate in *kolkhoz* (collective farms). Collectivization led to the establishment of schools for nomadic children that followed the families on their grazing pattern, and of colleges, which took in pupils during the winter when the parents migrated to the coast with their herds.

New industries have since been set up in the Chukchi area, like agriculture, fur treating and gold-mining. When practicing the traditional activities of fishing, hunting and herding, today the Chukchi use modern equipment, such as motorboats and rifles. They also use helicopters to follow the herds and move between towns and villages.

303 center and bottom right Using harpoons and rifles, hunting huge creatures like the gray whale is an extremely dangerous activity. Recently the Chukchi have received material aid in the form of more modern equipment, though this does not result in a greater impact on the environment. The Chukchi have traditionally observed environmental balances and notions of bio diversity, with the result that their hunting is ecologically sustainable.

304 top left *The upturned hull of a baidarka is being lined with walrus skins bound with tendons. This type of boat, similar to a kayak, is easily maneuvered, fast and handles well in the wind or a rough sea.*

304 top right *Inside his tent, a nomad hangs his fish to dry. Fish are an essential source of vitamins and minerals as imported foods do not provide the Chukchi with an adequate balanced diet.*

304 center *A reindeer herder prepares to leave his yaranga (tent) to attend to his herd in the inhospitable Siberian taiga. The Chukchi language has many terms describing traditional activities like herding: the reindeer has many names, depending on its color, sex, age and behavior.*

304 bottom *The tiny sled of this Chukchi child contrasts with the wooden one behind. Like the Inuit, the Chukchi use teams of dogs to pull them. It is thought that the ancestor of the husky was selectively bred by the Chukchi, who needed an animal able to haul modest loads long distances using as little energy and losing as little body heat as possible.*

Chukchi

304-305 The yaranga is made from a frame of wooden poles intertwined at the top and lined with reindeer skins. The circle of stones used to anchor the tent is a typical feature.

305 bottom A chavchu *('reindeer herder') surveys his herd in the tundra. The name* Chukchi *is derived from this term, as opposed to* ankalyn *('coastal people'), which refers to the maritime community of this people.*

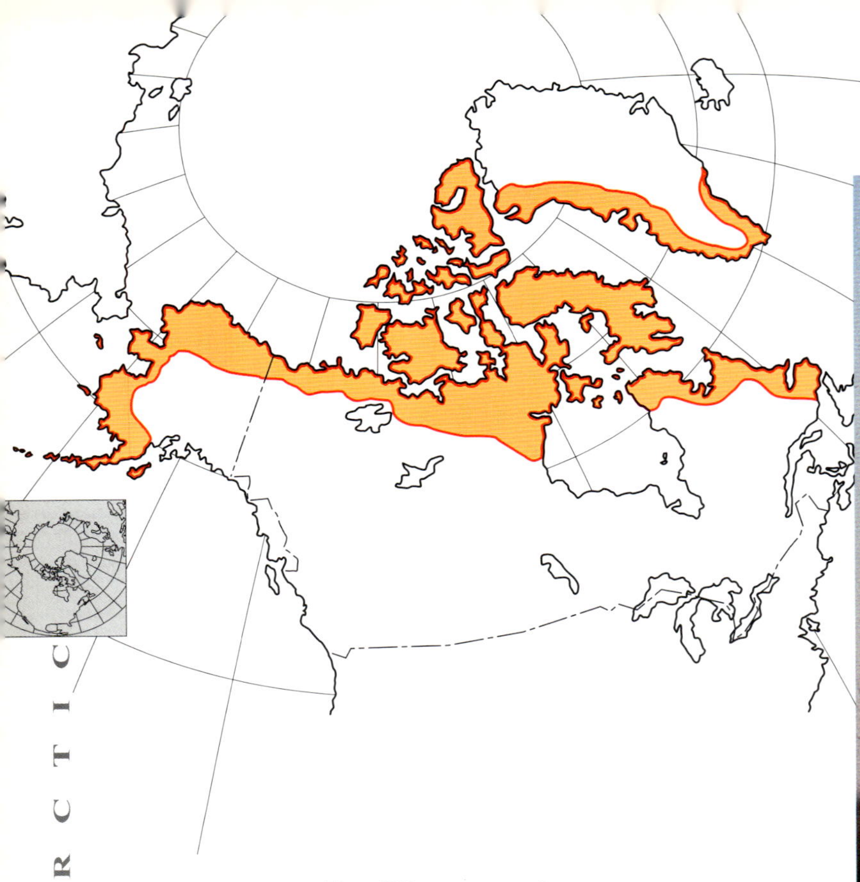

Inuit

ALASKA, CANADA AND GREENLAND

The term 'Eskimo', which means 'eaters of raw meat' in the Algonkian dialect, contrasts with the name used by the original hunters and fishermen of northern Siberia to describe themselves: 'Inuit', meaning 'the people'. These groups migrated from Siberia to the Arctic and sub-Arctic zones of Alaska between 10,000 and 5,000 years ago. Today the Inuit are spread across a vast area that stretches eastwards from the Bering Strait right across the Canadian Arctic coast to Labrador and Greenland, and, to the west, across Siberia.

Despite the geographic distance between the various groups – whose self-designations include Innuit in Alaska, Inughuit in Greenland and Yuit in Siberia – the Inuit are culturally analogous and speak similar dialects that can all be traced back to the same Eskimo-Aleut group.

The traditional economy of the Inuits is based on the hunting of polar bears, caribou, whales, beluga, seals and walruses. Adaptation to the harsh conditions of the tundra, covered by ice and snow for more than half the year, required clothes made of fur, eye protection against snow glare, sleds pulled by huskies, single-seater canoes lined with sealskin (*kayak*), larger, open boats used for fishing expeditions (*umiak*), harpoons, caribou-skin tents in summer, and semi-subterranean winter shelters (*igloo*) made from square blocks of snow and heated by seal fat burned in soapstone lamps.

Many of these items are still used and have only in part been replaced, for example, by motor vehicles and rifles in hunting.

To a certain extent hunting is still performed using the traditional means, for example, by the Inuit on the east coast of Baffin Island, who live in houses painted with seal blood. As many of the species these people hunt are protected,

306 A group of Inuit fishes in the partially iced over waters during the short Arctic summer. Traditional fishing equipment was bone hooks, bait made from bones and iron (bought), harpoons, bows and arrows.

306-307 To protect their eyes from the intense sunlight, for centuries the Inuit used wooden 'glasses' with a small slit that let through a minimum quantity of light.

307 right The igloo is one of the surprising inventions of the early Inuit to survive the circumpolar climate: resistant to strong winds, it is easily warmed inside and effectively retains the heat.

307 bottom left An Inuit woman slakes her thirst with a sliver of ice. She is a member of the Caribou people that lives in the Northwest Territories of Canada and is wearing a caribou fur (an American relation of the reindeer) under her tunic.

permission is required from the Canadian government. During winter hunts, the professional hunters still shelter in igloos, like their predecessors did for thousands of years, but they are able to remain in contact with their families through short-wave radio (Tundra net). Computers are found in schools, offices and houses, and, given the physical isolation of the Inuit villages, medical assistance is now available through internet.

In addition, a computer-based project has been created to gather and store as many traditions and tales of traditional Inuit culture as possible.

Besides cooperative hunting and fishing, other income-based activities practiced by Canadian Inuit are working in mines, oil wells and factories. Many, it should be added, live on government subsidies.

The harsh living conditions and isolation in part explain the spread of alcoholism and the use of drugs and the fact that Baffin Island has the highest rate of suicide in the world.

The Inuit in Greenland are Danish and live in villages dotted along the coast.

Not unlike what happens in Canada, the traditional economy on the world's largest island is supported by modern professions.

During the Soviet administration, the economic activities of the Asian Eskimos that live on Saint Lawrence Island in the Bering Strait were collectivized and the herding of reindeer was introduced.

308-309 *Protected by a thick caribou fur, a hunter waits for a polar bear. The Inuit are forced by nature to live exclusively on hunting and fishing, but they have great respect for their prey.*

309 top *A seal hunter in Greenland hurls his harpoon at his prey. The Inuit harpoon is a complex tool: it has a line attached to the hunter's arm and a mobile tip that prevents the rod from being pulled out of the prey's body.*

All Inuit groups have maintained their beliefs derived from ancient shamanic cults. The Inuit believe in the 'Sea Mother' and 'Man Moon' and that every living organism has a spirit. They have many religious taboos relating to hunting, which, if violated, cause damage and bring sickness and misfortune to the whole group. Still practiced today, propitiatory hunting ceremonies include dances to drummming, and songs and prayers that contain magical formulas. Amulets and talismans are used to beseech the protection of spirits in exchange for which certain taboos are respected, for example, the abstention from catching or eating particular animals. It is probable that these prescriptions had a practical value, like preventing indiscriminate hunting and the disappearance of certain species.

309 bottom *Tied in a fan shape to a hunter's* komatik *(sled), huskies pull their load across the ice-covered Baffin Sea. This form of transport is predominant among the Inuit though they use modern equipment such as rifles and radios to reduce personal danger. The frame of the sled is strengthened with caribou bone and horn, and the runners are lined with strips of bearskin to improve their glide.*

311 bottom Much loved and cherished by their parents, Inuit children can be adopted on a numerical basis to ensure that each family has the same number of children.

312-313 The hearth lies in the center of the tent. It burns on the kudlik *(soapstone plate) and provides the only source of light and heat and is also used for cooking.*

310-311 and 310 bottom right Completely blackened by soot due to the lack of an opening for the smoke, summer tents are made from a frame of curved poles (bottom).

310 bottom left Once the load-bearing frame is completed, the tent is lined with caribou pelts sewn to form a large circle.

311 top Given the almost complete absence of wood to burn, the Inuit use seal fat as a fuel.

INDEX

c = caption
bold = chapter

PHOTOGRAPHIC CREDITS

General Introduction
Page 1 D. Ball/Marka
Pagges 2/3 Marcello Bertinetti/Archivio White Star
Pages 4/5 Marcello Bertinetti/Archivio White Star
Pages 6/7 Gigi Toscano
Page 7 Marcello Bertinetti/Archivio White Star
Page 8 Tiziana and Gianni Baldizzone/Archivio White Star
Page 9 Marcello Bertinetti/Archivio White Star
Page 10 Gigi Toscano
Page 11 Marcello Bertinetti/Archivio White Star
Pages 12-13 Steve McCurryMagnum/Contrasto
Pages 14-15 Michele Vestmorland/Agefotostock/Contrasto

EUROPE
Introduction to Europe
Page 16 left Giulio Veggi/Archivio White Star
Page 16 right Nigel Dickinson
Page 17 Luciano Ramires/Archivio White Star
Pages 18 and 19 Marcello Bertinetti/Archivio White Star
Page 20 Giulio Veggi/Archivio White Star
Pages 20-21 Michel Cambaraz/Explorer/Hoa-Qui

Irish
Pages 22-23 Tim Thomson/Corbis/Grazia Neri
Page 22 bottom left Richard Cummins/Corbis/Grazia Neri
Page 22 bottom right Giulio Veggi/Archivio White Star
Page 23 top Peter Turnely/Corbis/Grazia Neri
Page 23 bottom David Turnely/Corbis/Grazia Neri
Page 24 top left Giulio Veggi/Archivio White Star
Page 24 center left David Turnely/Corbis/Grazia Neri
Page 24 bottom left Giulio Veggi/Archivio White Star
Page 24 right Giovanni Rinaldi/Il Dagherrotipo
Page 25 Gianluigi Sosio

Bretons
Page 26 top Charles Lénars
Page 26 bottom Bruno Barbey/Magnum/Contrasto
Page 26-27 Michel Renaudeau/Hoa-Qui
Page 27 bottom left Michel Renaudeau/Hoa-Qui
Page 27 bottom right H. Lesetre/Hoa-Qui
Page 28 top Charles Lénars
Page 28 bottom J.-M. Roignant/Hoa-Qui
Page 28-29 J.-M. Roignant/Hoa-Qui
Page 29 bottom left G. Morand-Grahame/Hoa-Qui
Page 29 bottom right J.-M. Roignant/Hoa-Qui

Andalusians
Pages 30 and 31 Antonio Attini/Archivio White Star
Pages 32 and 33 Antonio Attini/Archivio White Star
Page 34 top Nigel Dickinson
Page 34 center Nigel Dickinson
Page 34 bottom Nigel Dickinson
Pages 34-35 Nigel Dickinson
Page 35 Aisa

Walser
Pages 36 and 37 Giulio Veggi
Pages 38 and 39 Marcello Bertinetti/Archivio White Star
Page 40 Marcello Bertinetti/Archivio White Star
Pages 40-41 Luciano Ramires/Archivio White Star

Sardinians
Pages 42 and 43 Giulio Veggi/Archivio White Star
Page 44 top left Giulio Veggi/Archivio White Star
Page 44 top right Giulio Veggi/Archivio White Star
Page 44 bottom Giulio Veggi/Archivio White Star
Pages 44-45 Marcello Bertinetti/Archivio White Star
Page 45 top Giulio Veggi/Archivio White Star
Page 45 bottom Giulio Veggi/Archivio White Star
Pages 46 and 47 Giulio Veggi/Archivio White Star

Horsemen of the Pustza
Page 48 bottom left Silvestris
Page 48 bottom right Christian Sappa<
Pages 48-49 Sandro Vannini/Franca Speranza
Page 49 top Zefa/Hoa-Qui
Page 49 bottom Theo Hofmann/Silvestris

Rom
Page 50 top Peter Turnely/Corbis/Grazia Neri
Page 50 bottom left Nigel Dickinson
Page 50 bottom right Michael Boys/Corbis/Grazia Neri
Pages 50-51 Nigel Dickindson
Page 51 bottom left Nigel Dickindson
Page 51 bottom right Nigel Dickindson
Pages 52 and 53 Nigel Dickindson

AFRICA
Introduction to Africa
Page 54 left Marcello Bertinetti/Archivio White Star
Page 54 center Roger de la Harpe/Africa Imagery
Page 54 right Cristophe Ratier/NHPA
Page 55 Marcello Bertinetti/Archivio White Star
Pages 56-57 Peter Pickford/NHPA
Pages 58 and 59 Marcello Bertinetti/Archivio White Star

Berber
Page 60 top Bruno Barbey/Magnum/Contrasto
Page 60 bottom Bruno Barbey/Magnum/Contrasto
Pages 60-61 Bruno Barbey/Magnum/Contrasto
Page 61 top Bruno Barbey/Magnum/Contrasto
Page 61 center N. Thibant/Hoa-Qui
Page 61 bottom Harry Gruyaert/Magnum/Contrasto
Page 62 Xavier Richer/Hoa-Qui
Page 63 top Dennis Stock/Magnum/Contrasto
Page 63 bottom left Bruno Barbey/Magnum/Contrasto
Page 63 bottom right Bruno Barbey/Magnum/Contrasto
Page 64 top left Bruno Barbey/Magnum/Contrasto
Page 64 top right Bruno Zanzottera
Page 64 bottom Bruno Barbey/Magnum/Contrasto
Pages 64-65 Bruno Barbey/Magnum/Contrasto
Page 65 Bruno Barbey/Magnum/Contrasto

Tuareg
Page 66 Michael S. Lewis/Corbis/Contrasto
Page 67 top Charles Lénars
Page 67 center Giulio Veggi/Archivio White Star
Page 67 bottom Raymond Depardon/Magnum/Contrasto
Pages 68-69 Stefano Amantini/Atlantide
Page 69 Peter Adams/Marka
Page 70 top Tiziana and Gianni Baldizzone/Archivio White Star
Page 70 center Tiziana and Gianni Baldizzone/Archivio White Star
Page 70 bottom Luciano Romano
Pages 70-71 Tiziana and Gianni Baldizzone/Archivio White Star
Page 71 Tiziana and Gianni Baldizzone/Archivio White Star

Dogon
Pages 72-73 Luciano Romano
Page 72 bottom left Abbas/Magnum/Contrasto
Page 72 bottom right Luciano Romano
Page 73 top Michel Renandeau/Hoa-Qui
Page 73 center Michel Renandeau/Hoa-Qui
Page 73 bottom Michel Renandeau/Hoa-Qui
Page 74 top Michel Renandeau/Hoa-Qui
Page 74 center Patrick Ben Luke Syder/Lonely Planet Images
Page 74 bottom Michel Renandeau/Hoa-Qui
Page 75 Michel Renandeau/Hoa-Qui

Fulani
Pages 76 and 77 Marcello Bertinetti/Archivio White Star

Bororo
Pages 78 and 79 Tiziana and Gianni Baldizzone/Archivio White Star
Pages 80-81 Tiziana and Gianni Baldizzone/Archivio White Star

Surma
Pages 82 and 83 Gigi Toscano
Pages 84 and 85 Gigi Toscano

Maasai
Pages 86-87 Christophe Ratier/NHPA
Page 86 bottom left Jean-Louis Le Moigne/NHPA
Page 86 bottom right Christophe Ratier/NHPA
Page 87 top Roger de la Harpe/Africa Imagery
Page 87 bottom Roger de la Harpe/Africa Imagery
Pages 88 and 89 Marcello Bertinetti/Archivio White Star
Pages 90 and 91 Marcello Bertinetti/Archivio White Star
Page 92 top left Roger de la Harpe/Africa Imagery
Page 92 top right Roger de la Harpe/Africa Imagery
Page 92 bottom Roger de la Harpe/Africa Imagery
Pages 92-93 Roger de la Harpe/Africa Imagery
Page 93 F. Varin/Explorer/Hoa-Qui

Pygmies
Pages 94-95 Yves Gellie
Page 94 bottom AISA
Page 95 top Yves Gellie
Page 95 center Yves Gellie
Page 95 bottom Yves Gellie

Himba
Page 96 top left Anthony Bannister/NHPA
Page 96 top right Bruno Zanzottera
Pages 96-97 Anthony Bannister/NHPA
Page 97 top Yann Arthus Bertrand/Corbis/Grazia Neri
Page 97 bottom Anthony Bannister/NHPA
Page 98 top Bruno Zanzottera
Page 98 bottom left A. Dragesco/Panda Photo
Page 98 bottom right Roger de la Harpe/Africa Imagery
Page 99 A. Dragesco/Panda Photo
Page 100 A. Dragesco/Panda Photo
Page 101 top A. Dragesco/Panda Photo
Page 101 center Bruno Zanzottera
Page 101 bottom Bruno Zanzottera

Bushmen
Pages 102-103 Eric Vandeville/Gamma/Contrasto
Page 102 bottom left Anthony Bannister/NHPA
Page 102 bottom right Peter Johnson/Corbis/Contrasto
Page 103 top Peter Johnson/Corbis/Contrasto
Page 103 bottom Peter Johnson/Corbis/Contrasto
Page 104 top Peter Johnson/Corbis/Contrasto
Page 104 bottom left Anthony Bannister/NHPA
Page 104 bottom right Anthony Bannister/NHPA
Page 105 Gallo Images

Ndebele
Page 106 top left Lindsay Hebberd/Corbis/Grazia Neri
Page 106 top right Lindsay Hebberd/Corbis/Grazia Neri
Page 106 bottom M. Courtney-Clark/Hoa-Qui
Page 107 Daniel Lain/Corbis/Contrasto
Page 108 Lindsay Hebberd/Corbis/Grazia Neri
Page 109 top Roger de la Harpe/Corbis/Grazia Neri
Page 109 center Lindsay Hebberd/Corbis/Grazia Neri
Page 109 bottom Lindsay Hebberd/Corbis/Grazia Neri

ASIA
Introduction to Asia
Page 110 left Marcello Bertinetti/Archivio White Star
Page 110 right Antonio Attini/Archivio White Star
Page 111 Bohemian Nomad Picturemakers/Corbis/Contrasto
Page 112-113 Andrea Pistolesi
Pages 114 and 115 Tiziana and Gianni Baldizzone/Archivio White Star

Bedouin
Pages 116-117 Antonio Attini/Archivio White Star
Page 116 bottom left Antonio Attini/Archivio White Star
Page 116 bottom right Antonio Attini/Archivio White Star
Page 117 top Antonio Attini/Archivio White Star
Page 117 bottom Marcello Bertinetti/Archivio White Star
Pages 118 and 119 Antonio Attini/Archivio White Star
Pages 120 and 121 Antonio Attini/Archivio White Star

Palestinians
Pages 122 and 123 Marcello Bertinetti/Archivio White Star
Pages 124 and 125 Peter Turnely/Corbis/Contrasto

Haredim
Pages 126 and 127 Marcello Bertinetti/Archivio White Star
Pages 128 and 129 Marcello Bertinetti/Archivio White Star

Kurds
Page 130 top Chris Kutschera
Page 130 bottom Chris Kutschera
Pages 130-131 Zafer Kizilkaya
Page 131 bottom Chris Kutschera
Page 132 top Chris Kutschera
Page 132 bottom Zafer Kizilkaya
Pages 132-133 Chris Kutschera
Page 133 bottom left Chris Kutschera
Page 133 bottom right Chris Kutschera

Pashtun
Page 134 Steve McCurry/Magnum/Contrasto
Page 135 top left Steve McCurry/Magnum/Contrasto
Page 135 top right Steve McCurry/Magnum/Contrasto
Page 135 center Thomas Dworzak/Magnum/Contrasto
Page 135 bottom Steve McCurry/Magnum/Contrasto
Pages 136-137 Zafer Kizilkaya
Page 136 bottom left Marcello Bertinetti/Archivio White Star
Page 136 bottom right Marcello Bertinetti/Archivio White Star
Page 137 top left Heathcliff O'Malley/Gamma/Contrasto
Page 137 top right Steve McCurry/Magnum/Contrasto
Page 137 bottom Steve McCurry/Magnum/Contrasto

Rabari
Page 138 top Tiziana and Gianni Baldizzone/Corbis/Contrasto
Page 138 bottom Tiziana and Gianni Baldizzone/Corbis/Contrasto
Pages 138-139 Tiziana and Gianni Baldizzone
Page 139 bottom Tiziana and Gianni Baldizzone
Page 140 Tiziana and Gianni Baldizzone
Page 141 top left Tiziana and Gianni Baldizzone/Corbis/Contrasto
Page 141 top right Tiziana and Gianni Baldizzone
Page 141 center Tiziana and Gianni Baldizzone
Page 141 bottom Tiziana and Gianni Baldizzone

Ladakhi
Page 142 top left Gianluigi Sosio
Page 142 top right Marcello Bertinetti/Archivio White Star
Page 142 bottom Marcello Bertinetti/Archivio White Star
Page 143 Marcello Bertinetti/Archivio White Star
Page 144 top Andrea Pistolesi
Page 144 bottom Andrea Pistolesi
Pages 144-145 Christophe Boisvieux/Hoa-Qui
Page 145 bottom left F. Arvidsson/Explorer/Hoa-Qui
Page 145 bottom right Andrea Pistolesi

Gallong
Pages 146 and 147 Lindsay Hebberd/Corbis/Contrasto

Nishi
Page 148 top Lindsay Hebberd/Corbis/Contrasto
Page 148 center Xavier Zimbardo/Hoa-Qui
Page 148 bottom Lindsay Hebberd/Corbis/Contrasto
Page 149 Lindsay Hebberd/Corbis/Contrasto
Pages 150 and 151 Tiziana and Gianni Baldizzone

Apatani
Pages 152-153 Lindsay Hebberd/Corbis/Contrasto

Page 152 bottom Lindsay Hebberd/Corbis/Contrasto
Page 153 top left Lindsay Hebberd/Corbis/Contrasto
Page 153 top right Lindsay Hebberd/Corbis/Contrasto
Page 153 bottom Earl and Nazima Kowall/Corbis/Contrasto

Wancho
Pages 154 and 155 Lindsay Hebberd/Corbis/Contrasto

Bondo
Pages 156-157 Tiziana and Gianni Baldizzone
Page 156 bottom left Tiziana and Gianni Baldizzone
Page 156 bottom right Tiziana and Gianni Baldizzone
Page 157 left Tiziana and Gianni Baldizzone
Page 157 top right Lindsay Hebberd/Corbis/Contrasto
Page 157 bottom right Maurizio Leigheb

Sherpa
Page 158 top Roman Soumar/Corbis/Contrasto
Page 158 center Benelux Press/Hoa-Qui
Page 158 bottom Richard List/Corbis/Contrasto
Page 159 Benelux Press/Marka
Page 160 top left Earl and Nazima Kowall/Corbis/Contrasto
Page 160 bottom left Galen Rowell/Corbis/Contrasto
Page 160 right Nevada Wier/Corbis/Contrasto
Pages 160-161 Christine Kolisch/Corbis/Contrasto
Page 161 bottom Janez Skok/Corbis/Contrasto
Page 162 top Earl and Nazima Kowall/Corbis/Contrasto
Page 162 center left Shannon Nace/Lonely Planet Images
Page 162 center right Nevada Wier/Corbis/Contrasto
Page 162 bottom Christine Kolisch/Corbis/Contrasto
Page 163 Craig Lovell/Corbis/Contrasto

Tibetans
Pages 164 and 165 Marcello Bertinetti/Archivio White Star
Page 166 top left Mark Buscail/Housestock
Page 166 top center Marcello Bertinetti/Archivio White Star
Page 166 top right Marcello Bertinetti/Archivio White Star
Page 166 center Marcello Bertinetti/Archivio White Star
Page 166 bottom Marcello Bertinetti/Archivio White Star
Page 167 Marcello Bertinetti/Archivio White Star
Pages 168 and 169 Marcello Bertinetti/Archivio White Star

Mongols
Pages 170-171 Giacomo Pirozzi/Panos Pictures
Page 170 Dean Conger/Corbis/Contrasto
Page 171 top Dave Edwards
Page 171 center Bruno Zanzottera
Page 171 bottom Dean Conger/Corbis/Contrasto
Page 172 left Dean Conger/Corbis/Contrasto
Page 172 right Dean Conger/Corbis/Contrasto
Pages 172-173 Peter Oxford/Nature Picture Library
Page 173 How-Man Wong/Corbis/Granata Press
Pages 174-175 Zafer Kizilkaya
Page 174 bottom P. Wang/Explorer/Hao-Qui
Page 175 top Dave Edwards
Page 175 center Zafer Kizilkaya
Page 175 bottom left Colin Monteath/Hedgehog House/Hoa-Qui
Page 175 bottom right Bruno Morandi/Age/Hoa-Qui
Pages 176 and 177 Dave Edwards
Page 178 top Eve Arnold/Magnum/Contrasto
Page 178 center Thierry Falise/Gamma/Contrasto
Page 178 bottom Dean Conger/Corbis/Contrasto
Pages 178-179 Alain Le Garsmeur/Corbis/Contrasto
Page 179 bottom left C. Le Tourneur/Hoa-Qui
Page 179 bottom right Karen Su/China Span

Ainu
Page 180 top Martin Moos/Lonely Planet Images
Page 180 center Natalie Fobes/Corbis/Contrasto
Page 180 bottom Ian Berry/Magnum/Contrasto
Page 181 Kenneth Garrett

Miao
Pages 182-183 Xinhua/Chine Nouvelle/Gamma/Contrasto
Page 182 bottom Karen Su/China Span
Page 183 top Xinhua/Chine Nouvelle/Gamma/Contrasto
Page 183 center Xinhua/Chine Nouvelle/Gamma/Contrasto
Page 183 bottom Xinhua/Chine Nouvelle/Gamma/Contrasto
Pages 184-185 Patrick Aventurier/Gamma/Contrasto
Page 185 Karen Su/China Span
Pages 186 and 187 Tiziana and Gianni Baldizzone
Pages 188 and 189 Tiziana and Gianni Baldizzone
Pages 190-191 Karen Su/Corbis/Contrasto
Page 190 bottom left Dave G. Houser/Corbis/Contrasto
Page 190 bottom right Dave G. Houser/Corbis/Contrasto
Page 191 top Karen Su/China Span
Page 191 bottom Dave G. Houser/Corbis/Contrasto
Page 192 and 193 Karen Su/China Span
Page 194 top Alison Wright/Corbis/Contrasto
Page 194 center Steve Raymer/Corbis/Contrasto
Page 194 bottom Nevada Wier/Corbis/Contrasto
Pages 194-195 Jay Dickman/Corbis/Contrasto
Page 195 bottom left Alison Wright/Corbis/Contrasto
Page 195 bottom right Steve Raymer/Corbis/Contrasto
Pages 196-197 Steve Raymer/Corbis/Contrasto
Page 196 bottom left AFP/De Bellis
Page 196 bottom right Liz Thompson/Lonely Planet Images
Page 197 Lindsay Hebberd/Corbis/Contrasto

Padaung
Page 198 top Jan Butchofsky/Houserstock
Pages 198-199 Luca Tettoni
Page 199 top right Mark Downey
Page 199 bottom left Andrea Pistolesi
Page 199 bottom right Mark Downey
Page 200 top Jean Leo Dugast/Panos Pictures
Page 200 bottom Jacques Brun/Explorer/Hoa-Qui
Pages 200-201 Mark Downey
Page 201 bottom left Mark Downey
Page 201 bottom right Jan Butchofsky/Houserstock

Bali-Aga
Page 202 top Paul A. Souders/Corbis/Contrasto
Page 202 bottom Morton Beebe/Corbis/Contrasto
Pages 202-203 Richard I'Anson/Lonely Planet Images
Page 203 bottom left Yan Arthus Bertrand/Corbis/Contrasto
Page 203 bottom right Paul A. Souders/Corbis/Contrasto
Pages 204 and 205 Marcello Bertinetti/Archivio White Star

OCEANIA
Introduction to Oceania
Page 206 left Maurizio Leigheb
Page 206 right Paul A. Souders/Corbis/Contrasto
Page 207 P. Mazzanti/Marka
Pages 208-209 Maurizio Leigheb
Page 210 Australian Piacture Library
Page 211 Maurizio Leigheb

Dani
Pages 212-213 Luca Tettoni
Page 212 bottom left Maurizio Leigheb
Page 212 bottom right Luca Tettoni
Page 213 top Maurizio Leigheb
Page 213 center Maurizio Leigheb
Page 213 bottom Maurizio Leigheb
Pages 214 and 215 Maurizio Leigheb

Yali
Pages 216 and 217 Maurizio Leigheb

Una Pygmies
Pages 218 and 219 Maurizio Leigheb

Korowai
Pages 220 and 221 Maurizio Leigheb

Arapesh
Page 222 top Zafer Kizilkaya
Page 222 bottom Zafer Kizilkaya
Pages 222-223 Zafer Kizilkaya
Page 223 top right Woodfin Camp
Page 223 bottom Zafer Kizilkaya

Huli
Page 224 top P. Mazzanti/Marka
Page 224 bottom P. Mazzanti/Marka
Pages 224-225 P. Mazzanti/Marka
Page 225 Wendy Stone
Pages 226-227 Stuart Westmorland/Agephotostock/Contrasto
Page 227 Chris Rainier/Corbis/Contrasto

Aboriginals
Pages 228-229 Penny Tweedie/Corbis/Grazia Neri
Page 228 bottom left Penny Tweedie/Corbis/Grazia Neri

Page 228 bottom right Penny Tweedie/Corbis/Grazia Neri
Page 229 top Richard T. Nowitz/Corbis/Grazia Neri
Page 229 bottom Penny Tweedie/Corbis/Grazia Neri
Page 230 top left Australian Picture Library
Page 230 top right Matthew McKee/Eye Ubiquitous/Corbis/Grazia Neri
Page 230 center Penny Tweedie/Corbis/Grazia Neri
Page 230 bottom Penny Tweedie/Corbis/Grazia Neri
Page 231 Dallas and John Heaton/Corbis/Grazia Neri

Maori
Page 232 top Dave G. Houser/Houserstock
Page 232 bottom Anders Ryman/Corbis/Grazia Neri
Page 232-233 George Steinmetz/Contrasto
Page 233 bottom left Arno Gasteiger/Aurora/Grazia Neri
Page 233 bottom right Arno Gasteiger/Aurora/Grazia Neri
Page 234 top Arno Gasteiger/Aurora/Grazia Neri
Page 234 center left David Guttenfelder/AP
Page 234 center right Mark Baker/Reuters
Page 234 bottom David Guttenfelder/AP
Page 235 David Guttenfelder/AP
Page 236 top Maya Vidon/AFP/De Bellis
Page 236 center Gabriel Bouys/STF/AFP/De Bellis
Page 236 bottom STF/AFP/De Bellis
Pages 236-237 Maya Vidon/AP
Page 237 bottom Maya Vidon/AFP/De Bellis

Polynesians
Page 238 Jean-Bernard Carillet/Lonely Planet Images
Pages 238-239 Dennis Stock/Magnum/Contrasto
Page 239 top Marcello Bertinetti/Archivio White Star
Page 239 bottom Dennis Stock/Magnum/Contrasto

THE AMERICAS
Introduction to the Americas
Page 240 left Charles Lénars
Page 240 right Marcello Bertinetti/Archivio White Star
Page 241 Danny Lehman
Pages 242-243 Victor Englebert/Danita Delimont Agent
Pages 244 Dennis Stock/Magnum/Contrasto
Pages 245 Bob Rowan/Corbis/Contrasto

Native Americans
Pages 246-247 Thomas Hoepker/Magnum/Contrasto
Page 246 bottom Daniel Heuclin/NHPA
Page 247 top left Eve Arnold/Magnum/Contrasto
Page 247 top right Stephen Trimble
Page 247 bottom Buddy Mays
Pages 248 and 249 Dannis Stock/Magnum/Contrasto

Amish
Page 250 top McDonald Wildlife Photography
Page 250 bottom Bill Bachmann/Lonely Planet Images
Pages 250-251 Australian Picture Library
Page 251 bottom left Kevin Fleming/Corbis/Contrasto
Page 251 bottom right David Turnely/Corbis/Contrasto
Page 252 top left Kim M. Koza/Corbis/Contrasto
Page 252 top right Joe McDonald/Corbis/Contrasto
Page 252 center Richard Hamilton Smith
Page 252 bottom Joe McDonald/Corbis/Contrasto
Page 253 Richard Hamilton Smith

Huichol
Pages 254-255 Woodfin Camp
Page 254 bottom Woodfin Camp
Page 255 top Nicolas Reynard/Franca Speranza
Page 255 center Woodfin Camp
Page 255 bottom Woodfin Camp

Maya
Pages 256 and 257 Thomas Hoepker/Magnum/Contrasto
Pages 258-259 Thomas Hoepker/Magnum/Contrasto
Pages 260-261 Thomas Hoepker/Magnum/Contrasto
Page 260 bottom Thomas Hoepker/Magnum/Contrasto
Page 261 top David Alan Harvey/Magnum/Contrasto
Page 261 bottom Charles Lénars
Pages 262 and 263 Thomas Hoepker/Magnum/Contrasto
Pages 264 and 265 Thomas Hoepker/Magnum/Contrasto

Cuna
Pages 266-267 Danny Lehman
Page 266 bottom left Charles Lénars
Page 266 bottom right Danny Lehman
Page 267 top Danny Lehman
Page 267 bottom Danny Lehman
Page 268 top Danny Lehman
Page 268 bottom Danny Lehman
Page 269 Jack Fields/Corbis/Contrasto
Page 270 Dave G. Houser/Houserstock
Page 271 top Angelo Tondini/Focus Team
Page 271 center Dave G. Houser/Houserstock
Page 271 bottom Charles Lénars

Yanomani
Page 272 top left Alfredo Cedeño/Panos Pictures
Page 272 top right Maurizio Leigheb
Page 272 bottom Victor Englebert/Danita Delimont Agent
Page 273 Mark Downey
Page 274 top Victor Englebert
Page 274 center Maurizio Leigheb
Page 274 bottom left Maurizio Leigheb
Page 274 bottom right Maurizio Leigheb
Pages 274-275 AISA
Page 276 top left Nigel Dickinson
Page 276 top right Maurizio Leigheb
Page 276 bottom Maurizio Leigheb
Pages 276-277 Maurizio Leigheb
Page 277 Maurizio Leigheb

Peruvians
Pages 278 and 279 Marcello Bertinetti/Archivio White Star
Pages 280 and 281 Marcello Bertinetti/Archivio White Star
Pages 282 and 283 Marcello Bertinetti/Archivio White Star
Pages 284 and 285 Marcello Bertinetti/Archivio White Star

Aymara
Pages 286 and 287 Christophe Boisvieux
Page 288 top Victor Englebert
Page 288 center Victor Englebert
Page 288 bottom Stuart Franklin/Magnum/Contrasto
Page 288-289 Leo de Wys/Marka
Page 289 bottom Hubert Stadler/Corbis/Contrasto

ARCTIC
Introduction to the Arctic
Page 290 left Marcello Bertinetti/Archivio White Star
Page 290 right Bryan and Cherry Alexander/Alamy
Page 291 Marcello Bertinetti/Archivio White Star
Pages 292-293 Staffan Widstrand
Page 294 Marcello Bertinetti/Archivio White Star
Page 295 Pat O'Hara/Corbis/Contrasto

Saami
Page 296 top Nik Wheeler/Corbis/Contrasto
Page 296 bottom Marcello Bertinetti/Archivio White Star
Pages 296-297 Bryan and Cherry Alexander/Alamy
Page 297 bottom left Marcello Bertinetti/Archivio White Star
Page 297 bottom right Giulio Veggi/Archivio White Star
Page 298 top left Bo Zaunders/Corbis/Contrasto
Page 298 top right John Cleare/Alamy
Page 298 bottom Farrel Grehan/Corbis/Contrasto
Pages 298-299 Anders Ryman/Corbis/Contrasto
Page 299 bottom Marcello Bertinetti/Archivio White Star

Chukchi
Pages 300 and 301 Staffan Widstrand
Page 302 Staffan Widstrand
Page 303 left Staffan Widstrand
Page 303 top right Staffan Widstrand/Corbis/Contrasto
Page 303 center right Roman Poderni/R.P.G./Corbis-Sygma/Grazia Neri
Page 303 bottom right Roman Poderni/R.P.G./Corbis-Sygma/Grazia Neri
Page 304 top left Staffan Widstrand
Page 304 top right Colin Monteath/Hedgehog House
Page 304 center Natalie B. Fobes
Page 304 bottom Bryan and Cherry Alexander/NHPA
Pages 304-305 Staffan Widstrand
Page 305 bottom Steve Kaufman/Corbis/Contrasto

Inuit
Pages 306 and 307 Eugenio Manghi
Pages 308-309 Staffan Widstrand
Page 309 top Staffan Widstrand
Page 309 center Staffan Widstrand
Page 309 bottom Marcello Bertinetti/Archivio White Star
Pages 310 and 311 Eugenio Manghi
Pages 312-313 Eugenio Manghi
Pages 320 Marcello Bertinetti/Archivio White Star

320 *In the flat, frozen expanse of the Alaskan Arctic, an Inuit boy on a sled is wearing a warm caribou fur. Unlike other Arctic peoples, the Inuit continue to produce most of their clothes and tools using natural materials and following techniques they have tested and perfected over at least 5,000 thousand years.*